WOMEN
AND
WHITLAM

MICHELLE ARROW is Professor in Modern History at Macquarie
University and a Research Fellow at the Whitlam Institute. She
is one of Australia's leading contemporary historians and has
written for *The Conversation*, *Australian Book Review*, *Inside
Story* and the *Sydney Morning Herald*. Michelle is the author of
Friday on Our Minds: Popular culture in Australia since 1945 and
*The Seventies: The personal, the political and the making of modern
Australia*, which was awarded the 2020 Ernest Scott Prize for
history and was shortlisted for the Douglas Stewart Prize for
Non-Fiction in the NSW Premier's Literary Awards.

WOMEN
AND
WHITLAM

REVISITING THE
REVOLUTION

EDITED BY MICHELLE ARROW

NEWSOUTH

A NewSouth book

Published by
NewSouth Publishing
University of New South Wales Press Ltd
University of New South Wales
Sydney NSW 2052
AUSTRALIA
https://unsw.press/

A catalogue record for this
book is available from the
National Library of Australia

ISBN   9781742237855 (paperback)
        9781742238708 (ebook)
        9781742239644 (ePDF)

Internal design Josephine Pajor-Markus
Cover design Amy Daoud
Cover image International Women's Day march, 1975. Photograph by
    Anne Roberts. Mitchell Library, State Library of New South Wales,
    PXA 962/62
Printer Griffin Press

FOREWORD
THE HON TANYA PLIBERSEK MP

Gough Whitlam taught us two great lessons: first, that governments must be brave and bold. Second, that governments must be practical, and in touch with the daily needs of the people they seek to represent. You can buy *Blue Poles* and sewer western Sydney.

In popular memory, the Whitlam government can feel like a three-year blur of movement and change; of crashing through or crashing. But the truth is, progressive change came at the end of a long and difficult road. It required more than good intentions. Whitlam's reforms took years of hard, detailed policy work, much of it in the long, cold exile of opposition. And much of it was produced in partnership with those who would be directly affected by the policies. Or as we say today: nothing about us without us.

The work on women's policy was done by feminists inside the Labor Party, in concert with feminists outside it. It won't surprise anyone to learn that, in the 1960s and 1970s, feminism wasn't universally embraced within the ALP. Feminist activists, including many in the labour movement, worked through organisations like the Women's Electoral Lobby (WEL) to get women's issues on the policy agenda. WEL is still going strong, and in my own state of New South Wales played a leading role in the long overdue decriminalisation of abortion in 2019.

I describe these women as feminist activists, in the language of today, but at the time many considered themselves members of the Women's Liberation Movement. The reforms they advocated and then, in government, helped deliver, had liberation at their core; they had freedom at their core.

Freedom to choose to have and raise a child, without being thrown into poverty, with the Supporting Mother's Benefit.

Freedom to choose to delay or avoid pregnancy by listing the contraceptive pill on the Pharmaceutical Benefits Scheme, so women could exercise choice, whatever their means.

Greater freedom to leave an unhappy, or a violent marriage, with funding to women's refuges, rape crisis centres, and the introduction of no-fault divorce.

And freedom from a lifetime of being underpaid or excluded from the workforce. You can't be free if you need your father's permission to spend, or your husband's permission to borrow. You can't be free if you don't have the option to earn enough to support yourself.

We may still be striving to close the gender pay gap, but the first steps were taken when Gough reopened the Equal Pay case. Half a million female workers became eligible for full pay, and women's wages overall rose by around 30 per cent.

For the first time, under the Whitlam government, women became entitled to the minimum wage. For the first time, Commonwealth public servants became formally entitled to Maternity Leave. And ask any working parent about the importance of the Whitlam government's support for child care!

It may be hard to imagine now, but these liberating policies were bold, brave and, yes, often controversial. But each of them had a real, practical, meaningful impact on the everyday lives of Australian women. What seemed radical at the time strikes us as common sense today.

But it is not just women's policies that change women's lives. All policies affect women. And almost all affect women and men in different ways.

The Whitlam government understood that basic truth. Elizabeth Reid, adviser to Gough Whitlam, made the argument that all policies should be assessed for their impact on women.

Working for Bob Hawke in the 1980s, Anne Summers developed the Women's Budget Statement. When I was a minister, I used their great example, and our Cabinet documents included gender impact statements. Labor is committed to gender-responsive budgeting.

Targeted programs are important, but they're not enough to overcome structural disadvantage. Women's policy has to be underpinned by broad economic reform. I will never forget the way that people would stop Gough in the street when we were together, to thank him for their education. When he talked about the legacy of his government, one of the things he told me was that men usually thanked him for ending conscription. Women thanked him for making it possible to go to university.

Opening up universities and technical colleges to everyone wasn't one of the Whitlam government's women's policies, but the strongest beneficiaries were women. In Gough's three years of government, participation in higher education increased by 25 per cent. A generation of women and working-class men were liberated to make the most of their abilities. This was true in my family of working-class migrants. Without the Whitlam government's reforms, my parents could never have afforded to send me and my brothers to university.

Education has life-long and life-changing effects. Gough's reforms changed the lives of those who, for the first time, could continue their education. But the ripples of that change have been felt for generations. Their children, and now we can even say their grandchildren, continue to benefit. And each graduating class of women paved the way for the women who came after them.

When all Australians can reach their full potential, our country is stronger, smarter and better off. I was proud to support this legacy as Labor's shadow Minister for Education over six years. Just like I was proud to be federal Health Minister, with the privilege of defending and extending the legacy of so many Labor heroes such as Doug Everingham, Neal Blewett and Brian Howe.

The creation of Medibank, which became Medicare, was another nation-defining reform. It transformed Australia's health system and changed the lives of Australian women. Before Medibank, Australians who could not afford private insurance were locked out of proper medical care. Many were bankrupted if they became sick. And many in Australia's expanding outer suburbs faced long travel times to see doctors. As a former Health Minister, I know very well that when people can see their doctors, they can get better care sooner and lead longer, healthier lives.

When the Whitlam government created Medibank, many Australians got health care within easy reach for the first time. Funding new hospitals, and the Community Health Program, put health care in the expanding suburbs, where people lived.

When we talk about the Whitlam government's legacy for Australian women, the idea of universal access to health care through Medibank needs to be included. It means screening for breast and cervical cancers. It means vaccination programs that have made rubella a thing of the past. It means pre-natal and post-natal care that are now a norm and not a luxury.

The Whitlam government's focus on the suburbs, where so many young families lived, went beyond health care. As Neville Wran said, Gough 'found the outer suburbs of Sydney, Melbourne and Brisbane unsewered, and he left them fully flushed'. And we should never forget the impact of Margaret Whitlam's practical wisdom here. She lived in Cabramatta with a young family. She knew that concrete, achievable changes would make huge differences in the lives of women like her. Local swimming pools. Public libraries. Community playgrounds. She was a tireless advocate for the seemingly small but vital services and programs that so many Australian women, and their families, needed.

The third lesson of the Whitlam legacy I would reflect on is this: even when reforms have been carefully, painfully won, they can never be taken for granted. Today we have Medicare, not Medibank, because the Fraser government trashed it. Since then, we have seen Medicare under attack time and again by our opponents. The last time the Australian government published a Women's Budget Statement was 2013. The gender pay gap remains stubbornly high and we have slid from 15th down to 50th on the World Economic Forum's Global Gender Gap List.

We must build on the achievements of our predecessors, but we can never count those wins as permanent. Medicare came from Medibank. Medibank came from the Curtin and Chifley governments' health-care reforms. We must always fight to both defend and extend the victories won in the past.

Gough described the purpose of the Whitlam Institute as 'helping the great and continuing work of building a more equal, open, tolerant and independent Australia'.

As a Prime Minister, as a leader of the Labor Party, as a proud and ambitious Australian, Gough pursued this mission with his heart and soul.

That great work continues, as does the power of his example. As long as women are paid less than men, as long they retire with a smaller superannuation balance, as long as they feel unsafe at work or at home or in their communities, we need leaders who understand and prioritise equality between the men and women of Australia. And as long as this inequality exists, the Whitlam government will continue to inspire all of us who wants to build a fairer, smarter, more vibrant country.

CONTENTS

CONTRIBUTORS

Patricia Amphlett OAM professionally known as Little Pattie, enjoys a career that began in 1963. She had a succession of hits, joined Brian Henderson's *Bandstand* family and became a prominent force in the Australian music industry. Patricia's many industry awards include Best Female Singer, Most Popular Female personality, a *TV Week* Logie and Induction into the ARIA Hall of Fame. Recently, she received the MO Lifetime Achievement Award and the Australian Women in Music Lifetime Achievement Award. At age 17 Patricia was the youngest Australian to entertain our forces in Vietnam. Since then, she has devoted much of her time to Vietnam Veterans and their families. Patricia is a former member of the Council of the Australian War Memorial, former member of the ACTU Executive, former board member of the NFSA and former Federal President of MEAA. She is currently the patron of Forces Entertainment, a member of the Jessie Street Trust and a board member of the Whitlam Institute.

Gillian (Gil) Appleton is a writer and researcher. During her career she worked in various capacities for major government agencies and inquiries in film, broadcasting and cultural policy, and as an independent consultant. She served on many boards, including the Australian Film Commission, the Royal Botanic Garden Sydney, Penrith Performing and Visual Arts, the Eleanor Dark Foundation, Performing Lines, and the New South Wales Government's Arts Advisory Council (Chair 1999–2002).

Michelle Arrow is professor in Modern History at Macquarie University. She is the author of three books, including *Friday on*

Our Minds: Popular Culture in Australia Since 1945 (2009) and *The Seventies: The Personal, the Political and the Making of Modern Australia* (2019), which was awarded the 2020 Ernest Scott Prize for history. Michelle won the 2014 Multimedia History Prize in the New South Wales Premier's History Awards for her radio documentary 'Public Intimacies: The 1974 Royal Commission on Human Relationships'. In 2020, she was awarded a Special Research Initiative grant from the Australian Research Council for her current project, a biography of the writer and broadcaster Anne Deveson.

Craig Campbell worked as a historian of education at the University of Sydney from 1994 to 2009. Before then he was a public school teacher and teacher union leader in South Australia. In 1976 he met Jean Blackburn when they visited China on an educational tour early in that year. His more significant books, *Jean Blackburn: Education, Feminism and Social Justice* (2019), *A History of Australian Schooling* (2014) and *School Choice: How Parents Negotiate the New School Market in Australia* (2009) are each co-authored. Since leaving paid work, Craig has co-edited and written many of the entries in the online *Dictionary of Educational History in Australia and New Zealand* (*DEHANZ*). He and his partner of 45 years were recent beneficiaries of the right to gay marriage.

Marie Coleman AO is a retired public servant who has been active in the women's movement, particularly through the National Foundation for Australian Women, campaigning for paid parental leave, and establishing the #Gender Lens on the Commonwealth Budget.

Eva Cox née Hauser was born in Vienna in 1938, just before Hitler invaded and removed her family's citizenship as Jews. She spent eight years in England as a refugee, which included her being denied a drum in kindergarten as she was a girl. After two years in Rome with a father working for the UNRRA, settling refugees, she arrived in Australia in 1948, primed for the need for political changes. She retained this in her future activities as a feminist advocate as a sole parent in the Women's Electoral Lobby with a new BA (Hons) in Sociology. Her actions over the decades have earned her an AO and selection as presenter of the 1995 ABC Boyer Lectures on a Truly Civil Society. The latter predicted many of the problems faced today as *Homo economicus*, a very macho figure, took over economics and undermined society and women's contributions. She is still actively contributing to changes.

Sara Dowse's first novel, *West Block*, is based on her experience as head of the women's unit established in the Department of the Prime Minister and Cabinet to give bureaucratic support to Elizabeth Reid, Gough Whitlam's world-first prime ministerial Women's Adviser. She resigned from the service when, under Malcolm Fraser, the unit was transferred out of the department. Writing extensively on women's issues while embarking on her career as a writer, she drafted the women's policy for then Shadow Minister Susan Ryan, which was implemented by the Hawke government.

Cathy Eatock is a Gayiri/Badtjula woman, with traditional ties to the lands of central Queensland. Cathy is a PhD Candidate at the University of Sydney where her thesis is considering the capacity of the United Nations to support the recognition of Indigenous rights. Cathy is the elected Co-Chair of the Indigenous Peoples' Organisation-Australia (IPO) (2016–current). The IPO is a national coalition of Aboriginal and Torres Strait Islander organisations and individuals committed to advocating for the rights of Indigenous peoples. Cathy is also the elected Pacific

Representative to the Facilitative Working Group of the Local Communities and Indigenous Peoples Platform for the United Nations Framework Convention on Climate Change (2022–25).

Pat Eatock (14 December 1937 – 17 March 2015) was an Aboriginal activist and key member of the Aboriginal Embassy in 1972. Following the Embassy, Pat was the first Indigenous woman to stand for federal Parliament, in 1972, as an independent, though that bid was unsuccessful. Pat went on to be the first non-matriculated mature-age student to study at the Australian National University in 1973, where she graduated in 1977 with a Bachelor of Arts. Pat attended the Alternative Tribune to the International Women's Year World Conference in Mexico City in 1975 and the Women and Politics Conference in Canberra later that year. Pat worked in the public sector and as a lecturer at Curtin University on community development (1991–92), and at James Cook University in Aboriginal Studies (1997). From 1992 to 1996 she established and managed Perleeka Aboriginal Television, with her son Greg Eatock. In 2011, Pat was the lead litigant in a case against conservative columnist Andrew Bolt, in which she and others sued Bolt under the *Racial Discrimination Act* following a column alleging that fair-skinned Aboriginals had identified for monetary gain. The court found in favour of Pat and against Andrew Bolt, which led to a campaign by members of the Coalition to amend the Act.

Terese Edwards has held the position of CEO of the National Council of Single Mothers and their Children Inc. since 2009. Championing single mother families, Terese has appeared before parliamentary inquiries; co-produced a documentary; and presented at the Commission on the Status of Women at the United Nations, New York, in 2019. Terese addressed the Commission about her complaint, which alleges that Australia has violated single mothers' human rights by restricting access to social security. The first complaint of its kind, it is still being investigated. Terese is engaged in the women's and community sectors, assuming various roles, including the Deputy Chair of Economic Security 4 Women, and advisory member of the Australian Women Against Violence Alliance. She won the HESTA Unsung Hero award in 2019 and the International Women's Day Irene Bell Award (SA) in 2018.

Elizabeth Evatt AC was the first Chief Judge of the Family Court of Australia, from 1976 to 1988. Some of the positions she has held are: Deputy President of the Australian Conciliation and Arbitration Commission; Chair of the Royal Commission on Human Relationships, 1974–97; President of the Australian Law Reform Commission, 1988–93; elected member of the UN Committee on the Elimination of Discrimination Against Women (CEDAW), 1984–92, and Chair of the Committee, 1989–91; elected Member of the UN Human Rights Committee (monitoring body established under the International Covenant on Civil and Political Rights), 1993–2000; Chancellor of the University of Newcastle, 1988–99; Judge, World Bank Administrative Tribunal, 1998–2006; Commissioner, International Commission of Jurists, 2003–19; member of ICJ Australia; and Member, Women's Advisory Council, Corrective Services New South Wales since 2016.

Debra Hayes is an educator and educational researcher with a long-term commitment to equity and education. She is a Professor and Head of the University of Sydney School of Education and Social Work. Her recent co-authored books are *Great Mistakes in Education Policy* (2021) with Ruth Lupton, and *Jean Blackburn Education: Feminism and Social Justice* (2019) with Craig Campbell. Early in her working life, Debra taught in schools funded by the

Disadvantaged Schools Program and was deeply influenced by Jean Blackburn's education philosophies and policy legacies that shaped this program.

Julie McLeod is a Professor in the Melbourne Graduate School of Education and Pro Vice-Chancellor (Research Capability) at the University of Melbourne. She has previously been Deputy Director of the Melbourne Social Equity Institute, former co-editor of the journal *Gender and Education* (2012–16) and is currently a co-editor of the *History of Education Review*. She researches the history and sociology of education, focusing on youth, gender, educational reform and inequalities, with specialist expertise in research methods and graduate education. Julie previously held an Australian Research Council Future Fellowship (2012–17), and she is a Fellow of the Academy of Social Sciences Australia.

Iola Mathews OAM is a co-founder of the Women's Electoral Lobby, and a former journalist at *The Age*. Later she worked at the ACTU as an Industrial Officer specialising in women's employment, and was the advocate in the parental leave case, and equal pay cases for child-care workers and clerical workers. In 1996, she was awarded an Order of Australia Medal. She is the author of several books, including *Winning for Women: A Personal Story* (2019).

Camilla Nelson is Associate Professor at the University of Notre Dame Australia and EG Whitlam Research Fellow at the Whitlam Institute within Western Sydney University. Camilla is an internationally recognised media scholar. She is interested in voice and representation and how this shapes outcomes for people. A former journalist, Camilla has a Walkley Award for her work at the *Sydney Morning Herald*. Her most recent books are *Dangerous Ideas about Mothers* (2018) and *Broken: Children, Parents and Family Courts* (2021).

Professor **Heidi Norman** is a leading Australian researcher in the field of Aboriginal political history. In 2018 she commenced a large Australian Research Council–funded study of the social, economic and cultural benefits of Aboriginal land repossession in New South Wales. At the heart of her research is her support for Aboriginal peoples' rightful place in the nation, especially within political institutions, in society and in the economy as landholders. She is an award-winning researcher and teacher. She was awarded the University of Technology Sydney research excellence medal for collaboration (2015), National Teaching Excellence Award for her work in Indigenous studies (2016), and the inaugural Gough Whitlam Research Fellowship (2017–18). She is a descendant of the Gomeroi people from north-western New South Wales.

Tanya Plibersek is the Minister for the Environment and Water, and the federal Member for Sydney. Between 2013 and 2019, Tanya was Deputy Leader of the Opposition and Deputy Leader of the federal parliamentary Labor Party. From 2013 to 2016, Tanya was also the Shadow Minister for Foreign Affairs and International Development. From 2017 to 2022, Tanya was the Shadow Minister for Education and the Shadow Minister for Women. Tanya served as a Cabinet minister in the Gillard and Rudd governments. Tanya was Minister for Health, Minister for Medical Research, Minister for Housing, Minister for Human Services, Minister for Social Inclusion, and Minister for the Status of Women. Tanya holds a BA Communications (Hons) from the University of Technology Sydney and a Master of Politics and Public Policy from Macquarie University. Before entering Parliament, Tanya worked in the Domestic Violence Unit at the New South Wales Ministry for the Status and Advancement of Women. Elected to federal Parliament as the Member for Sydney in 1998, she spoke of her conviction that ordinary people working together can achieve positive change. Tanya lives in Sydney with her husband Michael and her three children, Anna, Joseph and Louis.

Dr **Elizabeth Reid** (AO FASSA FAIIA) is a feminist development worker, academic and writer. She taught philosophy at the Australian National University before being appointed as an adviser to Prime Minister Gough Whitlam in 1973 on matters relating to the welfare of women and children. Her development work since then has taken her to Africa, Papua New Guinea, the Pacific, Asia, the Middle East, the Caribbean, Central America, and Eastern Europe and the Commonwealth of Independent States. Elizabeth has worked as a national and international public servant with the United Nations, UN specialised agencies and UN regional commissions, and national governments. She has also worked with local and international non-government organisations and with faith-based organisations. She retired from field work in 2015 and now lives and works in Canberra.

Margaret Reynolds met Gough Whitlam in 1967 when he was campaigning in North Queensland and was immediately impressed with his commitment to reforming Aboriginal policy. As a young activist, Margaret was also inspired by Whitlam's vision of major change in opportunities for Australian women and for an end to conscription and the Vietnam War. She attributes many aspects of her long political career to being a member of the Whitlam generation. Margaret returned to university in the late 1970s and was elected to the Townsville City Council for four years in 1979 . She was elected to the Australian Senate in 1983, joining a small group of Labor women who continued to extend Whitlam's women's agenda, introducing sex discrimination and affirmative action legislation, as well as gender budgeting across all government departments. She was also strongly influenced by a range of the Whitlam Government's initiatives in education, local government and foreign policy.

Kim Rubenstein is a Professor in the Faculty of Business, Government and Law, and Director (Academic) of the 50/50 by 2030 Foundation at the University of Canberra. A graduate of the University of Melbourne and Harvard University, she is Australia's leading expert on citizenship and its formal legal status, and on law's intersection with broader normative notions of citizenship as membership and participation. This has led to her scholarship around gender and public law, which includes her legal and oral history work on women lawyers' contributions in the public sphere. She was the Director of the Centre for International and Public law at the Australian National University from 2006 to 2015 and the Inaugural Convener of the ANU Gender Institute from 2011 to 2012. She is a Fellow of the Australian Academy of Law and the Australia Academy of Social Sciences.

Marian Sawer is a former Head of the Political Science Program at the Australian National University and Leader of the Democratic Audit of Australia. She was made an Officer of the Order of Australia in 1994 for 'services to women and to political science' and has been a gender equality advocate inside and outside of government. She has published widely on democratic issues, including a history of the Women's Electoral Lobby.

Karen Soldatic is a Professor in the School of School of Sciences at Western Sydney University, Institute Fellow at the Institute for Culture and Society, and Honorary Fellow at the Whitlam Institute. Karen's research engages with critical questions of inequality, disability, race and ethnicity, and sexuality and gender diversity under settler-colonial regimes of power and within the global South and East. She obtained her PhD (Distinction) in

2010 from the University of Western Australia and has published widely on the Australian welfare state and social policy.

Ranuka Tandan is a young Nepali-Australian woman living on Gadigal land. She has extensive writing, editing and content creation experience after editing the student newspaper of the University of Sydney, *Honi Soit,* in 2020; publishing in *The Guardian*; and working in the Whitlam Institute's Public Affairs Team since graduating from Media and Communications at the University of Sydney. Ranuka has been involved in grassroots activism for the past five years and is passionate about fighting for social and environment justice, and erasing racial and gender inequality. She believes that the best way to do this is through collective action and looks forward to seeing the readers of this book on the streets!

Biff Ward was a founding member of Women's Liberation in Canberra in 1970. From her decades of activism, a highlight is the Women for Survival peace camp at Pine Gap in 1983. Another was the writing of her book, *Father-Daughter Rape* (1984). Her memoir, *In My Mother's Hands* (2014), was short-listed for the New South Wales and Western Australian Premiers' literary awards and long-listed for the Stella Prize in 2015. *The Third Chopstick: Tracks through the Vietnam War* (2022) takes the reader from her years of protesting to her captivating interviews with veterans about what was happening to them in Vietnam and afterwards. It concludes with Biff's love of Vietnam itself, the place, the people and their memories of the war. She lives on Ngunnawal and Ngambri country in Canberra.

Dr **Blair Williams** is an award-winning academic and is currently a Lecturer in Australian Politics at Monash University, following her tenure as a Research Fellow at the Global Institute for Women's

Leadership at the Australian National University. Her research focuses on gendered media coverage of women in politics, most recently published in *Feminist Media Studies, Politics & Gender* and *Parliamentary Affairs*. Dr Williams is currently working on several research projects, including an analysis of the gendered media coverage of women leaders' response to the COVID-19 pandemic, and an examination of the gendered double standards of Murdoch press coverage of political women. Dr Williams is highly visible in the media as a monthly columnist for the *Canberra Times*, federal political correspondent for Radio Adelaide, and a regular contributor to The Conversation. Her research and activism have featured in over 50 local, national and international platforms, including Radio National, SBS, the *Sydney Morning Herald*, BBC, Al Jazeera and *Le Monde*.

INTRODUCTION

MICHELLE ARROW

Most people with even a passing acquaintance with Australian politics know that 1975 was a seismic year in our political history. On November 11 that year, the Whitlam government was dismissed by the Governor-General, Sir John Kerr. Despite widespread outrage at Kerr's actions, Whitlam went on to lose the general election a month later. For most Australians, the Dismissal is indelibly linked with the image of Whitlam addressing the public on the steps of Parliament House (now the Museum of Australian Democracy). The image of Whitlam, a tall man, in a sea of men, declaring that 'nothing will save the governor-general', endures as one of the most famous in Australian history.

Yet few of us remember that weeks earlier, Parliament House was host to a different kind of political spectacle, one which spoke to a gaping absence in Australian public life. At the beginning of September 1975, women from all over the country converged at Parliament House for the Women and Politics Conference. More than 700 women, from organisations ranging from the Country Women's Association to Women's Liberation, attended.[1] The goal of the conference was simple: to encourage women to take part in political activity, not only as voters or party members, but in community organisations, lobby groups, and as citizens whose lives were shaped by political decision-making. The conference was diverse, and sometimes fractious. There were protests: some women at the opening reception wrote 'Lesbians are Lovely' in lipstick on the toilet mirrors and shouted slogans during Whitlam's opening address. The conference dramatised the fact that Australian women did not all share the same goals: Indigenous activists used the conference to raise awareness of their distinctive political demands. But the conference successfully expanded many women's political horizons and encouraged them to pursue political careers. It planted seeds that flourished in subsequent decades.[2]

Back in 1972, recognising women as distinctive political actors in this way would have been unimaginable. What made such an event possible in 1975? The women's movement played a crucial role: raising women's consciousness and expectations, and giving voice to their demands for freedom, equality and justice. But it is also clear that the Whitlam government was important in the transformation of women's political engagement and in their everyday lives. Fifty years since the election of the Whitlam government, this book examines the impact of the Whitlam reform agenda on Australian women.

This book began in the same place as the Women and Politics Conference. On 25 November 2019, a group of extraordinary women gathered at Old Parliament House to revisit Whitlam's revolutionary policy agenda for women. Hosted by the Whitlam Institute, and led by then-director Leanne Smith and Distinguished Whitlam Fellow Susan Ryan, the conference gathered many of the women who had played crucial roles in the Whitlam government's revolution for women. They discussed the ways women emerged as an important constituency for the Whitlam government, the scope and scale of what was achieved for women, and pondered what remained to be done. Women remain underrepresented in Australian politics, and gender inequality persists in almost every aspect of women's lives. This book aims to look to the past to help shape the future. It is the first book about the Whitlam era to focus entirely on the government's agenda for women: how it was shaped and enacted, what was gained and what remains to be done.

It is fitting that we mark the Whitlam government's achievements for women shortly after Australians elected a record number of women to federal Parliament, many of whom are part of the first Labor government since 2013. Large numbers of women – including a number of high-profile 'Teal' independents – were motivated to run for office in the wake of a turbulent period of women's activism on women's workplace rights, their unequal pay and conditions, and outrage at gendered abuse and violence. More than 41 per cent of the 227 seats across both houses of Parliament will be held by women after the 2022 election. This Parliament also has the highest-ever number of First Nations representatives: eight out of ten of these members are women. Perhaps most remarkable was the performance of the Teal independents, who defeated a swathe of male MPs in previously blue-ribbon Liberal seats. The only parties who went backwards in their representation of women were the Liberal and National parties: women now hold just 11 of the 57 Liberal–National lower house seats in the new Parliament.[3] These results reflect longer realignments in women's political allegiances. Women and younger voters played a crucial role in Labor's 2022 election victory, and women were far less likely to vote for the Coalition than men, according to exit polls.[4] Yet this was not always the case, and in order to understand women's political roles today, we need to briefly trace the history of women's changing political engagement, before the Whitlam era.

Putting women on the Whitlam agenda

For much of the 20th century, Australian women were not generally encouraged to take active roles in politics. Australia had been one of the first places in the world to grant white women full political rights at the national level (in 1902): not just the right to vote, but to stand for Parliament. Yet the first women were not elected to Australia's federal Parliament until 1943, and between 1943 and 1975, only a handful of women were elected to the House of Representatives or the Senate. Most of these women represented the Liberal or National parties and, indeed, for much of the 20th century, Australian women tended to vote for the conservative parties. The Labor Party was not especially welcoming to women: Australian historian Frank Bongiorno noted that in the 1960s and 1970s, the ALP was something of a 'bawdy masculine subculture with deep roots in Australian masculinity [...] from which women were absolutely excluded'.[5]

By the mid-1960s, the emergence of a new progressive middle class prompted a larger political realignment in Australia. These people were concerned with Aboriginal rights and reform of Australia's racist immigration policies, and were opposed to capital punishment, oppressive censorship and conscription. Many were part of the anti-war movement, with its critique of western imperialism and desire for sweeping social change. Women's changing relationship to work and education also changed their political needs and desires. In the 1960s, more married women were entering the workforce and higher education.[6] Yet child-care services did not emerge to meet the increased demand from working mothers, and even though the Commonwealth Conciliation and Arbitration Commission had granted women equal pay for equal work in 1969, most women continued to earn less than men.

By the late 1960s, a new political movement had emerged across the west, one with significant implications for Australian politics. The Women's Liberation Movement grew from women's experiences in the anti-war movement. Tired of being treated like second-class citizens by their male comrades, women's liberationists argued that women were an oppressed group, and that women's experiences in the private sphere amid a capitalist, sexist society, created the conditions for their broader oppression. One of the movement's most important insights was 'the personal is political': the insistence that one's private problems and grievances were neither unique nor personal, but structural, and political. As the American feminist Carol Hanisch wrote in 1969: 'personal problems are political problems. There are no personal solutions at this time. There is only collective action for a collective solution'.[7] This collective action would take many forms in the great flourishing of feminist activism in the 1970s, from establishing women's refuges to creating feminist culture. But it was women's political visibility in the lead-up to the 1972 election that ensured women's voices – and their votes – could not be ignored.

Many of the contributors to this book recall the power of the 1972 federal election candidate survey by the Women's Electoral Lobby (WEL). WEL had formed earlier that year to raise the profile of women's issues in the upcoming election. Working in pairs, women interviewed all the candidates for office and determined their views on issues of concern to women. The survey both trained women in political lobbying and exposed the widespread ignorance of women's issues by the (mostly) male candidates for political office. It also revealed a gap between the two major parties on issues of concern to women: several Labor candidates (including Whitlam himself) scored very well, while many Liberals (with the exception of Minister for Territories and member for Kooyong Andrew Peacock) rated poorly. The survey results also attracted widespread media coverage, with *The Age* suggesting that the 1972 election was 'the first in which the average woman is really interested. Much of this interest is due to WEL'.[8] The survey exposed the ways that Australian politics failed to speak to women as citizens with distinctive issues and needs.

Making policy for women

Astonishingly, in 1972 neither of the major parties had explicit platforms or policies relating to women. As ALP feminist trailblazer and Senator Susan Ryan noted, writing in 2020, the ALP policy program was detailed and extensive, but it lacked 'proposals for detailed investigations into the many disadvantages suffered by Australian women at that time, because of their gender'.[9] Whitlam's 1972 policy speech touched on just three issues of concern to women: equal pay for work of equal value, lifting the sales tax on contraceptives, and access to pre-school education for all children under five.[10] His famous policy 'Program' did, however, open the possibility of targeted action to improve women's lives. Its 'three great aims' were:

to promote equality;

to involve the people of Australia in the decision-making processes of our land;

and to liberate the talents and uplift the horizons of the Australian people.[11]

Susan Ryan was thrilled when she heard Whitlam open this speech with the words, 'Men and women of Australia', because, she realised, *'He means us too'*.[12]

No women were elected in Whitlam's first government. There was no Minister for Women, nor an Office of Women's Affairs. How would the government respond to the emergence of women as a distinctive constituency? In April 1973, activist and academic Elizabeth Reid was appointed as Women's Affairs Adviser to the Prime Minister. She quickly became a focal point for Australian women, receiving huge numbers of letters from women around the country. Reid felt that an important part of her role was to make government more responsive to women. Not only did this mean advocacy for policies that would help them, like improved access to child care, but also training the bureaucracy in the particularities of women's needs. She was also farsighted in her vision for changes that would reverberate far beyond her time in her role. In planning Australia's celebrations for International Women's Year in 1975, which included the Women and Politics Conference, she established three goals: to change attitudes towards women, to alleviate discrimination, and to encourage women's creativity.[13] Reid always had one eye on the far horizon of transformation, the other focused on women's everyday lives.

The Whitlam government achieved a staggering amount in just three years. Whitlam told the Women and Politics Conference that his government recognised that his policies for women aimed to

> give women the pre-conditions necessary for them to
> be able freely to choose the lives they want to lead. To
> do this they must have the possibility of a little peace of
> mind as well as the possibility of financial and emotional
> independence.[14]

Susan Ryan singled out three Whitlam-era reforms as especially significant for women, all of which helped fulfil these goals. Medibank, she said, improved the lives of all Australians, but especially those of women and children, the greatest users of health services. Second, the abolition of tuition fees for universities meant that older women who had been forced to leave school at 15 found they could study at university. She wrote, 'of all the letters and messages Gough Whitlam received during his long life, expressions of thanks from women who benefited for his no fees initiative outnumbered any other'.[15] Third was the single mother's benefit, which provided a minimum income for mothers who were alone with children for any reason. This meant that women who became pregnant without a partner or family support were no longer forced to have abortions or place their children up for adoption: a truly transformative social policy.

As well as appointing a Women's Adviser to a national government – a world first – the Whitlam government reopened the Equal Pay case; extended the minimum wage for women; improved the accessibility of contraception; funded women's refuges and women's health centres; funded community child care; introduced accessible, no-fault divorce and the Family Court; introduced paid maternity leave in the public service; and investigated the structural discrimination against girls in schools. For a government that came to power without a formal women's policy, this is an extraordinary list of achievements.

But there were gaps and shortcomings in the Whitlam revolution for women: after all, the government's time in office was cut short. The Royal Commission on Human Relationships was one of the most significant casualties of the premature end of the Whitlam government. This pathbreaking inquiry into private and family life, with a particular focus on reproduction and sexuality, was well underway when the Dismissal happened, and the incoming Fraser government cut the Commission's funding and time when it came to power. The Royal Commission's final report, with its deeply confronting revelations about the scale and extent of family violence and its airing of the unhappiness in many Australian households, was treated like a political football when it was released in 1977.[16] This report was one of the first government inquiries into family violence, foreshadowing broader public discussion of an issue that affects so many Australian women.

More significantly, the Whitlam government came to power just as the new ideology of neoliberalism was beginning to emerge across the west. Neoliberalism sought to shrink the size and role of the State just as women were making new demands on it for services and support. What this meant was that as the Whitlam government began to fund new women's services, like refuges, child-care and health centres, subsequent governments tried to unwind these new funding arrangements, or to subject them to the 'discipline' of the market, which undermined their quality. Unfortunately, many services for women remain underfunded, though their entitlement to state support was first established by the Whitlam government.

Introducing the collection

Women and Whitlam is arranged in five parts. Each part examines a crucial aspect of the Whitlam program and its impacts on Australian women.

Part one, Women and Political Influence, is introduced by the esteemed political scientist Marian Sawer. The authors in this section each had a different relationship to the Whitlam government: Elizabeth Reid was an activist and adviser, working inside and outside the government; Iola Mathews was part of the Women's Electoral Lobby; Biff Ward was a member of Canberra Women's Liberation; and Pat Eatock (introduced by her daughter, Cathy) worked within and across the women's movement and the Aboriginal Land Rights Movement, including the Aboriginal Tent Embassy. Their accounts of the era show how these groups each had different goals, but together, they formed an ecosystem which nurtured feminist reform, and feminist revolution.

In Part two, Women and the Law, introduced by legal academic and gender equality campaigner Kim Rubenstein, Elizabeth Evatt and Camilla Nelson trace the creation and impact of one of the Whitlam government's best-remembered reforms: the passage of the *Family Law Act* in 1975. The Family Court's inaugural Chief Justice, Elizabeth Evatt, reflects here on her work for the Whitlam government, which included chairing the ground-breaking Royal Commission on Human Relationships. Whitlam Institute Fellow Camilla Nelson offers new insights into the fraught and passionate debate over the passage of the *Family Law Act*. Writing in the shadow of the abolition of the Family

Court in 2021, both Evatt and Nelson reveal the transformative impact of that court, and its associated changes to family law.

Part three, Women and Social Policy, focuses on just four aspects of the Whitlam government's sweeping changes to social policy, and their implications for women: Marie Coleman (the first woman to head an Australian statutory authority) on women's health reform; Margaret Reynolds on the impact of Whitlam on women in regional Australia; Eva Cox on the first 'femocrats'; and Terese Edwards, CEO of the National Council of Single Mothers and their Children, on the introduction of the Supporting Mother's Benefit. Each blends the personal with the political, and each powerfully demonstrates the life-changing effects of policy that accommodated women's particular needs. The Supporting Mother's Benefit, in particular, transformed the lives of single mothers and their children, as Edwards demonstrates. The chapters are introduced by social scientist and disability policy expert Karen Soldatic.

Part four, Media, Arts and Education, centres on the ways that the Whitlam government's reforms in these areas changed the lives of many Australian women. Introduced by education academic Julie McLeod, these chapters demonstrate that the Whitlam government's policies aimed not just to improve women's material circumstances, but to expand their horizons and lift their aspirations, too. Debra Hayes and Craig Campbell focus on the government's role in changing the ways that girls were educated, and particularly the impact of Jean Blackburn's work on girls and education. Journalist Gillian Appleton remembers the deeply ingrained sexism of the media in the Whitlam era and the ways that activists used International Women's Year to confront it. Finally, Patricia Amphlett (better known as the singer Little Pattie) shows how the Whitlam government's new approach to funding the arts had multiple, transformative effects on artists and performers in a range of fields.

In the book's final section, introduced by historian and Whitlam Institute Fellow Heidi Norman, contributors look both forwards and backwards to ponder the legacies of the Whitlam revolution for women and ask: what remains to be done? Sara Dowse, who played a critical part in the revolution herself, considers the obstacles that may hamper further progress for women, especially the social and political transformations wrought by neoliberalism. Political scientist Blair Williams considers the ways that gender has shaped Australian political culture over the last decade, linking the misogynistic treatment of Julia Gillard to the explosion of women's anger in the 2021 March4Justice. Ranuka Tandan, who works at the Whitlam Institute, makes an impassioned call for an intersectional, socialist feminism that will carry all women forward.

A book like this cannot address every single aspect of the relationship between women and the Whitlam government. However, at a time when women are once again finding their political voice – marching for justice, calling out men's predatory behaviour and running for office themselves – this book revisits Whitlam's revolution for women in the hope it will not only inspire further research, but fuel the fight for equality and justice for all women. It brings together women from several generations to assess what has been achieved, and what needs to be done next. As Minister for the Environment Tanya Plibersek notes in her Foreword, while we can and must build on the advances of the Whitlam era, we must never take these earlier gains for granted. Looking back on this period of change can help us understand how these gains were made, and help us work towards a more just future for all Australian women.

PART ONE
WOMEN AND POLITICAL INFLUENCE

INTRODUCED BY MARIAN SAWER

Fifty years ago the stars aligned in southern skies. Women were on the move – the Women's Electoral Lobby (WEL) successfully intervened in the 1972 federal election and won policy commitments from the incoming Whitlam government. What followed was feminists moving straight from the women's movement into government, led by Elizabeth Reid, Whitlam's adviser on matters relating to women. Her ever-thoughtful approach to 'living the revolution' meant that government became the funder of consciousness-raising on a broad scale, reaching more diverse women than ever before.

Timing was crucial. At home, a reforming government was elected at a time when women were mobilised politically around the demands of women's liberation. Abroad, a new international normative regime was beginning to emerge. The UN's Commission on the Status of Women had become a significant actor, initiating the 1967 Declaration on the Elimination of Discrimination against Women and the proposal for 1975 to be International Women's Year (IWY). In Australia, IWY was to provide the framework not only for consciousness-raising on a national scale but also for many of the new demands that women were making of government to meet their needs for safety and justice.

This favourable opportunity structure at home and abroad was to be responsible for the distinctive way in which the women's movement was to operate through government in Australia, giving the world the new word 'femocrat'. One of the distinctive features of this relationship was that it was not at first mediated by the presence of women as elected politicians – in 1972 there was not a single woman in Australia's House of Representatives.

Other distinctive features were to be found both on the supply and the demand side of recruitment into government. On the supply side, 'looking to the State' to promote social justice was an Australian political tradition, quite different to the anti-state traditions that framed women's liberation theory in the United

States. On the demand side, as government started to grapple with the new policy domains opened up by the women's movement, experience in the women's movement became a legitimate job qualification. No wonder the world was amazed when the Australian government delegation to the UN's First World Conference on Women was led not by a traditional government spokesman but by someone speaking women's movement discourse about sexism.

The women who were part of this revolution of rising expectations believed quite rightly that they were changing the world and the world would never be the same again. As Iola Mathews writes in her chapter here, such beliefs were reinforced when Whitlam authorised the reopening of the federal Equal Pay case on his second day in office, the lifting of the sales tax on the contraceptive pill on the third day, and a substantial contribution to the UN Fund for Population Activities on the sixth day. In the 1974 election campaign, the Labor Party used a wonderful Bruce Petty cartoon of a woman soaring free of her shackles and told voters that one million women had got more in their pay packets as a result of the reopening of the equal pay case.

As Elizabeth Reid makes clear, not only was the Whitlam government responding to policy demands from already mobilised women, it was also helping with awareness-raising. IWY grants enabled the purchase of new gestetner machines by women's centres, for the more efficient dissemination of subversive messages, and also paid for awareness-raising projects in more traditional women's organisations, churches and trade union bodies.

The strategy of using a reforming government in this way was not without controversy. Sydney Women's Liberation members were bitter that IWY grants were not provided to struggling women's refuges. Guidelines directed that grants should not go to projects falling within the responsibility of a government department, such as ongoing funding for women's services. During the reception for the IWY Women and Politics Conference, the statue of King George V in in Parliament House was draped in a sign reading 'Women and Revolution Not Women and Bureaucracy'.

At the IWY conference itself there was naturally a session on Reform and Revolution. The speakers were Gail Wilenski and Wendy Fatin, both of whom were dedicated WEL members who said they saw reform as a tool of revolution rather than neutralising the revolution. Member of Canberra Women's Liberation Biff Ward writes in her chapter here that for her this was the main takeaway from the IWY conference, that reform could be a strategy for furthering the revolution rather than co-opting it.

Ward praises Elizabeth Reid's insistence that all the debate in the conference sessions be recorded, while so much of what was said at Women's Liberation meetings had been lost: 'Underneath whatever documents do remain was a heaving ocean of words, emotions, conversations, epiphanies, insights, theories, depth, wildness and action that coloured and energised the second wave of the feminist revolution'.

The diversity of voices recorded at the IWY conference workshops is a useful counterbalance to later ideas that sisterhood was achieved through the systematic silencing of the Other and the 'essentialising' of women as a homogenous group. The conference brought together those already active in mainstream or movement politics and those just starting to see their own experiences as political. Shared anger emerged, directed at the media trivialisation of women engaging with politics, triggering the famous march and sit-in at the *Canberra Times*.

One of the conference participants represented in this book, Pat Eatock, embodied the intersection of the feminist revolution and events bringing the claims of Aboriginal Australia to national attention. At roughly the same time as the establishment of WEL, the Aboriginal Tent Embassy was set up for the first time outside Parliament House and soon the new land rights flag became a potent symbol of Aboriginal political identity.

Eatock travelled from Sydney to visit the Tent Embassy, and becoming actively involved. She also addressed Women's Liberation members at the newly established women's house and returned there with her baby. She attended the many Women's Liberation and WEL meetings taking place – not only by choice, as she explains, but because she and the baby couldn't go to bed until the meetings ended. Not surprisingly, when she stood for the federal Parliament in 1972 with Elizabeth Reid as her campaign manager, she topped the WEL rating of ACT candidates on their knowledge of women's issues.

In 1975 Eatock collaborated with Carol Ambrus on a paper on 'Racism and sexism as determinants of the status of Aboriginal men and women in Australia' at the IWY conference and was also a rapporteur. While she regarded the conference as a whole as a triumph, she suffered personal hurt as a result of questioning of her Aboriginal identity. As her daughter Cathy Eatock recounts, this issue was also at stake towards the end of her life when she was the lead litigant in a successful racial vilification case against conservative commentator Andrew Bolt.

There is much to learn from the feminist activists of the 1970s. Notable is the strength of collectivism in the women's movement at the time. Leadership was eschewed as a dirty word. As Iola Mathews notes, even in WEL, hierarchy was eschewed in the early years and meetings were held with a rotating chair and consensus decision-making. In the novel *West Block*, Sara Dowse described attempts to import women's movement collectivism into the hierarchy of the bureaucracy.

Collectivism was a feature not only of organisational practice but also of policy solutions. Elizabeth Reid writes about how Women's Liberation members discussed the solutions to the suburban isolation and neuroses suffered by women: 'The solutions we were discussing in those times were collectivist and communal; for example, medium density housing, shared facilities such as laundry, or shared services, such as child care, cooking and cleaning. A sharp contrast to today's world where the policy response is increasingly individualised and personalised'.

The shift from collectivist to more individualised approaches to policy and practice reflected a counter-revolution that was under way. Milton Friedman, the apostle of market freedoms, made his first visit to Australia in International Women's Year, inspiring a new push to marketise the welfare state.

So just as the State was becoming more responsive to the diverse needs of women, this other revolution was taking place, lowering expectations of the State as a source of social justice. A 'business case' now had to be presented to justify gender equality policies.

The onset of neoliberalism brought policy directions inimical to the kinds of social transformation sought in the 1970s. Competition policy meant competitive tendering to provide community services, at the expense of the collectivist forms of social provision pioneered by the women's movement in women's refuges and women's health services.

Serious analysis of the gender impact of macroeconomic policy was also eventually abandoned by government. It would have shown the disproportionate impact on women of policies such as tax 'reforms' that benefited higher income earners while diminishing the revenue available for human services. While there was praise for frontline care workers during the pandemic, the status of the care economy remains at the heart of gender inequality.

However, reminiscent of the 1970s, anger over gender injustice boiled up again in 2021, bringing women in their thousands to protest outside parliaments. The chapters here tell of what can be achieved by sisterhood and solidarity, when combined with good strategy and political opportunities. The struggle continues.

WHITLAM AND THE WOMEN'S LIBERATION MOVEMENT

ELIZABETH REID

The context: The early 1970s

In the early 1970s, the Women's Liberation Movement swept through Australia like a bushfire.[1] It was one of the most important of the social movements of its time. Its influence was felt in virtually every aspect of Australian political, social and cultural life. It was a feminist movement, struggling to come to grips with the workings of power in our midst. At our fledgling Women's Liberation meetings, we gathered together the details of our lives, reflected on them, and formulated our demands. We were curious, rebellious and passionate, swept off our feet by our outrage at our place in the world and by the excitement of the times.[2]

In the early 1970s, Peter Wilenski, then Gough Whitlam's Principal Private Secretary, proposed to the newly elected Prime Minister that he bring someone onto his staff who could advise him in this emerging area.[3] Whitlam, although not necessarily aware of the demands of the movement, nevertheless was well aware of its issues. He had scored highly on the Women's Electoral Lobby (WEL) questionnaire on women's needs and concerns administered to candidates before the 1972 election. Prime Minister McMahon received one of the lowest scores of all. Pat Eatock, an Aboriginal woman who stood as an independent in the ACT and who was a member of Canberra Women's Liberation, gained a perfect score.[4]

Towards the end of his term in office, Whitlam stated that

> For most of this country's history women have lived without
> visible political power; they have been excluded from
> almost all levels of government in our society. [...] Women
> whether they be conservative, liberal or radical should be
> fully represented in the political power structure simply
> as a matter of right: not just because they are women, but
> because they are capable human beings with skills, abilities
> and creativity from whom the world has much to gain.[5]

Immediately on his election, Whitlam had addressed a number
of issues of concern to women. As Prime Minister–elect, he asked
for assurance from the Public Service Board that the provisions of
the 1951 International Labour Organization Recommendation on
Equal Remuneration for Work of Equal Value had been applied
within the Commonwealth Public Service and its agencies.[6] In
his first days as Prime Minister, he reopened the Equal Pay case
in the Commonwealth Conciliation and Arbitration Commission
and briefed Sydney barrister and later High Court judge Mary
Gaudron to present the Commonwealth's case. He appointed
barrister, and later Chief Justice of the Family Court, Elizabeth
Evatt a presidential member of the Conciliation and Arbitration
Commission. He abolished conscription, which had been the
concern of the Save Our Sons protest movement of women.[7] He
removed the sales tax on oral contraceptives, placed contraceptives
on the Pharmaceuticals Benefits Scheme and lifted the ban on
advertising contraceptives in the ACT. He also provided funding
for family planning development assistance programs.[8]

Women were on the agenda. But few were involved: women's
issues were rarely spoken about, or reported accurately or
objectively, and decisions were taken elsewhere.

The Women's Liberation Movement

The Women's Liberation Movement in Australia was a non-partisan political movement. Ours was a radical feminism, a commitment to a feminist revolution. It was a commitment to a kind of social change that was not just an inner journey, although it was that, but, necessarily, a political struggle, not for piecemeal reforms, but a struggle for a coherent set of changes that would change society and women's lives irrevocably. The structures oppressing women were to be assailed and dismantled; social, political, economic, linguistic and cultural life would become effectively unrecognisable.

We were very clear that our aim was not equality, which we understood, perhaps simplistically, as meaning women becoming more like men; equality is not the answer for as long as our society remains sexist. If pushed, we preferred the concept of equity, as it carries within it the concept of fairness in difference. We felt that what was really needed was a reimagining of equality: that men needed to spend more time as fathers, carers, partners and in the community.

Our approach was women-centred: our aim was to change the power relations in the world which harmed women, and to change them in such a way that women would be the negotiators and agents of their own changes, empowered and equipped for citizenship in a more caring, humane and fair world. We had a vision of a society based on kindness and the common good, rather than on competition and strife between individuals, groups and nations.

We wanted to do things differently. Kay Daniels, a member of the Hobart Women's Action Group, characterised the movement in this way:

As a movement it is an anti-leader, anti-hierarchy,
anti-bureaucratic organisation, because these approaches
give us the only way we have to get at one of the real
difficulties that lie behind getting involved in the
movement and social issues generally – women's inability
(albeit through conditioning) to accept responsibility
… to accept the responsibility that comes with freedom
and independence ,.. Women have to realise that they
have to earn membership. I think that full participation
at every level is the only way to break down the division
between organisers and spectators, and this was done at
the conference. In fact, although a structureless meeting
can indulge irresponsibility, encouraging full participation
is what asking women to 'come out' really means.[9]

To change how power relations operate in the world requires us to understand them. The historian Linda Gordon defined feminism as 'an analysis of women's subordination for the purpose of figuring out how to change it'.[10] We had a particular focus on the role of the housewife: a relentless role that was only performed by women. This was our challenge: to find alternative ways for humanity to cope with housekeeping and child-rearing. But to bring about the feminist revolution, we needed to understand what changes were necessary and how these changes could be brought about, that is, we needed a program. It had taken Whitlam more than 20 years of hard political work, thought, observation and experience to help develop the ALP platform. It was coherent, seamless and transformative.

Developing the theory

We too needed a platform that was coherent, germane and transformative. We wanted to end patriarchal oppression; to do this, we had to understand it. Impassioned debates took place in the Women's Liberation Movement about reform versus revolution, about wages for housewives, about radical lesbianism and a separatist movement, about the nature of sisterhood, about the landscape of patriarchy, of misogyny, and of sexism. At the Canberra Women's Liberation meetings, a topic for discussion was scheduled for each meeting and one of its members led the discussion.

The movement developed a set of practices for social transformation. The first of these was the principle of voice, that is, the active participation, of all women, not just the articulate or educated, in the discussions. The voices of all women were to be listened to, and the realities these voices were expressing were to be appreciated, reflected on, and incorporated into the analysis. The second practice, that of consciousness-raising, was based on the way women relate to the world, not as solitary selves but as being and growing in connectedness with others. Its premise was that women could come to understand societies and their structures *because of* the lives that each woman had led, not *despite* them. Other practices included the practice of sisterhood, the non-appropriation of other women's stories, and a non-hierarchical structure without 'leaders' or 'stars', particularly not media-created ones.[11]

The movement's practices led us from our individual experiences of the patriarchy to theory and to specific political actions. We began to formulate our demands, but the identification of a desired change was not sufficient: some actions could reinforce the status quo, some could be counterproductive, some inadequate. The aim of the movement was to end all forms of patriarchal oppression. But we were not just *against* the shackles of oppression; we were struggling towards a new sense of positive identity for women, both individual and collective. We were *for* the creation of safe spaces where women's agency, empowerment, sexuality and creativity could flourish, whether in the arts, the caring economy, reproduction, relationships, as politicians, artists, wives, workers or whatever.

The Women's Liberation Movement was demanding revolutionary political, economic, social and cultural change: an end to patriarchy, wherever and however it manifested itself. What reforms and revolutionary changes were required by such a revolution and how they could be brought about were what we had to determine. To this end we used, among other things, the concept of *sexism*.

When women talked about their experiences as women at a Women's Liberation meeting, we were describing the various forms of patriarchal control that we have personally experienced. We began to understand that what we are up against is a *system*, a system of male domination and sense of entitlement, of male control, in which women are subordinate and the hierarchical relation among the sexes is produced and reproduced.

Sexism is what causes women to be brutally bashed and beaten, to feel confined and constricted.[12] It is what causes women to be abused and raped, to seek backyard abortions, to be continually called on to nurture and care for others: sexism is what patriarchy does to women, whoever and wherever they are.

Our growing understanding of the nature of sexism made women's control over our bodies central to our liberation. Thus, taking back control over our sexuality, the right to abortion, the rejection of the institutionalisation of heterosexuality, and the ending of all forms of violence against women and girls, especially sexual and domestic violence, were central to our program.[13]

Reform, revolution and the State

But then what was the role of the State as distinct from the Women's Liberation Movement in the development of a revolution? Does the State have a role to play in ending the ideology of patriarchy? In the overthrow of the structures of sexism? In a conscious endeavour to change the attitudes of a nation?

These are difficult questions. Sexism and patriarchy are interlinked. Sexism can only be challenged and overthrown by changes in the attitudes of men to women, but, more so, by changes in the attitudes of women themselves. These changes in attitudes change the structures of sexism. Changes in the structures of sexism challenge and undermine patriarchy.

We, both the Women's Electoral Lobby and the Women's Liberation Movement, understood that unless reform measures were accompanied by attempts to change the attitudes which disadvantaged women, the reforms could easily be reversed. Reforms demanded may be necessary but not sufficient. Reforms such as equal pay for work of equal value, access to child care centres, to education and health, etc., are all vitally necessary because they tackle the disadvantage and discrimination that women experience. However, we argued, such reforms cannot be the only aim and end of social change for women. For the notion that there is a place, role or sphere for women has not been challenged, nor the notion that there should be distinct and separate spaces and roles for men and women.[14] It is conceivable that all these particular changes could happen, and women could still be disadvantaged and discriminated against.

Who is this 'we'? Does the Women's Liberation Movement, or the State, need to bring about a revolution and develop a revolutionary program? Should this be the imperative of both? Let Whitlam himself answer. At the first meeting of the National Advisory Committee for International Women's Year, on 11 September 1974, he said:

> Government legislation can only achieve so much, and I
> shall not pretend to you that any Government can achieve

immediately for Australian women the revolution required
to allow them to develop fully as individuals … For
instance, it must be said that, even if we were to remove all
the inequalities of opportunity and of status, it still would
not be enough. We have to attack the social inequalities,
the hidden and usually unarticulated assumptions which
affect women not only in employment but in the whole
range of their opportunities in life … This is not just
a matter for governments … it is a matter of changing
community attitudes and uprooting community prejudices,
and … this requires a re-education of the community …[15]

The Prime Minister himself had committed us to working together
towards a revolution and provided another attempt to capture our
understanding of sexism.

Special Adviser to a head of government

In April 1973, I was appointed Special Adviser to Whitlam on
matters relating to the welfare of women and children. I arrived
in Whitlam's office as a seasoned activist.[16] I also had an activist
lineage: both my parents were activists, in the trade union
movement, in the Labor Party, in the reform of the Catholic
education system. Women's Liberation had equipped me with
a radical conceptual framework, a feminist discourse, an ever-
growing list of concerns and passionate commitment. For the next
two and a half years, the women's movement operated, at least
in part, through the State to achieve a feminist revolution, along
with the needed feminist reforms, and the funding of feminist
services.

So, what was our revolutionary platform, a platform that
would address 'the social inequalities, the hidden and usually
unarticulated assumptions which affect women not only in

employment but in the whole range of their opportunities in life',[17] that is, would challenge the structures of sexism and bring about the required revolution? Even before the job of Special Adviser had been advertised, the Canberra Women's Liberation Movement had identified some of their areas of concern: the right to work, equal pay rate for the job, equal opportunity for work and education, free 24-hour child care, safe contraception, safe legal abortion on request, defining our own sexuality, and smashing the draft Criminal Code for the Australian Territories.[18] The draft code, tabled in Parliament in 1969, would have legalised rape in marriage, made even fewer abortions legal, made it a crime to take the abortion pill, and joint property within a marriage would legally have belonged to the husband.[19]

The wider Women's Liberation Movement was demanding 'access to contraceptives, abortion, divorce, women's health, equal pay, prevention of rape and battery of wives, [as well as expressing] a concern about beauty as oppressive'.[20] The Women's Electoral Lobby's first bi-monthly newsletter, *Broadsheet*, published in February–March 1972, proclaimed that reforms such as equal pay, equal opportunities, day care, contraception, abortion and prevention of ecological ruin were too urgent to wait any longer. They argued that women should vote as a bloc in the coming elections, on particular issues, not on party lines.

On taking up the job, the movement's principle of voice, that is, the active participation of all women, not just the articulate or educated, committed me to listening to what women – as many women as possible – had to say about their lives. In the months following my appointment, I travelled around Australia, listening to women talk about their problems, about the changes they wanted. The women who spoke out came from all backgrounds: migrant, Indigenous, rural, elderly, suburban, working, single, wealthy, married. We talked in factories, in housing estates, on farms, in schools, at women's meetings, in dairies, in jails, in universities – in short, wherever women were. I was deluged with letters. In a short time, I was receiving more letters than any member of Cabinet other than the Prime Minister.[21] At the same time, I began the long march into the halls and offices of Parliament and the bureaucracy to learn how to formulate, seek approval and implement the emerging policies.

From the letters and discussions, five areas of much-needed reform emerged: employment and financial discrimination, the education of girls, child care, social welfare and urban planning. These themes framed a program of work for us.[22] The letters that I received were often about different forms of financial discrimination, discrimination in taxation, or discrimination in housing or benefits. But there were other letters, heartbreaking ones, on the unnecessary and unwarranted medical examinations of girls, on women not being able to sit in judgment on men on juries in Queensland, and so on.

What surprised me most, on a recent re-reading of Women's Liberation Movement documents from those times, was our emphasis on the redevelopment of the suburbs and on the collectivisation of housework and care: 'In the area of urban planning, we must try to design living areas and work areas and community areas that are helpful to people instead of harmful. The effect of suburban living on housewives trapped in the home, isolated from others, is being shown in the cluster of illnesses known as the "suburban neuroses"'.[23] In an interview with journalist Dany Torsh, I said: 'I am really worried by the increasing incidence of ... alcoholism, drug taking, suicides, psychotic and neurotic behaviour in women, mainly in the suburbs. The social cost, the cost in human terms, is appalling'.[24] Today, the phrase, 'suburban neuroses', and the preoccupation, seem to have disappeared. The solutions we were discussing in those times were collectivist and communal; for example, medium-density housing, shared facilities such as laundry, or shared services such as child care, cooking and cleaning – a sharp contrast to today's world where the policy response is increasingly individualised and personalised.

These key areas were the *reformist* agenda, the areas of need that women, within and without the women's movement, had identified. We, the Women's Liberation Movement and Women's Electoral Lobby, still needed to sort out the policies which could bring lasting benefits to women from the ones which would just replace 'one set of inequalities by another'.[25] We weighed each proposed reform for the good or the harm it could cause: 'The question is what makes any specific reform positive rather than negative?'[26]

Putting principles into practice

My other gift from the Women's Liberation Movement was the beginning of an understanding of what we were up against and of the limit of lists of reforms. The intensive discussions and readings from those days provided me with some insight into what we were not trying to achieve. What we were struggling for was not some future post-revolutionary utopia, neither a socialist nor a utopian future society. *Our task was to create a revolution in the act of living it.* The revolution had to be something that we could do rather than something that we would aim for and hopefully someday arrive at. It was a revolution that had to occur in each person's heart and head, in each person's language and behaviour, and at the level of each society.

We had to live our revolution ourselves at the same time as fighting for it. It was not a case of reform versus revolution, but of working out how we could create a revolution that would unfold alongside our reforms, assisting us in determining which reforms might be more effective, and increasing their effectiveness. The first thing many of us did was to cease to be 'ladylike'. We started swearing; we insisted on our space in public bars and restaurants;

we started drinking boldly; and doing whatever else was considered at that time to be unladylike behaviour, but which we experienced as energising and transformative, as living our lives more freely. To this day, I cannot control my swearing! But I vividly remember the sense of freedom that it gave me.

What we felt was needed was something more diffuse, less tangible than a reform, rather a change in the way that women were perceived and valued, a conscious awareness that each one of us, regardless of religion, class, ethnicity, age, race, culture, ability, etc. – but particularly, regardless of gender – carries within them the seeds of sexism. For want of a better phrase, it was called a revolutionary consciousness. We still had a lot to learn! We needed to develop policies to address the necessity for a revolutionary consciousness. But which policies and how can one identify them?

We began by putting the practices of the Women's Liberation Movement into everything we did. We were committed to honouring the movement's principles of voice, consciousness-raising, and sisterhood and solidarity. We knew that *how* we did something was as important as *what* we did. For example, in the planning of the Women and Politics Conference, which was held in early September 1975 and hosted by the National Advisory Committee for International Women's Year, it was important that it be open to as diverse a range of women as possible, that interested women should be able to afford it, that all (over 700) voices should be heard, and that the program should be flexible, reflect women's interests, and be built around relatively unstructured small group work.

In order to ensure that women, particularly Indigenous, migrant and rural women, who lived far from Canberra, could attend, it was decided that no participant should pay in excess of the airfare from Melbourne to Canberra. To further minimise costs, accommodation was made available in the Australian National University at the rate of $5 per day. Additionally, special efforts were made to encourage women from minority groups, particularly Aboriginal and Islander women, to attend. In cases of hardship, these women were not required to make any financial contribution themselves. Free child-care facilities were available at the conference.[27] We tried to create the kind of society, in a microcosm, that we wanted to bring about in the larger world.

The Royal Commission on Human Relationships

One of the first occasions we had to identify an initiative that could significantly contribute towards the development of a revolutionary consciousness, indeed, to making the personal political, was the establishment in 1974 of the Royal Commission on Human Relationships.[28] Not only was great care taken with the selection of the commissioners and the formulation of its Terms of Reference, but much thought went into how we could maximise its impact on the attitudes and values of ordinary Australians. We wanted the Commission to reach out to those who had had no voice up until then, to give them the sense that they were being listened to, and then to reflect on what they were hearing and to let Australians know what was happening, usually out of sight, in such a way that they would see the impact of their own behaviour, see the underlying attitudes and values that caused the problems.

For Whitlam, the task of the Commission was 'to ensure that no area of need will be overlooked, that no social problem relating to women, whether they be married or not, with or without children, aboriginal or newcomer, English speaking or not, young or old, rural or urban, will be hidden away, forgotten or neglected'. It was, he added, 'the First Royal Commission in history to investigate such social problems'.[29]

The Commission was to inform and educate Australians about the extent and effects of these social problems and report back regularly to all Australians on our relationships with one another and our behaviour as citizens and members of our society. It had powers to investigate rape within and outside of marriage, violence to women and girls, family planning and fertility control, sexuality and gender, childbirth, the termination of pregnancies, and relationship education.[30]

The choice of commissioners ultimately assured the effectiveness of its work. All three – Justice Elizabeth Evatt, Anne Deveson and Bishop Felix Arnott – set to work identifying people with expertise for staff positions and creating a safe and respectful feeling in their office. The commissioners travelled all over Australia, talking and listening and reflecting. They held public hearings, creating safe spaces in which people gave testimony to trauma and violence and disappointment and shame. They answered phones, met with people one on one, even at times in their own homes, read huge piles of correspondence, held public forums, watched videos, read research papers, and more. They received over 1200 written submissions and heard testimony from over 400 people and talked with thousands more in informal discussions.

The first Interim Report of the Commission came out in January 1976. It set out the understanding of the commissioners of their terms of reference and the approach that the commissioners would take to the task. However, in early 1976, the commissioners were instructed to cut short their inquiry and to ensure that all work was completed by the end of 1976. Their Final Report came out in November 1977 in the middle of an election. Not one of its 511 recommendations, which covered almost every aspect of Australian society – human relationships and social change; sexuality and fertility, including unwanted pregnancies, adoption, abortion and fertility control; the changing nature of the family, including domestic violence, rape, child abuse, single parenting, and alcohol; and discrimination against women, Indigenous Australians, migrants, gay and bisexual men, and the handicapped – was ever implemented.

Nevertheless, the Commission and its commissioners, through the hearings and discussions, the research program, the Reports, and the recommendations, had a profound effect on the lives, norms and values of many Australians and on our nation's culture.[31]

International Women's Year

Another important initiative, chosen because of its potential to contribute to the changing of people's attitudes towards women, was the honouring of International Women's Year 1975. In 1972, the United Nations General Assembly proclaimed 1975 International Women's Year. On International Women's Day (8 March) 1974, the Australian government announced its own program to mark the year, and in September 1974, a National Advisory Committee was established. Its role was to publicise and coordinate the government's International Women's Year program, and to allocate funding to individuals and groups for projects that supported the three objectives of the year: to change attitudes, reduce discrimination and encourage women's creativity. Whitlam's approach to the year is best captured in his speech on International Women's Day 1975:

> International Women's Year, as all of you who fought and
> won and lost and came back to fight again will know, is
> not going to solve the problems of the world, the problems
> of women and of men and of children. It is, however,
> our responsibility, the responsibility of you the women of
> Australia and of us, your Government, to try to ensure
> that this Year the world will be given a shove in the right
> direction, a shove without which changes for the good of
> women, of all women, not just a few, might never occur.[32]

More than $3.3 million was allocated, mainly for grants to women's groups and organisations, to be spent in the course of the year.[33] The government's approach was outlined in a paper, *International Women's Year: Priorities and Considerations*, tabled in Parliament in December 1974.

The paper clearly stated that the funds were for projects which did not fall within the responsibility of any government department or other institution, which were once-only funding requests, or which could be finished within the life of the Committee. The Committee took responsibility to channel demands for ongoing funding requests into the appropriate department or institution, to argue the need for funding from regular budgetary sources with the department, and, in this way, to act as a catalyst for change within the bureaucracy; projects which 'lie within the responsibility of existing institutions', it noted, 'include, for example, child-care centres, women's health centres, women's refuges, family planning clinics, legal aid, distressed housing, rape crisis centres, interpreters for non-English speaking people, and so on'.[34]

Almost 700 grant applications were received, and a significant number of small, one-off projects in local communities were funded. For example, the National Youth Council of Australia was funded to publish and widely distribute a book by young women for young women, *If I Was a Lady and Other Picture Stories: A Mature Girl's Guide to Motherhood, Occupation, Education and Pleasure*. Another grant went to Lilla Watson and Julianne Schwenke to prepare a video tape on Aboriginal Women in Queensland. Another to the South Sydney Women's Centre in Redfern, Sydney, to help establish the women's centre.[35]

All applications supported were to contribute to changing people's attitudes, to the re-thinking of societal assumptions, beliefs, prejudices and opinions about women, their 'proper' roles and their capacities, that is, to our consciousness-raising objective.[36] As Whitlam himself said:

> My Government has not committed itself and will not commit itself to any program which it does not genuinely believe is both desired by the women of Australia and which will be of lasting benefit to them. During International Women's Year we are advancing and extending programs which we had already undertaken in response to the needs of women. But our overriding task and challenge for this year is to strike out at the attitudes which cause these difficulties and give rise to these problems.[37]

Priorities: Reforms and attitudinal change

Sara Dowse, the first head of the Office of the Status of Women, reflecting on the priorities of those times, said:

> The stated aim was to change community attitudes about the place of women in society, and each and every reform adopted was considered in light of how it would help in reaching this objective. A new childcare program was initiated, with a greatly increased allocation, because of its perceived centrality in enabling women to fully participate in society.
>
> … My main contention is that changing community attitudes about women was Reid's foremost consideration and influenced all our actions in the bureaucracy during that period. At the time, I admit, I wasn't entirely attuned to her vision – nor, needless to say, were her many critics within the movement.

I didn't see how important a few million dollars set aside
for International Women's Year could be, compared with
the $75 million, say, spent on childcare. Yet with hindsight
it is easy to see ... how that childcare program could be
undermined in subsequent years whereas the ripple effect
of IWY has been enormous. Likewise with 1975's Women
and Politics Conference, which galvanised women across
the political spectrum to plunge into politics, putting their
hands up for office at every government level. At the time,
however, the media had a field day with both. How can
[one] forget how demeaning the media was to everything
women did in those days?[38]

All these changes had a consciousness-raising dimension. Their
aim was to increase women's confidence and self-respect, which
would enable them to act as morally responsible agents, refusing
to accept abject and dependent lives. Once again, our 'personal'
experiences, be it 'man months', Ms, our sexuality, violence against
women, or women's involvement in politics, had become political.
As Whitlam said at the Women and Politics Conference: 'Women
are insisting more and more that the concerns of the home be
the concerns of politics, that the personal be political. Child care,
family planning, housework, and so on are now becoming issues
for the political arena. To this extent, women are in the process of
trying to re-define and re-describe the political'.[39]

Even before my resignation, in October 1975, it was clear
to Sara and to me that it was not possible, in the long term, to
be a bureaucrat and a feminist visionary. If your desire was to
contribute towards the expansion of a revolutionary consciousness,
you would be continually speaking truth to power. It would be
uncomfortable and would demand such extraordinary skills,
agility and judgment over time as to be incompatible with a career

in the bureaucracy. After the Women and Politics Conference, when the Prime Minister bowed to pressure from some of the men of his party and agreed to move me sideways into the bureaucracy, and so silence me, I resigned.

Were the achievements of lasting benefit?

The continuing life course of the achievements of those years has been uneven and unsteady, but almost everything has survived even if their origin has faded from political memory. Some illustrative figures might help. Commonwealth-supported child-care places increased from zero in 1969 to 246 000 in 1994, despite a decline in the Fraser years. By 2020, more than 1.3 million children regularly attended an approved child-care centre.[40] Sara Dowse considered child care to be the most important thing that was achieved because it signified agreement that 'society is responsible for children, not just women'.[41]

There were achievements in the field of services for women. For example, women's refuges expanded from an initial 11 in 1974 to 190 by 1988: an exponential growth that was funded by both state and federal governments. The refuges became entrenched as an important service for women experiencing domestic and family violence. And women's health centres grew in number from 2 in 1974 to about 65 by the early 2000s.[42] The women's health policy, which covered reproductive and sexual health, violence against women, ageing, mental health, women as unpaid or paid care providers, and the health effects of sex-role stereotyping, was drawn up as a result of the first national conference on Women's Health in a Changing Society.

The problems of women's health were seen to arise from the health system's culture with its sexist perceptions of women, and from the domination of the biomedical approach. The program was scrapped by the Fraser government but was reinstated by the

Hawke government. The violence of the police and of young male university students to women activists in the 1970s, as shown on the archival footage in the documentary on the history of women's liberation in Australia, *Brazen Hussies,* was shocking. Women are still subject to extraordinary levels of violence, with on average one woman losing her life to partner violence every week.

Women benefited immensely from the introduction of no-fault divorce laws, and the establishment of the Family Law Court, with its emphasis on mediated discussion rather than confrontation. The laws against rape were modified; rape in marriage was designated a crime, reversing the common law tradition that, as the property of their husbands, women could be raped by their husbands with impunity. Rape and a male sense of entitlement remain contentious and difficult legal, police and cultural issues, despite decades of activism and legal reform.

Looking forward

Whitlam placed new ideas as well as issues on the national agenda. He gave new meaning to the principles of democratic socialism in its passionate pursuit of the values of equality, democracy, liberty and social cooperation. The attainment of each of these values involved fundamental changes in our social organisation and our way of doing things.[43] Heated debate surrounds Whitlam's overall legacy, and his time in office seemed at times like being on a rollercoaster. However, in relation to policies affecting the lives of Australian women, there is no doubt that his legacy is strong and enduring.

Lasting political change, genuine social reforms, come about when they are based upon principles and ideas. For these ideas to reflect a democratic process, rather than an imposition, they must be communicated, clarified and argued in public. Then, they can contribute to political ideologies and provide moral choices about how to live our lives and to organise our social institutions. Without this, there can be no informed consent of the people.

It is important that we retrieve and rethink our heritage of social reforms, and our vocabulary within which they have been described, both as a political project and as a task for thinking politically in complex ways. As Whitlam said in the 1972 campaign speech:

> All of us as Australians have to insist that we can do so much better as a nation. We ought to be angry, with a deep determined anger, that a country as rich and skilled as ours should be producing so much inequality, so much poverty, so much that is shoddy and sub-standard. We ought to be angry – with an unrelenting anger – that our aborigines have the world's highest infant mortality rate. We ought to be angry at the way our so-called leaders have kept us in the dark – Parliament itself as much as the people as if to hide their own incapacity and ignorance.[44]

And as the *Report of the National Advisory Committee for International Women's Year* says: 'A viable and strong feminism does not whimper for women to be treated as human beings – it makes it impossible for this not to be the case'.[45]

WOMEN AND POLITICAL INFLUENCE: THE WOMEN'S ELECTORAL LOBBY AND EQUAL PAY

IOLA MATHEWS

I was fortunate to know Gough and Margaret Whitlam personally. It all began in the middle of 1971 when I was a young journalist, the education reporter at *The Age* in Melbourne. Sitting at my desk one afternoon, the phone rang and a stranger asked if he could discuss an article I'd written about a new progressive school called ERA, established by the Education Reform Association. His name was Race Mathews.

'I was hoping we could discuss it over dinner,' he said. 'I work for Gough Whitlam in Canberra, but I'll be in Melbourne in a couple of weeks.'

The name Whitlam caught my interest. He was the charismatic Leader of the Opposition, with radical new policies such as a national health scheme, a massive increase in federal funds for schools, free tertiary education and the abolition of conscription for the Vietnam War. The Prime Minister, Billy McMahon, was a figure of fun, and for some of us, Whitlam was the new Messiah.

I covered the receiver and turned to my colleague, Michelle Grattan, at the desk next to me and whispered: 'Do you know a guy called Race Mathews, who works for Whitlam?'

"Yes, he's nice.'

'Is he married?'

'No, he's a widower with children. His wife died about a year ago.'

I agreed to have dinner, and that was the beginning of a long courtship. Race was then Principal Private Secretary to Whitlam, working on speeches and policy development, and also a candidate for the seat of Casey in the federal Parliament. Race worshipped Gough, who was like a father figure, and I loved hearing Race's stories about Gough's rages when he was frustrated, his brilliance and his ever-present wit.

A typical story was after Race's first wife died and he was on a plane with Gough, travelling overseas. Race was writing a letter to his parents, who were looking after the children in Melbourne, and Gough took the letter and wrote on the bottom: 'This is your beloved Son, in whom I am well pleased'. It was typical of his self-parody and fondness for quoting from the Bible. When Race turned 33, Gough joked: 'Comrade, what have you achieved? At 33 Alexander had conquered the world and Jesus Christ had saved it'.

The Women's Electoral Lobby

Six months later, in February 1972, I had another life-changing phone call. It was from Beatrice Faust, a writer, feminist and political campaigner. She'd helped found the Victorian Council for Civil Liberties and was active in abortion law reform. She said *Ms.* magazine in the United States had published a survey of candidates for the White House and their attitudes to women's issues.

'We could do that for the federal election this year,' she said. 'I'm getting together a small group of women to discuss it. Would you like to come?' She mentioned issues like birth control and child care and said we could influence government policy. It sounded great.

The women's movement was spreading throughout the Western world, but I had not yet joined up. I'd been invited earlier to a Women's Lib 'consciousness-raising' group, but was turned off by the anti-male tone. I was young and free, and not interested in the frustrations of women who were angry with their partners for not sharing the domestic tasks and child care. Bea's approach was very different. She mentioned practical tasks and legislative reform, which sounded intriguing.

On Sunday, 27 February, we assembled in Bea's Carlton lounge room. There were ten of us, handpicked for our skills. Sally White and I were journalists with *The Age*, Carmen Lawrence (later Premier of Western Australia) was a psychologist; there were several sociologists and a librarian.

Bea Faust was then 34, a small, rather frail woman with chronic asthma, who sometimes gasped for breath. But she had a ready laugh, an indomitable spirit and a clear view of what was needed.

We drew up a list of issues that could be solved by legislation, including birth control, family planning, child care, equal pay, and equality in work and education. By the end of the meeting we'd agreed to survey all the candidates for the federal election and publish the results. It was very exciting. Overnight I became a feminist, and went on to work for women's rights for the next two decades.

We decided to call our movement the Women's Electoral Lobby (WEL). New members soon joined and groups were set up to research each issue. Helen Glezer, a psychologist, led a team that designed the questionnaire, tested it and oversaw the training of interviewers and the analysis and coding of results. Other groups looked after public relations, finance and the newsletter. General meetings of all WEL members were held regularly. I was on the coordinating committee and the public relations committee.

Bea Faust drove WEL forward in that first year, flinging out ideas at a rapid pace. She understood political lobbying better than most of us. She said WEL was not about her; it was a collective effort. She was right, but some WEL members who were also members of the Women's Liberation Movement criticised her dominant role in WEL. They objected to 'leaders' and 'hierarchies', which they said were the patriarchal way of doing things. So WEL had a flat structure, with no office bearers. Meetings were held with a rotating chair and 'consensus decision-making' rather than resolutions.

Many of the early meetings were taken up with philosophical discussions about our structure, which drove me mad. I just wanted to get on with the job, making things happen. Eventually, some of the Women's Lib members dropped out and the philosophical discussions eased off.

WEL spread quickly to Canberra and Sydney, and by the end of the year, membership was up to several thousand, with branches in all states and as far away as Darwin and Norfolk Island. Groups were formed in each electorate to monitor the candidates. It was the start of life-long friendships. Women who joined WEL said afterwards, 'It changed my life'.

It was a time of social and political change. The long-running conservative government under McMahon was faltering, and Whitlam was gaining popularity. In the months leading up to the federal election, WEL interviewed all candidates willing to participate, and quizzed them at public meetings. Two women conducted each interview; as one MP said, 'they hunt in pairs'. It was the first time a survey of all candidates had been attempted in Australia.

Most of the candidates were ignorant about women's issues, and gaffes were frequent. In the Sydney electorate of Bennelong, veteran politician Sir John Cramer was quoted as saying, 'A woman must be taught that virginity is the most valuable thing she possesses'. The leader of the Country Party, Doug Anthony, answered two questions about birth control and family planning, then refused to answer any more, saying WEL put too much emphasis on sex.[1]

In the middle of the year, Race and I decided to get married, and I got to know his three children, aged 10, 12 and 14. Soon afterwards, a telegram arrived for me at *The Age*. It was from Gough Whitlam and said simply, '*Nihil Obstat.* Delighted'.

A friend, Mary Featherston, invited us to have the wedding in her house, and my mother started organising the catering. She was anxious, however, because my parents and their friends voted Liberal, while ours voted Labor. She envisaged them standing on opposite sides of the room, not talking to each other.

On the night, however, everything turned out well. Halfway through the evening, my mother went up to Gough with her best friend. They were both short and peered up at him. 'Mr Whitlam', my mother said, 'I'd like to introduce my friend Jean Hardy'.

'Well, kiss me, Hardy,' said Gough, quoting Nelson's dying words to his friend Captain Hardy. Gough bent down and kissed her on both cheeks. As they walked away, Jean whispered to my mother, 'Isn't he gorgeous? I am not going to wash my face for a week'.

In Victoria, *The Age* assistant editor Creighton Burns agreed to publish the WEL survey. It appeared on 20 November 1972, in a green, four-page 'Women Voter's Guide'. Two Labor candidates in Victoria got the top mark, a perfect score of 40: David McKenzie in Diamond Valley and Gareth Clayton in Isaacs. The lowest score in the state was Peter Howson, the federal Minister for the Environment, Aborigines and the Arts, with minus 4.

The Prime Minister, Billy McMahon, got a score of 1, while the Leader of the Opposition, Gough Whitlam, got 33. Malcolm Fraser, a future Prime Minister, got 15. In general, Labor candidates did much better than the conservatives, and we spread the word with a poster that said, 'Think WEL before you vote'.

At the federal election in December, Whitlam became Prime Minister, and Race won the seat of Casey, in the outer suburbs where we lived. He was now an MP in the Whitlam government, and Gough and Margaret came to the electorate several times over the next few years, to help Race with his campaigns.

Many WEL members went on to be active in public life. At the federal level they included Elizabeth Reid, Women's Adviser to Prime Minister Whitlam; Sara Dowse, head of the Women's Affairs branch in the Department of the Prime Minister and Cabinet; Marie Coleman, head of the Social Welfare Commission and later the Office of Child Care; Gail Radford (formerly Wilenski), Director of the Equal Employment Opportunity Section in the Commonwealth Public Service; Justice Mary Gaudron; and Senator Susan Ryan. Winsome McCaughey led the community child-care movement, and at the state level there were many WEL women in prominent positions, as well as in local government.

WEL provided an instant political education for all its members through the survey of candidates, its general meetings or the many action groups. Publicity about WEL and the survey spread the word more generally.

Whitlam's reforms for women

By December 1972, the women's movement was in full swing, and Helen Reddy's song 'I Am Woman' was in the top 100. As soon as Whitlam became Prime Minister, he started implementing WEL's reforms for women. In his first week of office he reopened the federal Equal Pay case, removed the tax on contraceptives and announced funding for birth control programs.

Over the next three years the Whitlam government acted on practically every reform in the WEL questionnaire. The reforms for women were numerous, and nearly all had their origin in the

45 questions in the WEL survey, even the establishment of the Royal Commission on Human Relationships.[2] Whitlam ratified several International Labour Organization and United Nations conventions on the rights of women. For the first time, women were appointed to commissions, boards and delegations and as judges, arbitrators and diplomats. In higher education, the government abolished fees, introduced mature-age entry and the Tertiary Education Assistance Scheme (TEAS), which gave many mature-aged women the opportunity to get a degree for the first time.

Federal funds were allocated for family planning, sex education and child care. Women's services were funded, such as women's health centres, women's refuges, rape counselling centres, neighbourhood learning centres, play groups and the Working Women's Centre.

The Whitlam government introduced no-fault divorce and the Family Court. It increased pensions for widows and introduced the Supporting Mother's Benefit. In 1975 the government celebrated International Women's Year with grants for women's projects and a delegation to the IWY conference in Mexico City.

Why did Whitlam act on so many areas of interest for women? From the time he was elected to Parliament in 1953, he was passionately committed to human rights, which included women's rights. When elected Deputy Leader of the Opposition in 1960, he focused on new issues, including the political and economic participation of women, and equal pay.[3] By 1972, the women's movement was in full swing, and he recognised women's rights as a major political issue.

His wife Margaret was a great role model and instinctive feminist, whom he described later as 'my best appointment'.[4] In addition, he had advisers whose wives were active in WEL (Race Mathews in 1972 and Peter Wilenski in 1972–75). After April 1973, Elizabeth Reid was pivotal in focusing Whitlam on women's issues, in consultation with WEL and other women's groups, and women throughout the country.

From 1973 on, state governments picked up the lead of the Whitlam government, and over the next two decades, many areas of discrimination were abolished.

Equal pay

One of the key reforms of the Whitlam government was for equal pay. The WEL questionnaire included the following:

Q 35. Do you support the principle of equal pay for work of equal value?

Q. 36. Do you support the minimum wage for men to be extended to women?

Q. 37 Do you support an investigation in the value of female-dominated jobs?

These were carefully worded questions based on the wage-fixing system, which included national cases in the Conciliation and Arbitration Commission. In 1969 the Australian Council of Trade Unions (ACTU) had won a case for 'equal pay for equal work', but only 18 per cent of women workers had benefited from it, because most women were not doing the same work as men. In 1971 the ACTU followed up with a case for 'equal pay for work of equal value', but the McMahon government opposed it and the case stalled. WEL wanted the new government to support the case.

Whitlam was elected on 2 December, and two days later he authorised the reopening of the case and gave Mary Gaudron the brief to appear for the government. On 15 December the Commission granted equal pay for work of equal value, which led to a 30 per cent increase in women's wages. Whitlam later said this was his government's 'most striking and historically significant' reform for women.[5]

In 1973 the Whitlam government supported the ACTU's case to give women the same minimum wage as males. The following year, the Commission dropped the concept of 'family support' as part of the wage system. The ACTU was helped by an intervention from Edna Ryan for WEL, showing the exact number of women supporting a family. The minimum wage was then extended to some 300 000 women.

In the Commonwealth Public Service, the Whitlam government introduced three months' paid maternity leave and one week paternity leave, opened all jobs to both sexes and extended flexible working hours.

The legacy on equal pay

In 1975 the Whitlam government was dismissed, but its support for equal pay was taken up and expanded by future Labor governments.

Under the Hawke government (1983–91), Senator Susan Ryan, as the Minister Assisting the Prime Minister on the Status of Women, was responsible for the *Sex Discrimination Act 1984* and the *Affirmative Action Act 1986,* both of which helped to remove discrimination in the workplace and get women into better paid positions.

I was fortunate to go to the ACTU in 1984 to run the 'Action Program for Women Workers', working with key people in the Hawke government like Susan Ryan and Anne Summers, head of the Office of the Status of Women.

Under the 'Accord' between the government and the ACTU, during this time we won national cases to increase nurses' wages and conditions, to give outworkers in the clothing industry the same wages and conditions as factory workers, to implement equal pay across a range of female industries through 'award restructuring', and to extend parental leave provisions.

The Keating government (1991–96) passed legislation in 1992 to give superannuation to all employees, male and female. In 1993 it passed legislation that included the principle of 'equal pay for equal remuneration', which was an advance on 'equal pay for work of equal value', because 'remuneration' meant not just the award rate, but payments above the award.

Under the Gillard government (2010–13), there was a successful equal pay case for Social and Community Services workers (the SACS case) in 2012. A crucial element of the case was the support of the government, which pledged nearly $3 billion towards the pay increase. That's because the federal and state governments fund the non-government organisations that employ community service workers. The Rudd government introduced paid parental leave in 2010 and the Gillard government introduced paid partner leave in 2012.

Under Coalition governments, there has been little support for national equal pay cases, and only one has been successful. That was the eight-year case for degree-qualified early childhood teachers, run by the Independent Education Union in the Fair Work Commission. The decision, in April 2021, rejected the case for an Equal Remuneration Order, but granted substantial pay increases based on work value grounds.

What more needs to be done on equal pay?

I have discussed the long and ongoing battle for equal pay in my book *Winning for Women: A Personal Story* (2019). In 1985 the gender pay gap was nearly 19 per cent, and today it's 14.2 per cent, about $260 a week. That's progress, but it has fluctuated up and down for the past two decades. The gap is much wider in high-paid and senior jobs, and women are less likely to get over-award pay, bonuses and performance pay.

The gender pay gap measures only full-time work. The gap in *total* earnings is 32 per cent, because women are more likely to work part time and do less overtime, because of family responsibilities. The gap in superannuation is also big; women retire with a superannuation balance about two-thirds of men's. That's because women earn less, are more likely to work part time and have periods out of the workforce. We need to pay superannuation for employees on parental leave, and remove the tax breaks for high-income earners, who are mostly men.

We need a wide-ranging, national strategy to close the gender pay gap, and to strengthen the Fair Work Commission's ability to run pay equity reviews of low-paid female work such as child care, aged care and disability. Making the Workplace Gender Equality Agency publicly report the gender wage gaps in individual companies is another requirement. So is encouraging young women into non-traditional jobs. We need cheaper child care and improvements to paid parental leave and flexible work arrangements, for men as well as women. All these strategies have been widely discussed, but we need government commitment and funding.

Some lessons for young activists today

I was incredibly lucky to have been part of a movement which one writer has described as 'the only successful revolution of the twentieth century'. I was also fortunate to have known Gough and Margaret Whitlam and to live through the turbulent, exciting and transformative three years of the Whitlam govement and, later on, to work with the ACTU and the Hawke–Keating governments.

Looking back on 50 years since I joined the women's

movement, there are some lessons I can pass on to young women today.

First – you need collective action. You can achieve some reforms alone, but a great deal more with collective action. When I joined WEL, women who had been chafing against discrimination found they could achieve much more by working through Women's Lib or WEL. Later, when I worked for the ACTU, I was no longer an individual voice, but was able to represent women workers at the national level, and occasionally at the international level. So I urge you to get involved in a group such as your union, a progressive political party, or an organisation fighting for social change.

Second – get the plan right before you start action. In WEL, it was essential to get the questionnaire right, so it was very specific and tied to government action. At the ACTU, the 'Action Program for Women Workers' had been carefully worked out so that each section could be implemented by the ACTU working with the new Labor government. So take time to work out the plan and then get broad support for it.

That's what Gough did. With his colleagues and staff, he spent years developing his policies, arguing for them and explaining them to the public. Medicare is a good example. Politicians are reluctant to do that nowadays, in case their policies are attacked. But it's the right way to go.

Third – do your research and talk to the experts. A good starting point on women's issues is the National Foundation for Australian Women, which publishes a 'gender lens' on the budget each year.

Fourth – follow your passions. When I found myself out of work in the early 1980s, I took on voluntary work in the area I was passionate about, reforms for women at work. In that way I met new people and developed new skills and knowledge, and that eventually led to job offers.

Finally – never give up. Some things can be achieved quickly and some things take a long time. When I joined WEL, we campaigned to get contraceptives advertised, but the influence of the churches made it impossible. Years later, with the AIDS epidemic, everything suddenly changed. Progress comes in stages, not all at once.

Take your inspiration from the Australian coat of arms. It features the kangaroo and the emu, which were chosen to symbolise a nation moving forward, based on the fact that neither animal can move backwards. So keep moving forward!

SISTERHOOD
BIFF WARD

The party

Why me? I thought when asked to write about women and the Whitlam government. This is the domain of those who were directly involved and the feminist academics who have researched and theorised about it since. I am none of those things.[1] I was always a Movement junkie, my focus on grass roots awareness-raising, in creating new feminists, on increasing our numbers.

But in terms of the Whitlam government, I did remember a particular party. I could write about that, I thought. Maybe it would lead to other memories.

It was early 1973, and the new Prime Minister, Gough Whitlam, had decided to create a special position: a Women's Adviser, reporting directly to him. A week of interviews and activities was set aside for the selection process, part of which was a Saturday night party held at the home of a member of the Prime Minister's staff in the Canberra suburb of Hughes. It was an ordinary 1970s three-bedroom house in which the living room and dining room were one L-shaped space with a door into the kitchen, which had a second door leading to the entrance hallway. In other words, it was a circuit plan which I remember from my own home at that time where the children might start a game of chasing, round and round, with squeals and yells and laughter.

Maybe that party was the last night, a moment to relax after the formalities of the week. All the 18 short-listed applicants were at the party, as were many Labor parliamentary luminaries, including Gough himself. I was not an applicant but had been urged to come to the party by someone who was, as had a few other Canberra Women's Liberation women.

At one level it was an ordinary party for those times: men in safari suits, women in attire that ranged from floaty Laura Ashley dresses through to jeans and T-shirts, quite a lot of drinking, loud loud talk and a high-energy group in the kitchen where some sat on the sink or benchtops. But there was a frisson of difference that night, one I struggle to put into words even after these many years.

The women mostly knew each other – from Women's Liberation–based conferences with their associated meals and parties and dances, from friendships that had developed over the three previous years, from projects we'd considered or worked on together. We were a tribe, and although we had no secret handshakes, no special looks, there were invisible threads connecting us as we moved among these men, a sure and certain knowledge that we and our new agenda were the reason we were all there and that we had these men ever so slightly on edge. They were newly in government (after 23 years in opposition) and just beginning to get used to being the stars of the show wherever they went. That night, they were sidelined by the short-listed women.

Years later, when I was myself a femocrat for four years (the founding Equal Opportunity Officer at the University Of South Australia, 1984–88), I wrote a poem which included the lines:

We've been studying them all our lives
They've only just noticed we exist
And they don't know where we come from

The party felt like one of those moments when the patriarchy noticed us – a question mark in invisible ink hovered over proceedings. As I left the party, I saw Elizabeth Reid in deep conversation with two or three of the large men in suits, as she had been all evening. She had done her homework thoroughly, I later discovered, and got her head around many arcane government protocols, including how policy was developed into legislation, so she was no doubt engaging in conversations which were beyond the realm of most of us at that time.

I reference this party because, as my only experience of that week-long selection, it has become a benchmark for me. There was a sheen of unreality to the whole event: the slight awe of the men in the presence of our coven-like togetherness, the slight diminution in the men's power that night and a tremulous shiver in the air. What did the change mean? Where would it lead?

And what had produced this moment?

Starting in 1969–70 in Sydney, Women's Liberation had established 'women's houses' around the country, one in nearly every major city. The core feature was always a meeting room with other spaces designated for office, printing (one of the old gestetners always present), screen printing and artwork, and a rudimentary kitchen. Some 'women's centres', as they tended to be called, had a bedroom with a resident member who doubled as de facto caretaker.

The activities in these houses formed the intellectual and cultural driving force that flowed into the zeitgeist of possible programs being picked up by the new government, particularly by the office of the Prime Minister. While there are several claimants to being the catalyst that suggested the position of Women's Adviser, I incline to the nexus of Peter Wilenski, Principal Private Secretary to the PM, with his partner, Gail Radford, who was a member both of Canberra Women's Liberation and of WEL, as being the source of the idea.

The combination of Women's Liberation, with its well-spring of ideas harvested from sharing the lived experience of women, and WEL, the river of female outrage that swelled to push the issues into politicians' faces, meant we spread like an unexpected flood into public consciousness. While Women's Liberation and WEL still existed as separate entities, it was around this time that we became the women's movement.

None of us had planned or even pictured a development such as that of Women's Adviser. It was, after all, the first such position in the world. Hundreds of applications were received, some say 362 women and some 40 men, some say more. Virtually all the short-listed candidates were members of Women's Liberation and/or WEL. Naturally this was the case because who else had knowledge of these 'new' issues and insights?

The new doorway

In the newspaper *MeJane,* created and edited by the Sydney Women's Liberation group at Glebe, the editors quite rightly interrogated the creation of the position and how it might relate to the women's movement. They were concerned about how one woman could be seen to represent all women: a pertinent question. The Canberra group, on the other hand, meeting in one of the suburbs closest to Parliament House, didn't, as I recall, see the position as an issue requiring discussion. Most of us hardly thought about it at all, except for a few, particularly Helen Shepherd, who walked into Elizabeth's office with offers of help. While this assistance was eagerly taken up at first, it fell away when Elizabeth undertook her extensive travel program to hear from women all over the country.

In general, our Canberra position was that Elizabeth was one of us, and she'd moved into this unimaginable new job. We simply trusted, we knew, that she would be doing whatever she could for the betterment of all women.

In recent years, Elizabeth has written that the continuing existence of Women's Liberation was crucial to her ability to operate as Women's Adviser to the Prime Minister. She saw it as the incubator of the ideas powering the movement of women for change. The Canberra group, geographically closest to her, had no conscious notion of this, though with hindsight it is obvious.

Building on this observation of hers, some academics appear to assume that there was a recognisable bifurcation that needed negotiating and that we made decisions about how we and her office might interact. Nothing could be further from the truth. We were used to women moving on. In 1972–73 some of our members had joined WEL, some had begun lobbying in universities to develop Women's Studies courses and others were getting active around various 'family planning' systems, which were the gateway to our solutions about women having control of their own bodies. Others were at the start of the long journey to bring gender awareness into schools. During Elizabeth's tenure, Sara Dowse, a founding member of our group, became head of the Women's Affairs Section in the Department of the Prime Minister and Cabinet, charged with undertaking implementation of the policies that had resulted from Elizabeth's consultations, and to assist with her mail, which was, in volume, second only to the PM's. Other leading feminists from Women's Liberation and WEL took jobs in Elizabeth's and Sara's offices. Later, in 1975, Susan Ryan entered Parliament as an ALP Senator for the ACT. Members leaving our group was seen as us growing, expanding, finding niches from which to continue our work.

As these women entered this new arena, the rest of us went on doing what we'd been doing before – attending our weekly meeting, discussing an endless array of topics and gasping in outrage at the multitudinous examples of sexism we were uncovering. In that we continued as before, it's true that we were maintaining the powerhouse of ideas and demands that had generated the position in the first place. On that basis, I completely understand Elizabeth's appreciation that we were there, continuing to grow the movement and develop analyses of issues such as rape and domestic violence. I can see now that this was crucial to the efficacy of her job, to her ability to reference 'the women's movement'.

As for our sisters 'inside' the power structure, we knew they were part of us, that they had the same goal: an end to sexism, a women's revolution.

Women's Liberation principles within and without

In taking their Women's Liberation consciousness into these jobs, these women mostly took with them Women's Liberation principles of operation. I'll list these in the order they make sense to me: in fact, they evolved from our ways of working and were identified over time, a kind of naming praxis.[2]

The first of these was 'consciousness-raising', which meant that as we talked and shared our lived experiences, patterns and commonalities of systemic sexism became apparent to us. We called this consciousness-raising and used it to rename and reframe our lived experiences as issues that were common for many or most women and that needed to be addressed by the whole society.

This led to the insight that 'the personal is political', the discovery that our lives are positioned within structures of power. For example, a woman having to procure a 'backyard' abortion is a political issue, as is a woman being raped and unable to get redress through the justice system, as is unequal pay, and so on.

Thirdly, 'direct action' was the natural response to the injustices we were uncovering. For example, demonstrating at the 1971 ACTU Congress to demand equal pay, writing a booklet about safe sex that was given out at the gates of several high schools, setting up a refuge, and establishing WEL.

Fourthly, 'sisterhood is powerful' drew all these together in expressing our sense of solidarity and trust in women's voices that underpinned our connections with each other and, potentially, with all women.

I will add a fifth, 'no stars', which came out of the experiences many of us had had on the (male) left, of listening to the men while we made the coffee and noticed how they jockeyed for 'the right line' or 'the winning argument' and made enemies of those who were actually closest to them on the political spectrum. We did not want to replicate such ludicrous practices. In fact, we were trying to *'be the revolution we wanted to see'*. The means of getting there was as important as the ends.

Elizabeth never made herself a star. In 2019, the *Canberra Times* published an article with the headline, 'This Canberra Woman Is the Feminist Hero You've Never Heard Of'. A nice footnote to her lifelong adherence to Women's Liberation principles.

We also held to the maxim: 'no woman is liberated until all are liberated', which grew out of our perception that sexism (a term coined in those years of the early '70s) affected all women everywhere even if they were not aware of it. We envisaged dismantling the infrastructure that made it possible to oppress and discriminate against a single woman: we were truly aiming for a revolution.

Around that time and in the years following, people would ask, 'Aren't you liberated yet?', as though it was a personal title you could claim. In the face of such crassness, it was well-nigh impossible to explain how far there was to go, how big our vision was.

Elizabeth's approach within

Elizabeth applied these Women's Liberation principles in the job, as far as she was able. Her first focus was to travel all over Australia, listening to groups of women in as many different settings as she could possibly manage. She tells me she was scrupulous about asking open questions, about trying not to influence the outcomes. (As a lover of open questions myself, my toes curl in delight.) This process of consulting also served as a means of women coming together in groups to talk about things that had never been aired before and, in that process, finding common ground. It was, in fact, a mass form of consciousness-raising, a spectacular application of our principles.

Another focus was International Women's Year in 1975 and what this could mean for Australia. In the year before, an International Women's Year secretariat had been set up in the Department of the Special Minister of State to administer funding for one-off projects that were designed to improve women's and girls' lives. Elizabeth knew well that most applications would come from the grassroots, essentially from the projects that the women from Women's Liberation or WEL were involved in. Some groups seemed to apply without understanding that the National Advisory Council for International Women's Year, which was assessing the applications, was mandated to justify the expenditure of funds. (If proposals lay within the remit of existing government entities and needed ongoing funding, they were not eligible for a one-off International Women's Year grant.)

It was a moment of grassroots passion meeting The System, and it raised tensions on both sides. This period of confrontation led to some unfair attacks on Elizabeth personally.

It is interesting to reflect that when a Canberra group applied for funds to open a refuge, they knew how to apply: they interviewed people, gathered statistics, made a case and were granted the monies forthwith. In hindsight, some of us have wondered if simply living in Canberra where a spouse, neighbour, friend or acquaintance was a public servant, had conferred on us a knowledge of government and how it operates at a visceral level, almost by osmosis.[3]

The International Women's Year secretariat was also charged with organising the Women and Politics Conference with several international speakers, as the culmination of the year. Historically, this turned out to be Elizabeth's undoing, although I prefer to see it as her crowning achievement. When she brought together nearly a thousand diverse Australian women in Canberra for several days with some incendiary speakers and audience contributions, of course there were individuals and interest groups who engaged in wild bursts of self-expression which, in the end, brought her down. Elizabeth's chapter in this book elegantly traces the philosophical tensions between her Women's Liberation politics with its focus on wanting *all* women's voices to be heard and the political needs of the government to maintain face and look respectable for 'the sensible middle', as democratic governments must always do.

But to start with, so far removed was I from what Elizabeth and her team were doing, that I perceived the Women and Politics Conference as having nothing to do with me/us. By pure chance, I bumped into Elizabeth in the street and she said she hoped I was coming. When I demurred, she spoke forcefully to the effect that the conference was for all women and she really wanted Women's Liberation to be there.

'Give a paper,' she said, 'on anything you like'.

I drilled down, looking for what I thought we as a movement might need at that juncture. I decided it was a review (though I didn't have that language back then), a stop-and-reflect session for active Women's Liberation members. I envisaged consideration of the political pros and cons of what we were doing and questions such as 'What now?' and 'Where to from here?' I expected about 10 or 12 to show up.

My title was read in a different light from the one I intended. Two hundred women came and packed out a large lecture theatre at the ANU. They literally wanted to know Why Women's Liberation? What was it about? The intense inward-focusing session

I had planned zapped out the window and the workshop became a mass consciousness-raising event instead. Revisiting my 'paper' now, I see a set of columns entitled Theory, Practice and Reality, laced with words such as structurelessness, tokenism, existentialist and egalitarian, and am both amazed and bamboozled. Women criticised my language for not including all women, which was absolutely true. I hadn't even thought of the issue because I had envisaged a chat with seasoned activists. However, with the help of some Canberra sisters, we fielded the questions and confusion as best we could. Reading the transcript now, I notice the intensity of the discussion about women having the confidence to speak in public, about women having a voice (the eternal cry of the marginalised). Throughout that hour or two, I could feel the familiar yin and yang of resistance and conversion that occurred among groups of women new to Women's Liberation in those days swirling through the room.

Gail Radford also gave a paper, 'Reform and Revolution'. It was a big issue at the time, with revolution seen as the goal of Women's Liberation (pretty accurate), and reform, getting things done, being seen as the remit of WEL (pretty accurate also). In a delicious dance in her paper, Gail claims both: reform as a strategy for furthering the revolution. Nowadays, this double helix is obvious to all. At the Whitlam and Women Conference in 2019, that was the main takeaway for me: the historic collapsing together of Women's Liberation and WEL, like two sisters agreeing in old age that they were always headed in the same direction, but just chose to take different paths.

I had assumed that there was no record of those papers, only to find that Elizabeth had insisted on every session being recorded. A brilliant decision, because many of the discussion sections among these papers constitute one of the few records of how free-ranging and exploratory, how personal and political, our discussions could be.

Generally, history resides in documents: records on paper, words or diagrams or photos, of what is purported to have happened. While Women's Liberation started creating documents from a completely blank slate in 1969–70, principally local newsletters and the Sydney-based newspaper, *MeJane*, there were only sporadic effort to keep records of our meetings. A handful of individuals, like Julia Ryan in Canberra Women's Liberation, kept a record of our meetings in a special journal, with an eye to a future history. Underneath whatever documents do remain was a heaving ocean of words, emotions, conversations, epiphanies, insights, theories, depth, wildness and action that coloured and energised the second wave of the feminist revolution. Generally speaking, these conversations were not recorded at the time.

The Australian National Library's Women's Liberation Oral History collection captures some of this turbulent exhilaration. The 2020 film, *Brazen Hussies*, not only does this as well, but the director, Catherine Dwyer, also shapes the material into a coherent narrative – a huge achievement.

As a creative writer, I'm interested in this endeavour to capture the essence of change, the ambience of transformation, the ineffable twists and slides in progress. While movement demands and achievements are markers, they leave out all those reaching, swooping, cascading, soaring conversations that gave birth to them.

Herstory as history

The refuges and rape crisis centres came out of consciousness-raising conversations. The need for places to go that were safe. They were seen as necessary to help women *now,* the day they needed it. It became known as the 'women's services' arena and it attracted workers mostly from Women's Liberation, some from WEL and a slew of women who wanted 'to help' and became feminists in the process. Some argued that refuges were bandaid solutions, that we needed policy and cultural change to eradicate the problems.

At the same time, the Women's Adviser position and all that it spawned in the bureaucracy became another major area of feminist endeavour so that Women's Liberation and WEL women found themselves working in various bureaucracies. In later years, these streams of feminists working for change overlapped when refuge workers found themselves lobbying feminist bureaucrats for funding and when those same bureaucrats, in even later years, consulted feminist academics who supported the cause of the refuges.

The Whitlam years helped the women's movement to create a flurry of activities, both within and without The System, that formed the bedrock of the feminist platform and launching-ground from that day to this. Part of that activity flowed from that original Women's Adviser position and the ways in which Elizabeth used it.

Looking backwards and forwards

These reminiscences have raised a question for me – about sister-hood. The film *Strong Female Lead*, concerning Julia Gilliard's term as Prime Minister, and retired politician Kate Ellis' book, *Sex, Lies and Question Time*, and writing this chapter, have made me reflect on the issue of support for women in jobs of great import.

The film and the book are startling in their revelations. Kate herself and other Labor women in Parliament with Julia wish now they had supported her better, wish they had spoken out when she was traduced and humiliated, much of it in highly sexualised ways. One of the most egregious and repulsive was the Liberal National Party fundraiser menu, which served up Julia Gillard quail.[4]

It was 'labelled tacky and scatological' by a leading Labor man when it was actually far far more than that. It was an excrescence of deeply seated misogyny (literally, *hatred* of women) and it's completely unimaginable in reverse.

After reading Kate Ellis' memoir, I am left wondering if there is a parallel between Julia's female colleagues and our own response to Elizabeth's embattlement, especially by the media. Why did those Labor women not speak out in support of Julia? And why weren't half a dozen of us with Elizabeth on her last day, as she walked across the forecourt of Parliament House with the press following her like jackals? (A scene I only remembered when I saw the film *Brazen Hussies* for the first time.) A phalanx of sisters? Why hadn't we been an ongoing sounding-board during her tenure, a personal cheer squad? An 'outside force' consciously and actively supporting those 'inside' the palace of power?

My only answer to this question is sisterhood, how important it is. When we ourselves are fearful of power, we leave these women out in front alone. And, historically, don't they cop it?! Sisterhood is about *supporting a woman as a woman*, and can be done even when we disagree with her politics or actions.

It is noteworthy that the same old issues of bodily integrity – domestic violence, coercive control and sexual predation – that spurred so much of 1970s feminism, are still the touchstones for the landslide of fury among women right now.

Today, sexism in all its complexities is understood as never before. I am awed by how younger women have broadened and deepened the language and insights we bequeathed them. I am awed by their ability to conceptualise and organise. In their challenge to be truly inclusive (we failed), I offer them the Women's Liberation principles and picture them cleaving to the notion of sisterhood. It is our secret handshake and our strength.

We need all the strength we can muster because the goal is still revolutionary – to end sexism. US feminist theorist Susan

Griffin wrote decades ago, 'There is a world without rape [and violence in all its forms] because that world is in our minds'. We can see it; it empowers us. A new strategy for some of the young women heading today's revolutionary surge is refusing to play nice, giving a new face to this relationship with male power – and don't we cheer them on!

Standing up for and with each other is called sisterhood, and it's very powerful.

THE PERSONAL IS POLITICAL
PAT EATOCK AND CATHY EATOCK

The women's movement in the early 1970s aligned with my mother Pat's growing political activism against the appalling conditions in Aboriginal communities and had reflected her personal experiences back at her within a broader feminist analysis. Pat's introduction to the Canberra women's movement was a revelation of feminist consciousness, which she recalled as the 'the most fantastic, stimulating period of my life'.[1] It gave voice to her frustrations as a self-described suburban housewife, where she had five children in quick succession, the eldest seven years old in 1964 and the youngest, Ronald, seriously mentally disabled due to a staph infection as a newborn. In 1971 Pat fell pregnant with her sixth child. By now seven years old, Ronald could not distinguish crying from laughter, and with an unusual physical strength for his age, he had previously hit his siblings with an iron bar for a reaction. Both Pat and her husband shared their concern that he may inadvertently harm a baby. But with abortions illegal at that time, it was a panel of men that determined Pat didn't qualify for a legal termination, available to mothers where their physical or mental health was threatened, but rather had recommended she put the expected baby up for adoption. Forced to choose between children, it was a 'Sophie's Choice' decision that devastated Pat and led to the institutionalisation of young Ronald and severed what was left of a strained marriage.

Having made forays into the Aboriginal movement in Sydney, Pat had travelled to the Canberra Aboriginal Embassy in early 1972 to assess the support required from Sydney. During the trip, Pat and Bobbi Sykes, who was to become a prominent member of the Aboriginal Embassy, were invited to address the Canberra Women's Liberation Movement on land rights and the concerns of Aboriginal women at the newly established Women's House at Bremer Street, Griffith. It was following this presentation that Pat arrived back in Canberra with the baby and a suitcase at Bremer Street, where Pat's contributions to the consciousness-raising sessions was drawn from her lived experience. The need for abortion reform, women's refuges, the lack of a welfare payment for deserting mothers, discussions on the entrenched oppression and narrowly defined role of women, exposed the middle-class theory of the Canberra feminist movement to the actuality of a working-class woman leaving a marriage without resources. While Pat was energised by the atmosphere of sisterhood, consciousness-raising and feminist political debates, those present heard firsthand of the challenges, surrounded by bags of nappies. She later claimed that her and the baby's constant presence had contributed 'the most impetus for the establish-ment of the women's refuges in Canberra'.[2]

Pat's involvement with the Canberra women's movement melded with her experiences of direct action through the 1972 Aboriginal Embassy. The Aboriginal Embassy had been established in response to Prime Minister McMahon's rejection of land rights in his announcement of 50-year leases where Aboriginal people could prove an economic benefit, which had followed a determination against Yolngu land rights in the *Milirrpum v Nabalco Pty Ltd* (1971) case against a proposed bauxite mine. This also followed the raising of land rights as a core Aboriginal issue with the Gurindji Walk Off at Wave Hill Station, which had remained unresolved since 1966.[3] Pat had joined the Embassy following her participation at the Federal Council for the Advancement of Aborigines and Torres Strait Islanders Conference in Alice Springs, where after a session on land rights, Pat had sought direction on what to inform those on the east coast. She was given the Arrernte term Ningla-A-Na, which, as explained to Pat by the Elders, meant, 'we are hungry for our land, as a baby is hungry for the milk of its mother's breast'.[4] It was subsequently taken up as the anthem for the land rights movement, in its abbreviated form, 'we are hungry for our land'.

However, the Embassy also protested broader Aboriginal issues. The Minister for Aboriginal Affairs, Peter Howson, and the Australian government recognised that the term 'Embassy' also implied recognition of a sovereign Aboriginal people.[5] On 5 February Aboriginal activist and journalist John Newfong distributed a Five-Point Plan, which called for self-governance through a Northern Territory Parliament, land and mining rights in the Northern Territory, land rights over Aboriginal reserves and settlements, the protection of sacred sites, designated land in capital cities and compensation for lands not returnable, and an annual percentage of the gross national income.[6] Gough Whitlam, as Leader of the Opposition, having visited the Embassy on 8 February 1972, confirmed a commitment to support land rights and 'the protection of all those areas of spiritual significance to the original inhabitants of this country'.[7] The public support of the Embassy by Whitlam and other Labor Party members likely contributed, in part, to the subsequent election victory of the Labor government.

Pat became one of the Embassy's core group that withstood the 'storm trooper' force used to dismantle the canvas structure. It was Pat who, on 20 July, had forewarned the Embassy participants and student supporters that the police were about to move on them. Having secured an office assistant position within Aboriginal Affairs, Pat had been transferred to the less contro-versial Government Printing Office, after an article she had written on the forced relocation of the Wallaga Lake Aboriginal Mission had surfaced. Though ostensibly a less controversial location, it was there she overheard that the police were waiting on the printing of the amended Section 12 of the Trespass on Commonwealth Lands Ordinance, which would make camping illegal and allow the police to move on the Embassy. Despite the possibility of charges and a potential jail sentence, Pat feigned being sick to leave work and phone through messages to those at the Embassy and to rally students at the ANU to fortify their lines. The warning increased the Embassy numbers from five or six to a core group of around 30, which swelled to 70 or so with the arrival of students.[8]

The success of the Aboriginal Embassy relied on the unity of mob from across the continent, with women a key part of its core group, coming together to defend the Embassy and assert Aboriginal rights to land and sovereignty. They were met by a 'paramilitary force' of 150 police who barged through the interlinked arms defending the fragile canvas frame.[9] As the tent was moved away, the Embassy sign was retrieved and waved jubilantly overhead, confirming though the tent may go, Aboriginal sovereignty could not be removed. The violent images of police beating their way through the protesters sent shock waves through the Australian community and reverberated globally.[10] Pat recalled how they had been met by a 'gestapo squad' of hundreds of police, whose brutality in the ensuing melee resulted in nine protesters requiring medical treatment, including a cracked rib, eight arrested, and five police requiring treatment for bites and abrasions.[11]

An ACT Supreme Court injunction was taken out on 21 July by Pat, and other Embassy members, Ambrose Golden-Brown, Billy Harrison and Allan Sharpley, which challenged the ordinance.[12] By 23 July, around 200 protesters re-erected the tent and were met with a further escalation of violence by 360 police marching in tight formation.[13] The protesters again linked arms around the Embassy, with chants of 'Land rights now'. The unity of collaborative action, the ferocity of the police and the realisation, so eloquently expressed in Pat defiantly holding the

Aboriginal Embassy sign aloft as the tent was dismantled, that police could beat them and forcibly remove the tent but they could never suppress Aboriginal sovereignty and their just claims. Justice Fox, on 25 July, found Section 12, having been hastily compiled, was an 'unsatisfactory piece of legislation'.[14] Pat and others attempted to negotiate a formal alternative site for the Embassy with diplomatic status; however, the letters sent by Pat to Prime Minister McMahon, seeking to avoid further violence and potentially deaths, were ignored.[15]

By Sunday, 29 July, an estimated 2000 participants and supporters marched from the Australian National University to Parliament House, where the tent was re-established, surrounded by three separate rows of protesters with arms interlinked, with more defenders jammed between each row.[16] By late afternoon, in a bid to avoid violence, the protesters agreed to allow the tent to be pulled down, allowing only a few officers through. As the canvas was removed it exposed Pat and several protesters sitting with their arms outstretched, holding their hands high, making the peace sign.[17] On 12 September the government's appeal of the court finding again found that the Ordinance had 'not been notified in accordance with the provisions of the act'.[18] When the government attempted to amend the Ordinance in Parliament to finally give it legal force, a former Liberal minister, Jim Killen, crossed the floor to vote with the Labor Opposition to prevent the re-gazettal of the Ordinance.[19] It was an omen of the upcoming election.

For Pat, the federal election of 2 December 1972 provided a further opportunity to promote Aboriginal concerns; her proposal for a Black Power member to stand for Parliament was directed back to her, for her to stand. She stood for the ACT seat, Canberra being the heart of the Australian government, and where the strong Labor following of the sitting member, shadow minister Kep Enderby, would not threaten the expected outcome of the election: a change of government.[20] Though Pat sought the protest vote, she rejected the single-issue mantra, adopting the issue of Aboriginal rights against racial oppression, seeking land rights, addressing the appalling infant mortality rate, unemployment, the need for housing and seeking dedicated seats in Parliament.[21] However, she also actively campaigned on women's rights, repealing abortion laws, equal opportunity for women in employment and education, political representation, family planning and child care. These issues, in Pat's view, could not be ignored.[22] Liz Reid came on as Pat's campaign manager, supported by Eileen Hailey, an active member of the Canberra women's movement, and others. With Pat, the baby and Liz sharing Liz's house, they developed a close friendship, grounded on mutual feminist perspectives.[23] But Pat's standing for election strained allegiances among the Labor Party members of the feminist movement.

Pat was pleased to be the only candidate to score 100 per cent in the emerging Women's Electoral Lobby's survey of election candidates, which stimulated media interest.[24] However, a second Labor break-away candidate stood as an independent against abortion with backing from the recently formed anti-abortion group the Right to Life Association, which effectively undermined the protest vote as Labor voters grew concerned at the potential split of the Labor vote.[25] The reality of limited funds meant that how-to-vote slips were carefully reused, and though the campaign resulted in an overall vote of less than 2.5 per cent, Pat was informed she had received a large number of second preferences.[26] Despite the comparatively low number of votes, the campaign had successfully raised the critical issues of women's and Aboriginal rights, both of which were significantly progressed by the incoming Labor government. While seeking 'a big stick' with which to pressure the government, Pat believed 'a small and stinging twig' had been sufficient.[27]

The Whitlam government established the new Department of Aboriginal Affairs, doubled Aboriginal funding and established self-determination as an overarching Aboriginal policy.[28] The National Aboriginal Consultative Committee was established to facilitate Aboriginal decision-making in policy. The Woodward Commission into Aboriginal Land Rights, established in 1973, asserted in its second report that, 'to deny Aborigines the right to prevent mining on their land was to deny the reality of their land rights'.[29] An Aboriginal Loans Commission and *Aboriginal Land Fund Act* were established in 1974. In 1975 the *Racial Discrimination Act* was enacted, and Prime Minister Whitlam returned 1250 square miles (more than 3000 square kilometres) to the Gurindji people, who had walked off Wave Hill Station years before demanding the return of their traditional lands.[30] The *Aboriginal Land Rights (Northern Territory) Act* was enacted in 1976 under the Fraser government. It was a significantly weakened version of legislation that had been put in train by the Whitlam government, and it failed to achieve national land rights.[31] As Pat would outline decades later, 'there have been huge changes but as far as concrete benefits it's practically nil, there are people who still die in this country just because they are Aboriginal'.[32]

The women's movement equally secured unprecedented transformative developments with the establishment of the Supporting Mother's Benefit,[33] the funding of women's refuges and Liz Reid's appointment as Women's Affairs Adviser to Prime Minister Whitlam.[34] However, some elements of the women's movement were suspicious of altering from an activist course to being perceived as more aligned with government. The resulting division among the women's movement caused Pat some consternation. Pat felt the position provided opportunity to shift women's concerns from an external pressure group to more directly influencing government decision-making.

In 1975 Pat's selection as one of ten delegates to attend the International Women's Conference was one of the highlights of her life.[35] The Conference, held in Mexico, was socially and politically exhilarating. Coming from what she termed 'a humble background', Pat recounted going down a glass lift on the external side of a hotel in San Francisco where they whooshed straight through trees and garden which covered the roof of the 11th floor, to the foyer floor below. Yet it was the Conference that gripped Pat and confirmed to her that the feminist debates within the Australian women's movement were leading feminist analysis globally.[36] The Australian women's movement had previously contested and taken a position on many of the issues raised at the conference, where Pat considered the US delegates to be hindered by their focus on internal divisions.[37] Pat also attended First Nations sessions and, following the conference, travelled up through New Mexico, Arizona and California visiting reservations and interviewing First Nations women on their own experiences. However, despite these insights, Pat was disappointed that she faced difficulty reporting back to the women's movement on the conference or the similarity of experiences she found among the First Nations communities of the United States.[38]

One of the key achievements for the feminist movement in Australia was, according to Pat, the Women and Politics Conference in 1975, where 800 women from all regions and political persuasions converged.[39] Pat was asked to be a rapporteur on a session on Women and the Electoral System, given her experience as a federal candidate. However, at the opening of the Conference in the Kings Hall of Parliament House, Pat had been verbally abused by some of the Aboriginal women attending, which left her confused and personally devastated.[40] The tensions had followed into the Conference, which impeded her participation and required Pat to review eight hours of recorded sessions before formally reporting back.[41] It was not until Evelyn Scott crossed her path during the Conference that Pat was informed her own biological sister had alleged Pat wasn't Aboriginal. Pat's sister had lived with their Scottish mother in Cardwell, North Queensland, as an active member of the Country Women's Association and was involved in the local council, through the denial of her Aboriginality. When attending the previous Aboriginal and Torres Strait Islander Women Conference in Townsville, Pat had been collected from her sister's and brother in-law's leased garage. It was on a later petrol stop by other participants of the Conference that Pat's sister had denied her Aboriginal heritage, desperate to maintain the lifestyle she had fabricated.[42]

Aboriginal participants at the Women's and Politics Conference were resistant to what they perceived as a middle-class process: a vocal group of Aboriginal women, frustrated at the slowness of change on the ground, jeered and chanted throughout Whitlam's opening address.[43] Many Aboriginal women believed the women's movement's focus on men's domination didn't address the entrenched racial oppression they experienced, where they felt they could not afford the luxury of dividing the Aboriginal movement along gender lines.[44] However, though Pat agreed with the need for women to be at the forefront of the Aboriginal rights struggle, she took a more nuanced position. She believed that addressing the intersection of racial and gender oppressions was required for her liberation, with both aspects integral to her identity. In response to questions raised in a meeting between Aboriginal women and feminists, documented in the film *Ningla-A'Na*, Pat had suggested 'we didn't have to attack black men, we could examine what white men were doing to black women and organise around that'. That input, however, was edited out because the male director sought to highlight divisions between feminism and the Aboriginal movement.[45]

The rumours questioning Pat's heritage, she was informed, contributed to her difficulty in securing work, despite her being one of the few Aboriginal people at that time with a university degree, and culminated in her retreat to the North Coast of New South Wales where she reflected on the impact of the women's movement on her.[46] As an Aboriginal woman who had always assessed her own and other's situations against a broader feminist and political analysis, Pat recognised the inseparable nature of how her personal experiences informed her analysis, expressed so comprehensively in the feminist adage she often referenced, 'the personal is political'.

What follows is an extract from Pat's autobiographical essay about these years, originally published as 'There's a Snake in My Caravan' in Jocelynne A. Scutt (ed.), *Different Lives: Reflections on the Women's Movement and Visions of its Future* (Ringwood: Penguin, 1986). I thank Jocelynne for granting permission to reproduce the chapter here.

There's a snake in my caravan

There's a snake in my caravan and I don't know what to do. A nasty dull-black sinuous thing that has made its home in the back of a large electric fridge that's in storage, with other furniture, in the caravan annex. It has bitten my dog (which barely survived) and forced me to install my latest batch of hijacked hitch-hikers in the front bedroom of the little old farmhouse where I live. If I could pluck up the courage to get after it with the '12 bore', the only result would be a dead caravan. The snake would then settle down to a snug winter and a productive spring in its comfortable, new, all mod. cons. accommodation. I can envisage the scene sixty years from now: my daughter, Amanda, then seventy-five, leaning on her walking stick while gesturing expansively at a tangled heap of aluminium and steel, a tatter of canvas still fluttering defiantly through the bracken and weeds, as she explains to *her* hijacked hitch-hikers 'there's a snake in the caravan, so you'll have to stay up at the house'.

With just a cursory glance and a swish of its tail that snake has reduced me to utter powerlessness. Inadequate, ineffectual,

I fall into the pit of what must be the ultimate of peculiarly female 'downness': I am no longer in control of my life. My caravan, the private space in which I write, is denied me. Yet this feeling of powerlessness is all too familiar. In 1971 I was a suburban housewife, the mother of five children. The youngest, then seven years old, was severely retarded and epileptic. Then I became pregnant again.

In those days, one could get a legal abortion only on grounds that the pregnancy presented a danger to the physical or mental health of the mother. Unaware that I would have qualified for a termination on medical grounds, and having lived the previous seven years on the brink of a total breakdown, I signed myself into a mental institution. I did not have an abortion. I was told that I was 'too sane'. I had not come in dripping blood. They suggested I 'have her adopted'. This decision, made by *others*, was the beginning of my conscious desire for *real* control of my life.

I had been married for fifteen years. The fifth child was placed in an institution for the intellectually handicapped just one month before the youngest was born. Married life was soured even before the handicapped child, whose illness created a social and economic barrier to our ending the marriage. [...]

Being of mixed racial origins, my identity resolved and focused on my Aboriginality more and more throughout the years. Childhood and marriage (to a first cousin on the Aboriginal side of the family) led to an incredibly isolated existence providing no real protection against continuing racist barbs. However, during 1971 I was increasingly active in the Aboriginal land rights movement, visiting a number of Aboriginal reserves throughout New South Wales. At Easter, 1972, I attended the National Land Rights Conference in Alice Springs.

The land rights movement would not have survived had it not been for the role of Aboriginal women.[47] The Gary Foleys, Paul Coes, Mick Millers and others fought long and hard throughout the 1970s, and into the 1980s. But the strength of nameless hundreds of women, tempered by years of direct conflict with bureaucracies (police, welfare agencies, schools) in defence of their children, played an important role in the development of Aboriginal organisations and the general demand for land rights. Yet while the land rights issue has passed from the hands of the young male militants of the late 1960s and early 1970s to the National Aboriginal Conference (predominantly mature males), Aboriginal women have consistently demanded that the needs of women be taken into account in land rights. So far, little has been achieved.

In April 1972, I took the baby and left my home in Sydney's outer western suburbs, daughter joined me, and in December 1973 the remaining children came to Canberra for the Christmas holidays, and stayed.

I participated in the activities which saw the brutal but triumphant demise of the Aboriginal Embassy in Canberra in August 1972, and stood as an independent 'Black Liberation' candidate in the 1972 federal elections in the ACT. In 1973 I became the first non-matriculated mature-age student at the Australian National University.

As a child I had been fascinated by the distant white gleam of buildings at the University of Queensland at St Lucia. I gradually realized that working-class kids don't go to university. At least not unless you were a 'real brain'. High school didn't enter my thinking because, in my day, you didn't enter high school until you were thirteen or fourteen. I left school at fourteen, beginning a 'career' in factory process work. Years later I realised how lucky I was to be in school at all. Until 1948 (the year I was ten), any principal could refuse to accept any Aboriginal child into his school.

When a friend first suggested I go to university, I laughed. I laughed again when Liz Reid suggested it in 1972. After dropping out for a year in 1975, I completed my degree in 1977 at the age of forty. Six years after arriving in Canberra, I worked for more than two and a half years as a project officer in the Department of Social Security's 'Aboriginal Unit'. The frustrations of working in the bureaucracy, together with health and other problems, led to my resignation in January 1981. For the next two years I lived in 'rural retreat' near Grafton.

To grasp the real impact of women's liberation on my life requires an awareness of the tremendous dynamism of the women's movement in 1972 and my relationship with the Bremer Street Women's House in Canberra. Early in 1972 Bobbi Sykes and I were invited to speak to a group of Canberra women about land rights, the Aboriginal Embassy, and other issues of concern to Aboriginal women. It was the day Canberra Women's Liberation took formal possession of the Bremer Street house. This was my introduction to Women's Liberation. One week later, I arrived in Canberra, penniless, with a five-month-old baby – to stay. After three weeks, still penniless, Amanda and I moved into the Bremer Street meeting room, having passed from hand to hand among some of the 'sisters' in a vain attempt to find a less inconvenient niche for us.

The atmosphere at Bremer Street in 1972 was electric. Hardly an evening passed without some sort of meeting, with twenty to sixty women. Consciousness-raising was a twice-weekly event. General meetings, action groups, and the embryonic Women's Electoral Lobby (WEL) had a weekly time and space. Days were filled with the comings and goings of newsletter production, the preparation of leaflets, classes in screen printing, the establishment of the feminist library, or just dropping in.

I was an active participant. Not only by choice, but also because baby Amanda and I couldn't go to bed until the meetings ended. We stayed for about six weeks. Then, when I lost my recently acquired public service job as a temporary clerical assistant because of my activities in the Aboriginal Embassy, I also lost my accommodation in a government hostel. Amanda and I returned to Bremer Street.

If nothing else, I can claim to have done much to assist the establishment of a women's refuge in Canberra. The physical presence of the Green Valley housewife, her baby, the nappies and disorder, and the endless recitations of my latest trauma as I fought for recognition of entitlements as a *deserting* wife with the ACT [Australian Capital Territory] welfare authorities were concrete evidence of the urgent need for a 'real' women's refuge. (In 1972 only 'deserted' wives were entitled to welfare.)

[...] 1972 had been an extremely traumatic year. Separated from my children, I was often in despair. When meetings closed, usually in the early hours of the morning, I was left alone to cry myself to sleep: no future, no place to go. Too 'working-class' proud to ask for charity, I fed the baby sugar-water while humorously describing my latest battle with welfare. During the first nine weeks I received only two $10.00 food vouchers. Few women at the meetings noticed. I understand, but still resent, the pressures put on me to 'move on'. Three or four weeks is insufficient time for a woman in crisis to get back on her feet.

The advent of the Women's Electoral Lobby caused the numbers of women at the house to grow rapidly. Consciousness-raising sessions were divided in two. The activity-oriented, newer, WEL women did not always succeed in grasping the 'personal is political' ambit of feminist theory. The potential growth of consciousness-raising 'rap' groups bogged down for lack of leadership and inspiration. And hard-core feminists were avoiding discussions about the role and validity of the position of adviser to the Prime Minister on women's issues, the appointment of Elizabeth Reid to that position; and the relationship of the Canberra women's movement to both the position and the incumbent.

The last 'rap' I attended was on 'my mother and me'. Many

women sat silent, making no contribution. I suspect that the articulate, competent, well-educated Canberra women felt more threatened by the processes of consciousness-raising than I. I could only benefit (in the long term) by discarding the 'shit' elements of my socialised role as a woman, housewife and mother. By society's chauvinistic criteria, my 'inadequacies' and 'unworthiness' had constantly been confirmed to me. Through consciousness-raising, I came to realise a new and autonomous self [...]

The Elizabeth Reid situation did not improve my relationship with the Canberra women's movement. I was closely identified with Liz who had been a tremendous support to me in 1972, not only as campaign manager, but by sharing her home with the baby and me for many weeks prior to the election, and raising funds for my campaign. Labor Party feminists were attempting to block Bremer Street involvement in my election campaign, using their influence to prevent any direct or specific endorsement of me from the Women's Electoral Lobby. Other 'sisters' stood back and observed my campaign, amazed at my impertinence and gall.

In 1975 I was selected together with nine other women of all backgrounds to attend the International Women's Year Conference in Mexico City. Even my few remaining feminist friends were disturbed that this may have been an example of 'special patronage'. Well, whether by intention or not, the Canberra women's movement actively destroyed any validity that my experiences in Mexico may have had, by the simple expedient of not listening when I returned. Two attempts were made to organise meetings on my behalf to discuss the conference, one at the Women's House, one with the ANU Radical Feminist Group. Neither attempt even went so far as a date for discussion. The message was loud and clear: the women's movement of Canberra just did not want to know what had happened in Mexico.

The information they rejected, the great news from Mexico in 1975, was that Australian feminist theory was leading the world.

Liz Reid, Laurie Bebbington (the radical lesbian activist from the Australian Union of Students), Pat Giles (trade unionist and now ALP senator from Western Australia) and other Australian women caught and held the centre stage of world interest as their theory of feminism related to practice in their fields. At the same conference, American feminists were booed from the stage when, with chauvinistic arrogance, they attempted to align the weight of the international conference on one side or other of their internal schisms and disputes.

The Canberra women's movement was predominantly middle class, educated and articulate, with an intimate knowledge of the public service structure and the complexity of its mechanisms. They participated in legislative reforms by submissions on family law reform, anti-discrimination legislation and others, and giving evidence at enquiries such as the enquiry into poverty by Henderson and the Australian Council of Social Service. However, as time passed, many chose action in fields like child-care, the women's refuge, abortion counselling and the rape crisis centre. Others took a more 'revolutionary' stance or withdrew under the guise of having to 'sort out your own problems before you can solve the problems of society'.

The political assessment of the 'correct direction' for the women's movement unfortunately led many Canberra women into 'concrete' activity or to a 'self'-centred encounter group/ meditation direction, and away from the 'reformist' submissions and other legislative processes where their unique talents could be fully used. Those women who did persist from within the bureaucracy were seen to be vaguely 'invalid'. They were either not *real* feminists, or not really 'Canberra'.

I see the grand finale for the women's movement as being the Women and Politics Conference in 1975. I was an official rapporteur on the 'campaigning' session of the conference, but throughout that week I was under constant attack from my

Aboriginal sisters. Tolerance – if not complete forgiveness – was extended to me for my political consciousness of my working-classness and femaleness, as well as my Aboriginality. But then a sister started a rumour that I was not Aboriginal at all. This charge was not made easier by originating from a sister-by-blood (my biological sister) in a futile attempt to retain her Queensland country town eminence as a member of the Junior Chamber of Commerce and president of the local Parents and Citizens Association. (Years later my mother accused me of 'destroying' my sister's life by 'coming out' as an Aborigine: my sister was forced to retreat into the anonymity of Brisbane's suburbia!) Fortunately, all but a few die-hards accepted the truth when confronted with it.

Personal traumas aside, the Women and Politics Conference was a triumph of feminist sisterhood. Over 800 women of almost all political persuasions found that their female identity gave them more in common than an arbitrary division of party politics and ideology. That this groundwork was not followed up was *the* tragedy of the more recent years of feminism, even surpassing the competition for, and distrust of, the funding hand-outs of 1975–7 [...]

So where do I go from here? Despite having written the foregoing on my experiences of women's liberation and feminism in Canberra, I confess to being greatly in their debt. I would have survived without them. I would have broken out of my marriage somehow. But I certainly would never had gone to university, and I would have been socially, emotionally and psychologically 'other' than I am today. I value the few steadfast friendships, the two or three sisters, I retain.

Despite many snakes – in differing forms, but invariably male – the changes in my life have, for the most part, resulted from my own decisions. Or, at least, the limitations on my freedom of choice have been more covert, more indirect, than in earlier days. The women's movement has done more for me than simply encouraging me to redirect my guilt from poor housekeeping skills to my inability to deal with a snake. By the way, if *you* have a snake in your caravan and you don't know what to do, try ratsac in milk! A woman told me …

Pat's life and career after 1975

The aspersions regarding Pat's Aboriginality continued, at a time when government agencies sought more visual mascots of their Aboriginal employment efforts, which may have also impacted Pat's capacity to secure employment. Her public service career had commenced as a Project Officer in the Department of Social Security's Aboriginal Unit (1978–81), before she moved to the north coast of New South Wales. Following her return to Sydney, after applying for 17 positions, she landed a position in the Equal Employment Opportunity Unit of the New South Wales Department of TAFE (1987–89), but in 1988 the incoming Liberal government cut staffing of the unit from 16 down to two.[48] In 1991–92 she lectured in community development at Curtin University, Western Australia. By December 1992, Pat had returned to Sydney and was instrumental in establishing Perleeka Aboriginal Television, with her son Greg. Perleeka produced films for community television, trained Aboriginal film-makers and aspired to establish a national Aboriginal TV channel. However, with the election of the Howard government in 1996, Perleeka lost its federal funding. Pat subsequently took a position teaching Aboriginal Studies at James Cook University in 1997, before moving back to Sydney in semi-retirement.

Pat remained engaged in Aboriginal politics, and was appointed Chair of the Aboriginal Rights Coalition, established by her son Greg and daughter Cathy in response to the racially targeted and punitive Northern Territory Intervention. The Aboriginal Rights Coalition organised 2000 people to protest at the opening of Parliament in 2008. However, the most satisfying endeavour in the later part of Pat's life was winning a racial discrimination case in 2011 against journalist Andrew Bolt and his publisher the Herald & Weekly Times, which Pat led with eight other litigants.[49] Bolt's articles in the *Herald Sun*, entitled 'It's so Hip to be Black' and 'White Fellas in the Black', had alleged Pat and other fair-skinned Aboriginal people had fabricated their Aboriginality for career advantage. Though Pat had been warned by her doctor not to travel to Melbourne to give evidence because of her heart condition, she was determined to affirm her Aboriginality to the court, how she had been removed from the white section of the school because of her father's racial heritage, that she had fought her way through school as a result of that difference, and that she had publicly identified as Aboriginal from the age of 14.[50] Judge Bromberg determined that the articles had breached Section 18C of the *Racial Discrimination Act*, finding the articles 'reasonably likely to offend, insult, humiliate or intimidate' the claimants with the denigration motivated by 'the race, colour or ethnic origin' of the litigants.[51] Further, the articles failed to meet the exceptions of Section 18D in being undertaken in 'good faith', given they contained 'erroneous facts, distortions of the truth and inflammatory and provocative language'.[52] Pat passed away on 17 March 2015, satisfied that justice had been served against the behemoth might of Andrew Bolt and Rupert Murdoch's News Corp. Her political-feminist values and indomitable spirit remained steadfast until she joined our ancestors.

PART TWO
WOMEN AND THE LAW

INTRODUCED BY KIM RUBENSTEIN

In this far-reaching collection, the chapters by Elizabeth Evatt and Camilla Nelson highlight the ways that law acts as a framework for ensuring the protection of human rights while shaping the lived experience of Australian citizens. The Whitlam government, perhaps for the first time, made women's experiences central to formulating law and legislation itself and, thereafter, to the process of administrating, adjudicating and judging law in practice.

In her Introduction, Michelle Arrow contextualises this shift, noting 'for much of the 20th century, Australian women were not generally encouraged to take active roles in politics' – despite being 'one of the first places in the world to grant white women full political rights at the national level (in 1902): not just the right to vote, but to stand for Parliament'. Indeed, when thinking about 'active roles in politics', we think first and foremost of politicians and, often, of their pursuit of election or re-election to either the House of Representatives or the Senate. But once elected, the role politicians play is centred around law and Parliament's constitutional function as the legislative body *making* legislation. If women are not legislators, then their lived experience is less likely to be incorporated into the outputs of Parliament – the laws thus enacted. No wonder, then, that Elizabeth Evatt writes, '[a] significant obstacle to achieving reform for women was the almost complete lack of women in Parliament, in the judiciary and in senior levels of the public service'.

This further narrows Arrow's point as women were not encouraged to be active as law-makers, nor were they encouraged in those pre-Whitlam days to be active *practitioners* of law. So, while a law degree granted a rich quill of professional tools for active citizenship when drawn by men, in the case of women, a law degree had a more threatening character. As the legal academic Mary Jane Mossman writes of the first women lawyers in the late 19th and early 20th centuries, while 'the role of women doctors could be explained as an extension of women's roles in the "private sphere"'; by contrast, women lawyers were clearly 'intruding on the public domain explicitly reserved to men'.[1]

Traversing the earlier history of women entering the profession, we can see the immense struggle involved. Flos Greig, for example, was the first woman to enter any law faculty in Australia, in 1897, and she completed her arts/law degree at the University of Melbourne in 1903. She began her law degree before women possessed the right to vote or stand for Parliament and without any certainty that she would be admitted to practise law upon graduation from university. While Greig was studying in Melbourne, Ada Evans enrolled in the Sydney University Faculty of Law, when the Dean was absent on leave and could not prevent her entry, as he was not accepting women law students. Evans continued her studies and in 1902 (a year before Greig) became the first Australian woman to complete her law degree. Flos Greig and her supporters began a campaign in Victoria to allow women to enter the legal profession and in April 1903 the Parliament of Victoria passed the *Women's Disabilities Removal Act 1903* (sometimes referred to as the 'Flos Greig Enabling Act') to specifically allow women to practise law. Greig went on to practise law for the remainder of her life, while campaigning for causes including children's welfare, women's suffrage and adult education, before her death in 1958, aged 78.

More can be read about these trailblazing women lawyers, who I referred to in my presentation at the conference from which this book emanates, in the online exhibition 'Australian women lawyers as active citizens'.[2] The collection highlights how the study of law can be foundational to not only practising law but for thinking about law and its impact on policy, and then vice versa, how policy can be translated into law. This requires women to be equally present in Parliament, in the judiciary and in senior levels of the public service – the places in which policy plays out, is implemented, executed and adjudicated upon.

Lawyers like Elizabeth Evatt, herself a trailblazer, and the other women she refers to in her chapter, including Justice Roma Mitchell, appointed to the South Australian Supreme Court in 1965, and Kemeri Murray, appointed to the South Australian District Court in 1973, demonstrate Whitlam's concept of law as an expression of both human rights and lived experience.

Elizabeth Evatt is a case study of this entwined thinking. As she notes, one of Whitlam's earliest acts, in December 1972, was to invite her to take up an appointment as a Deputy President of the Commonwealth Conciliation and Arbitration Commission, which made industrial awards and set the basic wage. But '[t]aking up this appointment meant a significant disruption to my family'. The lived experience enmeshed here emphasises its double relevance – not simply to human rights law and the way it regulates people's lives affected by it, but also to the lived experience of *law-makers* – with their lives being a lens through which decision-making occurs. If we don't have sufficient women in positions of law-makers administering law or judging laws, then this lens, influencing decision-making, is necessarily narrowed.

Elizabeth Evatt also headed the Royal Commission on Human Relationships. The Commission had extensive terms of reference – all with a bearing on the law as lived experience – including topics like responsible parenthood, sex education, relationship training, fertility control, family planning services, factors and pressures affecting women's decision to seek an abortion and medico-legal determinations on the subject of termination.

Evatt was aided by Jane Mathews as counsel assisting the Commission. Mathews later became the first woman appointed a judge in New South Wales, and the first woman appointed to that state's Supreme Court. Mathews' own experience before each of her roles, as counsel assisting and her later appointments, presents a rich source of study for anyone with an eye to the impact of lived experience on judicial and quasi-judicial decision-making and temperament, equally true, of course, for anyone bringing that eye to Evatt herself.[3] In this, Evatt's chapter may well be the ideal starting point.

Her chapter is revealing of the work of the Royal Commission on Human Relationships in gathering vast amounts of evidence brought by women before the Commission. It also covers the influential work undertaken by the Women's Electoral Lobby in the lead up to Whitlam's election.

There is no more far-reaching example of how women's lived experiences influenced the law reform agenda of the Whitlam government than the introduction of the *Family Law Act 1975*, which fundamentally recast divorce law, removing its fault-finding premise. With Evatt's appointment by Whitlam to head up the Family Court on its establishment, we have a poignant view of women's lived experience coming together in this chapter. We are privileged to have Evatt's account and reflections about this key period of law reform in Australia.

Camilla Nelson's rich chapter further extends the centrality of women's lived experiences to law reform. She explains that the 'historical reality of a male-dominated society tended to keep the focus of the law reform debate on men's complaints. But a re-emergent women's movement was organising in this period, and by 1972 the Women's Electoral Lobby (WEL) was demanding real policy solutions to the real social problems women faced'.

WEL directly articulated the need for government to understand how equality fundamentally included issues of marriage and family, money and property. By highlighting the direct experiences of women, it was able to advocate dismantling systemic discrimination against women so embedded in the fabric of family law at that time. Nelson's chapter shares the painful experiences of women under this paternal fault system – including where, for example, women were not eligible for a divorce based on 'habitual cruelty' because a judge determined 'she could have avoided being assaulted by her husband' had she modified her conduct 'by being dutiful, restraining her outbursts of temper and exercising self-command'.

Like Evatt's chapter, Nelson's similarly amplifies the significance of thinking about law through a human rights framework. We learn more about WEL's lobbying of government in laws about employment, education, women's health and control over fertility. WEL also pushed for active combating of violence against women and their children, and for the provision of family support services, including child care.

We are reminded too of the significance of the role of women legislators – including Labor members Joan Child, Jean Melzer and Ruth Coleman, and Liberal member Kathy Sullivan. As Nelson states, 'on the floor of the Parliament, they brought a different perspective … which, as the records of the all-male Senate Committee eloquently demonstrate, had included a startling number of unchallenged chauvinistic assumptions and insults'.

Added to the mix were the women judges adjudicating Family Court matters – including Evatt and Justice Peg Lusink. Nelson also writes of the reforms to procedure altering the nature of the court experience for litigants: 'An air of informality grounded the new court: judges sat on the same level as parties, rather than behind a high bench, and barristers appeared without wigs or robes. The rules of evidence were also relaxed, so the court had greater discretion to accept evidence related to credibility, character, and tendency'. Some of the consequences of these changes, and the personal experiences of the judges themselves, also bear out the significance of lived experience on both the content of the law and the adjudication of it. Readers interested in this aspect of the Family Court's early days are able to listen to reflections of that period in the oral history of Justice Peg Lusink.[4]

Ultimately, this section indelibly extends and recasts the

phrase 'the personal is political' to the 'personal is legal'. The more women legislators there are, and the more women's lived experiences are fundamentally built into developing legislation, the more law has the potential to address inequalities more broadly. And this is a heartening aspect to the present – given the 2022 federal election results with many more women in Parliament.

Finally, Evatt's and Nelson's chapters are of a piece in focusing on the ongoing issues when thinking about law as human rights and how the range of women's lived experience is still insufficiently factored into policy development and implementation. However, the extent of women legislators, women public servants and judges as adjudicators of the law could also be claimed as a consequence of other initiatives during the Whitlam years, importantly, access to education and legal education. Many of the oral history interviews recorded as part of the Trailblazing Women and the Law project, housed in the National Library of Australia, specifically refer to the Whitlam government's initiatives as relevant to their careers.[5]

These and the many women who follow these trailblazers provide some hope that it is more likely those lived experiences – taken so seriously during the Whitlam government's period of reform – become an embedded frame for thinking about the exercise of power in society. If that does eventuate, we better guarantee law being used as a tool for justice and not oppression.

WHITLAM, WOMEN AND HUMAN RIGHTS

ELIZABETH EVATT

Bringing Australia into line

Gough Whitlam often mentioned that during his time in government, he had sought to bring Australia into the international human rights community. This meant ratifying international human rights instruments and adopting their standards. One of his earliest acts in government, on 18 December 1972, had been to sign the two major UN Covenants, the Covenant on Civil and Political Rights, and the Covenant on Economic, Social and Cultural Rights. As those instruments were not yet in force, his attention had later focused on the Convention on the Elimination of Racial Discrimination, which was already in force. The enactment of the *Racial Discrimination Act* by the Whitlam government in 1975 enabled Australia to ratify that Convention, with highly significant consequences.[1]

The reforms initiated by the Whitlam government to advance women's rights can be seen as part of Gough Whitlam's commitment to human rights and to the ratification and implementation of international human rights standards. I consider here some of these reforms in this light. I deal mainly with issues with which I was closely connected at the time.

At the time of the 1972 election, I had been living in London with my family for some years, working in law reform, and in particular family law reform. Even at that distance it became clear early on that the Whitlam government intended to introduce a range of reforms which would promote the rights and interests of women. A significant obstacle to achieving reform for women was the almost complete lack of women in Parliament, in the judiciary and in senior levels of the public service. The House of Representatives was all male, until the election of Joan Child as a Labor member in May 1974. The Senate included two Liberal women, Nancy Buttfield and Margaret Guilfoyle.[2] In May 1974 they were joined by Labor senators Ruth Coleman and Jean Melzer. There were no women in the Whitlam Cabinet, and very few in the higher levels of the public service; the longstanding marriage bar, which required women to give up their jobs once they married, had ended only in 1966. Faced with this situation, and recognising that to deliver progress for women he would need to have first-class advice, Whitlam appointed Elizabeth Reid into a high-level position to advise him on the needs and interests of women. He also appointed Marie Coleman to head the National Social Welfare Commission – the first woman in Australia to head a national statutory authority.

In a gesture showing his commitment to the equal right to participate in public life, the Whitlam government acceded to the Convention on the Political Rights of Women on 10 December 1974, Human Rights Day.[3]

In 1972 only one woman held judicial office in Australia, Justice Roma Mitchell, who had been appointed to the South Australian Supreme Court in 1965. In 1973 Kemeri Murray was appointed to the South Australian District Court, the second woman in Australia to be appointed to the judiciary. The federal judiciary was exclusively male. One of Gough Whitlam's earliest acts in December 1972 was to invite me to take up an appointment as a Deputy President of the Commonwealth Conciliation and Arbitration Commission, a quasi-judicial body whose role was to make industrial awards and to set the basic wage (its successor is the Fair Work Commission). Taking up this appointment meant a significant disruption to my family, while offering a great opportunity to be part of the progressive reforms which were being rolled out. As might be expected, the media coverage of the appointment placed great emphasis on family and domestic issues.

My appointment was followed later by the appointment of Mary Gaudron as a Deputy President of the Commission, and Judith Cohen and Pauline Griffin as commissioners. These appointments were the first steps along a road whose end – parity – is not quite in sight. The number of women in the judiciary, federal and state, continues to grow. Women make up more than one third of the Fair Work Commission members; though doubts have been raised about whether women share equally in the Commission's important decisions.[4]

Equality in employment

The principle of equal pay for work of equal value had been accepted by the Arbitration Commission a short time before the election of the Whitlam government, leading to an overall rise in women's wages. However, the claim for an equal minimum wage had not been granted. Whitlam briefed Mary Gaudron to apply to reopen the National Wage and Equal Pay case before the Commission, which finally accepted the principle of an equal minimum wage in 1974. This enabled Australia to ratify the International Labour Organization's Convention on Equal Remuneration.[5] The fight has continued to ensure that work predominantly done by women was properly evaluated and to overcome the discrepancies in actual pay between men and women.

Whitlam was quick to ratify the ILO Convention (No. 111) concerning Discrimination in Respect of Employment and Occupation, in June 1973. National and state committees on discrimination in employment and occupation were established to resolve allegations of discrimination in those areas. The committees worked by conciliation, and had no enforcement powers. Comprehensive national legislation outlawing discrimination in employment on the ground of sex would have to wait until 1984, following Australia's ratification of the Convention on the Elimination of All Forms of Discrimination Against Women (CEDAW) in 1983.[6] Whitlam responded to the claim by women for paid maternity leave by enacting the *Maternity Leave (Commonwealth Employees) Act 1973*, to give Commonwealth public servants paid maternity leave for 12 weeks (with 40 weeks unpaid).

The Royal Commission on Human Relationships, 1974-77

Central to the claims of the Women's Electoral Lobby in the 1972 election was fertility control and access to legal abortion. Equality and independence required that women have the right to choose freely whether and when to have children.[7] Whitlam moved quickly to remove sales tax from contraceptive pills and to subsidise them under the Pharmaceutical Benefits Scheme. The government went on to provide funding for newly established women's health centres and family planning services.

Abortion was more difficult; it was dealt with by state and territory laws, under which it was a crime, except in South Australia, where legislation enabled abortions to be carried out legally in prescribed circumstances. Judicial decisions in New South Wales and Victoria enabled a doctor to perform an abortion where they considered there was a risk to the woman's physical or mental health, though the threat of prosecution was not entirely removed. In some states women risked injury or death in order to end an unwanted pregnancy.

The federal government could not reform abortion law, except in the territories, which were still under Commonwealth jurisdiction. In May 1973 two Labor members of the House of Representatives introduced a Bill to reform the abortion law of the ACT. After much debate, Gough Whitlam voted in favour of the Bill, but it failed to get a second reading on a conscience vote. During the debates, Race Mathews MP moved that a Commissioner be appointed to inquire into the social, educational and legal aspects of sexual relationships. Malcolm Fraser put up a counter-proposal. His motion was accepted; by then it was September 1973.[8]

There was no further action until April 1974 when the government announced that there would be a Royal Commission to inquire into and report on the family, social, educational, legal and sexual aspects of male and female relationships. I was asked to chair the Commission with fellow commissioners Bishop Felix Arnott, then Anglican Archbishop of Brisbane, and Anne Deveson, writer and journalist. At that time I was deeply involved as a presidential member of the Arbitration Commission in the negotiations for a new building industry award. However, I was persuaded that the Royal Commission would provide a tremendous opportunity to explore important social issues in changing times. The building industry award was completed a few months after the Commission began its work.

The Royal Commission on Human Relationships was announced on 21 August 1974 and began its work soon after. The terms of reference were extensive, and referred specifically to matters such as responsible parenthood, sex education, education in relationships, medical education in regard to fertility control, family planning services, factors and pressures affecting women's decision to seek an abortion, medico-legal determinations relating to termination, and so on.

The Commission encouraged wide community interest and participation around a number of key social and legal issues. Open procedures enabled the voices of many Australians to be heard, and provided a real opportunity for women to put forward their concerns about laws and policies which they considered had failed them. Some 1200 written submissions, several hundred witnesses in formal hearings, and many hundreds more in informal sessions, helped the Commission to identify major areas of concern to the community, within the scope of its terms of reference. Research reports were commissioned on topics such as medical education, abortion, attitudes to sexuality, rape, disability, domestic violence, child abuse, migrant women. The Commission aimed to lay down principles to guide reform in areas of vital interest to the community, including many of great concern to the women's movement.

After the Dismissal of 11 November 1975, the incoming Fraser government allowed the Commission to continue, but with restricted resources. The final report was submitted at the end of 1977. Its many recommendations for law reform, policies and programs have been described as a feminist reform agenda, though it has taken many years for some proposals to be implemented. Jane Mathews, counsel assisting the Commission, later became the first woman appointed a judge in New South Wales, and the first woman appointed to the Supreme Court of New South Wales.

Abortion

On the issue that had led to its establishment, the Royal Commission recommended that abortion should be decriminalised when carried out in the first 22 weeks of pregnancy and beyond that date in certain defined circumstances. Abortion law reform remained a matter for the states and territories, and many years of effort by the women's movement were needed to bring about reform. It was not until 2019 that all states had decriminalised abortion.[9]

Along the way, women had to fight attempts to remove termination procedures from Medicare rebates, and overturn the restrictions on access to the drug RU486 (mifepristone) imposed by the government in legislative amendments to the *Therapeutic Goods Administration Act* introduced by Senator Brian Harradine. Effective access to safe and legal abortion, where the life or health of the pregnant woman or girl is at risk, is now recognised as part of international human rights, though it remains under attack in many countries.[10]

Violence against women, rape and sexual abuse

In the 1970s, the plight of women trapped in violent relationships, with no resources to draw on, and often with children, had prompted feminists to establish women's refuges, such as 'Elsie' in Sydney founded by a group led by Anne Summers. The Whitlam government recognised the significance of this issue, and began funding women's refuges in its second term. This was the first time that the federal government had paid attention to the issue of family violence.[11]

The issue of violence against women was raised in many submissions to the Royal Commission on Human Relationships.[12] Researchers organised a phone-in, and a study was carried out of over 100 women at 'Elsie'. The evidence showed that family violence (that is, between spouses or partners, or against children) was a widespread problem, prevalent in every social group. It had an enormous effect on family relationships, and caused severe mental and physical damage to women and children.[13]

The Commission recommended an increased level of funding by the federal government for women's refuges, covering all costs including salaries, halfway houses and flats. It recommended more effective protection and community support for women and children; and educating and training health and social services personnel and police to deal with domestic conflict.[14]

Many submissions to the Commission raised concerns about the way rape and other sexual offences against women were handled by the legal system. In the 1970s the police investigation and the court procedures that followed were gruelling and retraumatising for victims. As a result, many women did not report these crimes or press for prosecution. If there was a prosecution, the woman/victim had to face an intimidating court experience in which her character would be attacked. Marital rape was not recognised as a crime. The Commission's recommendations included specialised police units and medical panels, better support for women in court, and limits on cross-examination.[15] Many changes in law and practice have been made in the intervening years, including the recognition of rape within marriage in 2012.[16] Most recently, the New South Wales *Crimes Act* has been amended to provide that consent to sexual activity must be communicated by words or actions.

Violence against women and sexual abuse were recognised internationally as human rights issues by the 1990s and are now part of the work of the Australian Human Rights Commission.[17]

Discrimination and equality

The Royal Commission received many submissions on the issue of discrimination against women.[18] Women wanted greater legal protection against discrimination not only in employment, but in *all* areas: health, education, the law and in the provision of goods and services. It was only in 1975 that South Australia enacted the first anti-discrimination legislation, the *Sex Discrimination Act 1975*, which covered employment, education and the provision of goods and services.[19]

The Royal Commission recommended comprehensive national legislation against discrimination on the grounds of sex and marital status.[20] It also recommended universal paid maternity leave, which Whitlam had already extended to the Commonwealth Public Service.[21]

Comprehensive Commonwealth legislation outlawing discrimination against women in the workplace and more widely in employment, education and the provision of goods and services had to wait until Australia had ratified CEDAW in 1983. The Minister for Women, Susan Ryan, introduced the *Sex Discrimination Act 1984* to implement the Convention. But Australia had to enter a reservation in respect of article 11(2)(b) of the Convention which calls for maternity leave with pay or comparable social benefits. It was not until 2011 that Australia had a national paid parental leave scheme, as required by CEDAW.

Divorce, family law and equality in marriage

The agenda for the women's movement in 1972 included divorce law reform and equal rights in marriage and divorce. The Commonwealth had taken over the field of divorce from the states in 1959. It had brought together all the various grounds of divorce under the former state legislation in the *Matrimonial Causes Act 1959*. These grounds, 14 in all, were largely based on fault. A woman who left her marriage would have very little legal protection. The law was saddled with historic inequalities between husband and wife, father and mother. It was an era of private detectives and 'blackmail' divorce.

Before the 1972 election, Labor Party policy had included divorce law reform.[22] The matter had been under consideration by the Senate Standing Committee on Legal and Constitutional Affairs.[23] After the election of the Whitlam government, Attorney-General Lionel Murphy, who had been a member of the Senate Committee, took over divorce reform with enthusiasm. First, however, in July 1973, he appointed a woman as the first civil marriage celebrant. This was the first of many such appointments, and they proved very popular. These days, around 80 per cent of marriages are performed by civil celebrants.[24]

In December 1973 Senator Murphy introduced a Bill in the Senate providing for a radical modernisation of divorce and family law, based on no-fault principles and on gender equality. The Bill was reintroduced after the 1974 double dissolution, and was referred to the Senate Standing Committee. This time the Bill included provision for a federal Family Court.

After the Senate had passed the Bill, Whitlam introduced it in the House of Representatives on 28 November 1974. In doing so he said that public opinion polls showed overwhelming support for the reforms contained in the Bill, including the proposal for a no-fault ground of divorce based on one year's separation.[25] He was an enthusiastic supporter of the legislation and of no-fault divorce. He had resisted the Anglican Archbishop Marcus Loane's attempts to pressure him to direct a vote against the legislation, pointing out that there would be a conscience vote.[26]

After a free vote in both houses, the *Family Law Act* received assent on 12 June 1975. The Act removed the remnants of legal inequality between husband and wife, such as the question of guardianship of children, bringing Australia into line with human rights principles.[27] It provided for a single no-fault ground of divorce – irretrievable breakdown of marriage, evidenced by one year's separation. The provisions dealing with children, property and maintenance were based on the principles of the equality of husband and wife, mother and father, and the recognition of the homemaker role. Women would be entitled to an independent domicile. The welfare of the child would be the paramount consideration, and the wishes of children over 14 would be respected.[28] Emphasis was placed on conciliation, counselling and resolution of disputes. In most cases each party would pay their own costs. Provision was made in the Act for parties to apply for legal aid under the legal aid scheme which the Whitlam government had established. This benefited many women, who seldom had access to resources.[29]

There was resistance in some quarters to the introduction of no-fault divorce. Some religious groups and conservative women's groups argued that it would destroy the sanctity and security of marriage if one party could walk away from the relationship and then divorce an 'innocent' partner. On the other hand, there was considerable support in Parliament and in the community not just for no-fault divorce, but also for the other provisions of the new Act.

The Act set up a new federal court, the Family Court of Australia. It also provided an option for states to set up their own Family Courts. There would be a Family Law Council to advise on family law issues and an Institute of Family Studies to conduct research.

Commenting on the Act, Whitlam said that 'Australia will have the most enlightened matrimonial and family law in the world. The medieval concepts of guilt and fault will be removed from divorce proceedings ... By recognising the fundamental status of marriage as a profoundly personal human relationship, ... the Bill will give fresh and meaningful stature to the institution of marriage itself'.[30]

The Family Court of Australia was established as a free-standing court, dealing exclusively with family law matters. The judges were to be appointed specifically for their suitability for dealing with family law matters. The court would have counsellors and welfare officers in addition to legal staff, and would provide mediation to help the parties to reach a civilised determination of their issues. The court premises would be relatively informal, and proceedings were simplified with the aim of keeping costs low. It was referred to at the time as a 'helping court'. Judges would not wear judicial robes, and the judge's bench was at a relatively low level.

The *Family Law Act* was proclaimed in August 1975, and was due to come into force on 5 January 1976. When Gough Whitlam invited me to head the court, I was immersed in the work of the Royal Commission on Human Relationships. As I was reluctant to abandon the Commission, it was agreed that I should continue with both roles. There followed a period of intense activity until the work of the Commission was completed; my court duties meant that a heavy burden fell on Anne Deveson and the support staff.

Five judges were appointed to the court in August, and further appointments were to be made before the Act came into force. However, the dismissal of the Whitlam government prevented this, and the incoming Fraser government had a caretaker role until after the 13 December election. The efforts of Senator Ivor Greenwood to unproclaim the *Family Law Act* failed. When the Act came into force, Attorney-General Robert Ellicott had the task of making appointments to a court for which the government had little enthusiasm. The appointments came slowly, while a backlog of cases built up quickly. Many people had been waiting for the new legislation to come into force.

The Family Court and its legislation have always been surrounded by a certain amount of controversy. Some sections of the community have been unwilling to accept no-fault divorce, the concept of equality between husband and wife, or that decisions about children should be based on the children's interests and needs. There has always been an element of patriarchal resentment and anger directed to the court. Widespread gender-based violence against women and murder of women by their partners has been paralleled in personal threats to judges, bomb threats, actual bombings and murders.

Over the last 45 years, the Family Court has assumed additional jurisdiction to cover all children, whether or not their parents are married,[31] disputes between de facto partners, and same-sex relationships and marriages.[32] Provisions have been added about superannuation, child support and child abduction.

Though the original *Family Law Act* did not refer expressly to violence, family violence and child abuse became major areas of concern for the court.

There remain difficult issues relating to the overlapping jurisdiction of the Family Court and state courts in relation to the protection of children from abuse.[33] Other problems relate to the lack of resources and a reduction in the court's in-house counselling and mediation services, the build-up of unacceptable delays in dealing with cases and increasing costs, exacerbated by lack of access to legal aid and the increasing complexity of matters.

To these problems has been added the most recent blow, namely the merger of the Family Court with the Federal Circuit Court, which for some years had been dealing with a range of family law matters under the Act in addition to its other jurisdictions, such as migration issues. While this merger has brought all matters within one two-tier court (and thus closer to the original concept), this has been done at the great cost of losing the identity of the Family Court of Australia, which was established to administer the *Family Law Act*. An institution originally set up with special resources to provide support to families in troubled times is in danger of turning into one more court.

A lasting legacy

This is not the place to argue out the issues. The important point to note is that way back in 1974 and 1975, a totally new framework was envisaged for dealing with marital breakdown, and a court was set up with in-house counselling and mediation services. That the dreams were not fully realised does not mean that they had no validity. I have not wavered from my support for the general principles of the *Family Law Act*. The model it established was admired around the world, and remains one of the great legacies of Gough Whitlam and his Attorney-General, Lionel Murphy.

'EVERY DIFFICULT FEMALE': WOMEN AND THE FAMILY LAW ACT

CAMILLA NELSON

Few legislative changes have provoked as much ongoing controversy as the *Family Law Act 1975*, which removed the social stigma attached to family separation by establishing 'irretrievable relationship breakdown demonstrated by a twelve-month separation' as a single ground for divorce.[1] For the first time, the Act recognised marriage as a relationship between two equal human beings, with equal rights and responsibilities – previously, this had not been the case. Historically, women had been constructed in common law as subservient to men. And although, to quote a 1962 court decision denying the 'relief' of a divorce to a female victim of 25 counts of domestic assault, 'The development of the law of domestic relations both at common law and by statute has been consistently in the direction of putting a wife on the same footing, so far as possible, as her husband'. The words 'so far as possible' made it abundantly clear that the law did not consider men and women to be equal.[2] Without the 'relief' of a divorce – and a finding that she was not 'at fault' for the breakdown of her marriage – a woman and her children could be rendered ineligible for welfare support, access to public housing, and the payment of financial maintenance. Before 1975, married women had no right to a share in the family assets if those assets had been listed in their husband's name, and often – if relatives were unwilling to take them in – no place to go if they left.

The Whitlam government's family law reform agenda intervened in the patriarchal structure of 1970s society, attempting to establish a more equitable foundation for the family. Crucial to its success was the integration of legal change with a radical social and economic vision, which included access to legal aid, providing genuine equality before the law by making legal representation accessible for those who could not afford it; the Supporting Mother's Benefit, for women who could not stay in abusive marriages and relationships; as well as funding for women's support services and a string of women's refuges that were being established by a re-emergent women's movement across the country. For the first time, a woman's unpaid labour as wife, mother and homemaker was to be taken into account in the division of family assets, forcing a historic shift in the recognition of women's unpaid domestic labour as an economically valuable contribution to society. Although women's gains under the new laws were incremental and uneven, the reforms changed the lives of many women who were living in violent marriages and relationships – as well as women whose marriages were fraught, or simply not working – by giving them both a legal and an economic pathway out.

Some groups – including the Women's Electoral Lobby – supported the change.[3] Others – including Catholic clerics and conservatives – dubbed the Family Law Bill 'a Casanova's charter', alleging it 'made a farce of marriage', and put the institution of the family 'in danger'.[4] 'Struggle Looms on No Guilt Divorce', warned the *Sydney Morning Herald*, followed by, 'Family Law Bill Backed, Attacked'.[5] 'Pernicious Attack on "the Family Unit"', announced the Adelaide *Advertiser*, followed by 'New Bill "to Destroy Marriage"'.[6] Opposition to the Bill largely centred on the desire to retain the attribution of 'fault' in marriage breakdown, with religious groups opposed to exorcising what the *Nation Review* archly dubbed 'the ghost of the fiery pit' from the law.[7] One Catholic bishop told the *Sydney Morning Herald* that the Bill threatened to introduce 'Hollywood-style' divorce, constituting 'the greatest blow against the Australia we love'.[8] 'Guilt is Vital in Divorce', the Melbourne *Herald* reported, on a similar theme.[9] Petitions were tabled in the House of Representatives and the Senate. Letters were sent to the editors of newspapers in every metropolitan centre. Religious groups held vigils on the lawns outside Parliament, including a mock wedding ceremony organised by Fred Nile's Festival of Light, featuring a bride dressed in a full-length wedding gown and veil.[10]

Debate on the Family Law Bill was shaped by the moral panics of the 1960s and 1970s, including the spectre of the 'permissive society', the changing status of women, and the alleged disintegration of the family. 'NSW No.1 Divorce State', ran the headline to an article in the *Sydney Morning Herald*, with a follow-up story warning 'Australians are now being divorced at a rate of nearly one an hour'.[11] 'Man Divorced Five Times', ran another headline.[12] Meanwhile, the *Western Australian* raised the spectre of intergenerational cycles divorce, reporting 'Inquiry Hears Divorce Runs in Families'.[13] Some news outlets blamed the women's movement directly. 'Divorce Rise with Wives Earnings', ran *The Australian*.[14] 'Job Equality Seen as Divorce Cause', reported the *Canberra Times*.[15] Even the normally cerebral *National Times* ran a feature on alleged divorce trends in the United States, claiming, 'Once Husbands Did all the Running Away from Marriage; Now Wives are Catching Up'.[16] Some media outlets gave the debate an apocalyptic twist, with one headline in *The Australian* baldly declaring, '[Magistrate] Fears Ghastly Horrors of Sodom'.[17]

But the social realities that underpinned mid-20th-century divorce were more complex than the gender stereotypes that drove the headlines. Desertion was the most common ground for divorce at the time the old laws were repealed. These cases mostly involved women who had been left by their husbands to raise their children on their own.[18] The difficulties of deserted wives were compounded by the legal requirement that they sue their husbands in the magistrate's court to the point of having them jailed for non-payment of family maintenance in order to show, as barrister Anna Frenkel told the *Sydney Morning Herald* in 1973, that 'they are destitute and that their husband has left them – before they are eligible for a deserted wives pension'.[19] If a deserted wife refused to sue, or if her husband could not afford to pay her maintenance when she did, as a solicitor explained in the *Nation Review* in 1976, then there was a significant chance that her husband may well end up in jail, and the wife and children could still be 'faced with the spectre of immediate starvation'.[20] 'When a deserted wife comes to my office and tells me she has to issue a maintenance summons against her husband but that he cannot afford to pay,' the solicitor continued, 'the law does not authorise me to advise her to tell her husband to disappear. But conscience would never sanction anything else'.[21]

Men's refusal – or inability – to pay maintenance led to the establishment of the Divorce Law Reform Association in late 1960s Sydney, with branches soon appearing in other states and territories. The association claimed a 40 per cent female membership, but it was described by Frenkel as an organisation that 'consists of many very bitter men who say women take advantage of the present laws in their claims for maintenance'.[22] The *Nation Review* was less polite, labelling the association a group of 'male chauvinists' with a disregard for the fact that 'under the present western rules of conduct the male, usually unhampered by the physical charge of a child or children, is generally in a better financial condition to make a fresh start'.[23] The Divorce Law Reform Association created and sold wildly popular 'Do-It-Yourself Divorce Kits' to couples who could not afford legal representation. They regularly advertised in newspapers, under taglines including 'the Legal Profession and Especially Judges have a Shocking Record', 'Avoid Family Tragedies Caused by Judges Decisions', 'No Lawyers in Family Matters' and 'Destroy the Divorce Laws Before They Destroy You'.[24] The association mounted a successful legal action in South Australia, calling into question every Maintenance Order that had been awarded by a South Australian Court since 1959. Members frequently appeared in the news, or wrote letters to newspaper editors, under headlines such as 'Bid to Right Injustice to Defaulters',[25] 'Divorced Men Aided to Escape'[26] and the 'Law Forces a Man into Slavery'.[27]

In the 1970s, the historical reality of a male-dominated society tended to keep the focus of law reform debate on men's complaints. But a re-emergent women's movement was also organising in this period, and by 1972 the Women's Electoral Lobby was demanding policy solutions to the real social problems women faced. The harsh treatment of women fleeing domestic abuse was a particular focus for Women's Liberation groups. In Sydney, members of Women's Liberation led by Anne Summers broke into vacant premises in Glebe and established 'Elsie', the country's first female refuge for women and children fleeing domestic violence. Family violence and the lack of services for affected women and children was also a focus for the Royal Commission on Human Relationships – established in 1973 and led by Elizabeth Evatt and Anne Deveson. The Royal Commission established a phone-in, inviting the public to 'telephone our office over a 2-day period about violence in family life'.[28] Their report concluded that family violence is a 'problem the community has been reluctant to face'.[29] They added, 'Our evidence leads us to believe that family violence is common in Australian society; it occurs across lines of class, race and age. The damage done to women and children is often severe'. Evatt's report also canvassed the newly enacted *Family Law Act*, pointing out the benefits of a legal regime that finally understood family breakdown was a social problem 'requiring assistance and support rather than punitive measures against one party or the other'.[30]

But the scope of the social, cultural and economic changes ushered in by the *Family Law Act 1975* can only be fully understood when they are set against the astonishing iniquities of the divorce laws that the Act replaced – comprising a common law tradition that proudly traced its lineage all the way back to the ecclesiastical courts of the Middle Ages; embodying centuries of political and religious tradition that enjoined husbands to control their wives, if necessary, by force.

Exorcising 'the ghost of the fiery pit'

Garfield Barwick, Attorney-General in the Menzies government, and later the longest-serving Chief Justice of Australia, created Australia's first uniform divorce law in 1959. The *Matrimonial Causes Act* – then known as the 'Barwick Act' – did not substantially change the historic gender inequalities that underpinned matrimonial law, but amalgamated various state Acts into a single national code. Effectively, laws that had been written in the colonial period, buttressed by 19th-century attitudes to women, were repurposed, with a handful of concessions, for use in the modern world. To obtain a divorce under the Barwick Act, separating couples had to demonstrate grounds. This included 13 long-established fault-based grounds – namely, adultery, desertion, refusal to consummate, habitual cruelty, rape, sodomy or bestiality, drunkenness or intoxication by drugs or frequent convictions, imprisonment, attempts to murder or unlawfully kill or inflict grievous bodily harm, failure to pay maintenance, failure to comply with a restitution order, insanity, or presumption of death – and one new 'no-fault' ground, being separation for a period of more than five years (with the proviso that none of the previously named 'marital offences' were committed within this period).[31]

Cases were heard in the Supreme Courts of the different states. At trial, one spouse would be found to be 'at fault' for the breakdown of the marriage, and the other spouse would generally do better with their claims for maintenance and care of the children. Moreover, under the 'restitution' provisions supported by the Act, judges could – and did – order women to return to abusive husbands. Marital rape was not a crime. And a 'nagging' wife could be held to be responsible for any assaults that were subsequently perpetrated against her by her husband.[32] Alternatively, if sufficient evidence of 'fault' could not be found, or if collusion between a separating couple could be proved, then the 'relief' of a divorce would be refused. Unhappy couples were known to collude by manufacturing evidence of adulteries they had not in fact committed, going so far as to stage infidelities by hiring a private investigator to photograph one of them in a motel room with another partner. Trials were conducted in a glare of media publicity. They functioned as a warning to other married couples and a source of public entertainment, with newspapers like the Sunday *Truth* publishing salacious stories under headlines such as, 'Ice Follie Star Went Cold on Her Husband After 2 Months' or 'Singer Off Key: She Kissed Me and then Left, Says Police Constable'.[33]

But the tabloids' focus on society divorces, PIs and photographers masked a more brutal reality. To secure a divorce on the ground of 'cruelty', for example, a wife had to prove that 'cruelty' – defined as grave physical violence – had been 'habitual' for a period of 'not less than 12 months'. Before the Barwick Act, each state had taken a different approach to family violence, with some barely recognising 'cruelty' at all. The Barwick Act made a small concession to shifting social attitudes to women by omitting the traditional legal requirement for a woman to produce corroborated evidence of 'frequent assaults and cruel beatings' – that is, repeated grave physical injuries – across a 12-month period and leaving the term 'habitually cruel' undefined. Judges were theoretically free to use their own discretion in applying legal precedents. But as legal academic Colin James argues, in practice, judicial attitudes to domestic violence hardened through the 1960s, as judges reacted to moral panics around the escalating divorce rate. Some judges used their discretion to draw on precedents that dated back to earlier in the century when judicial tolerance for men's violence was higher, and women's interests were more precarious, in an attempt to re-establish male control in families.[34] The requirement that a wife must endure 12 months of 'habitual cruelty' to be eligible for a divorce was eventually tested in the High Court in 1968. In the case known as Tilney, appealed from the Full Court of the Supreme Court of Queensland, the High Court found that although the conduct of the husband met the exacting test of danger to life, limb and health that legal precedent apparently required, the wife was still not eligible for a divorce, because the danger had only been sustained for a period of seven months 'at the most'.[35]

Judge Selby, of the New South Wales Supreme Court, raised the matter of Tilney in his evidence to the Senate Standing Committee on Constitutional and Legal Affairs, after Lionel Murphy, as Leader of the Opposition in the Senate, referred an inquiry on the 'injustices and iniquities of divorce laws' to the committee in December 1971. The Senate Committee, which contained both government and opposition members, invited public submissions, advertised its hearings in the press, and collected evidence. But 'habitual cruelty' was only discussed by this all-male committee as a kind of afterthought. Selby said:

> MR JUSTICE SELBY – … And perhaps just one other
> thing, which I had not mentioned, but now it has been
> brought up I feel that it is a matter that might be looked
> at … There was a case in the High Court a few years ago
> where it turned out that the woman had only been bashed
> for – I think it was – 9 months [sic]. The High Court said:
> 'Well, it is bad luck, but the Acts says 12 months. You have
> not got a ground for divorce.

CHAIRMAN – Stick it out for another 3 months!

SENATOR BYRNE – In other words the referee cannot stop the fight at the end of 9 rounds, it has to go the full count of 12.

MR JUSTICE SELBY – The full 12 rounds. I feel that if cruelty is to be retained as grounds for divorce – and I think it should – it should be merely in those words – that the respondent has been physically cruel, or words to that effect. Twelve months bashing is a fair bit to ask.[36]

For family violence to be treated as more than just an afterthought – or as analogous to a boxing match – women had to get organised.

In 1972 the Women's Electoral Lobby, led by Beatrice Faust, set about polling politicians on their beliefs about women's rights, including 'if they had any' (that is, whether they had given the matter a single thought). 'The men running the country are only tin gods,' Faust told the *National Times*. WEL scored Gough Whitlam at 39 out of a possible 45. They scored Liberal Deputy Leader Billy Snedden at minus 3.[37] In the aftermath of the 1972 election, a handful of WEL members took up positions as ministerial staff and were trumpeted in the media – perhaps with a hint of panic – as 'The Women Who Govern Labor'.[38] When the Family Law Bill was being drafted between 1973 and 1974, WEL representatives met with the Attorney-General, Lionel Murphy, to urge improvements.

'Caught in a cleft stick'

Murphy met with WEL representatives to discuss the Family Law Bill on 1 March 1974.[39] In the wake of the meeting, WEL wrote back to the Attorney-General to express their support for the proposed legislation 'as an enlightened attempt to simplify the procedure for dissolution of marriages which have broken down irretrievably'. They particularly supported the property provisions, which, for the first time, gave equity to women by recognising unpaid maternal labour as an economic contribution to the family, also allowing adjustments to be made for the children's future needs. But they raised concerns about the ongoing impact of social and economic discrimination against women and the consequences for older women who – historically – had been denied the opportunity of work and education. They said:

> ... the Bill perpetuates a situation where women are caught in a cleft stick. The Bill deprives a separated wife of her traditional right of support whilst at the same time our society curtails her opportunities to support herself and her children on the grounds that she is being supported. Today 48% of married women work, they are concentrated in low skill monotonous jobs which offer low pay, little prospect of advancement and no security.[40]

WEL's submission clearly flags the need to bring an expanded idea of equality to bear on the issue of marriage and family, money and property, connecting family law to wider social and economic issues, including access to education and child care. It draws attention to the wider context in which, for example, job advertisements were uncritically divided into men's (better paid) and women's (poorly paid) work. Even the public service – though it had stopped retrenching women when they married – was running separate men's and women's entry exams. Young women – in organised acts of defiance – were applying to sit the men's examinations and being turned away.[41]

Groups like WEL and Women's Liberation were not compliant recipients of the government's largesse, but actively intervened in the government's agenda. In a meeting of Sydney Women's Liberation, for example, reported in the *Nation Review*, 200 activists gathered at the Balmain Town Hall to express frustration at the long campaigns that had been required to secure funding for 'the women's refuges, health centres and rape crisis centres – all of which the Sydney Women's Liberation Movement had set up during the preceding year'. Speakers talked about the bureaucratic barriers they had encountered. Although they empathised with Whitlam's adviser Elizabeth Reid, when told to seek funding from other government departments, they worried from 'bitter experience that persuading bureaucrats to depart from their traditional interpretations of their responsibilities was a heart-breaking and usually futile exercise'. They even expressed concern that the Prime Minister's speech at the opening of the Leichhardt Women's Community Health Centre had suggested that funding had 'always been promptly and freely available' when members of the women's movement had fought hard for its release. They complained that government departments regularly referred women in distress to 'Elsie', oblivious to the fact that its founders had 'trekked around three departments' before getting funding, which they protested was inadequate, and even 'miserly'.[42]

Family law reform was controversial because it transgressed what were still considered to be firmly established boundaries between private and public life, by bringing allegedly private concerns – including not only marriage and children, but also sex, violence and family dysfunction – into the public domain.[43] On some of these broader social issues, Murphy remained 'unconvinced'.[44] At the end of their letter, WEL insisted: 'The hearing of custody and financial matters require humane and unintimidating judges. It is submitted that women would make extremely appropriate judges in this area'.[45] And on this issue, they were wholly successful. Female barristers and solicitors were elevated to the bench, and Elizabeth Evatt – then leading the

Royal Commission on Human Relationships – was appointed as the new court's first Chief Justice.

Despite their reservations, WEL ultimately embraced the government's family law reform agenda because – in a revolutionary way – it swept aside centuries of gender injustice encoded within a body of common law that had historically treated women and children as property. As Canberra Women's Liberation group told the *Canberra Times*, 'The Bill introduces, for the first time, a beginning of a definition of marriage as a relationship between two equal human beings. It presents no legal impediment to equality of rights and obligations ...' Far from placing women at an 'advantage', older laws that allegedly aimed to 'protect' women, actually oppressed women, and 'in effect compound her difficulties'.[46]

Once the Bill was drafted, Murphy reached out to speak to women directly. In an interview headlined 'New Style Divorce', which ran in the *Australian Women's Weekly* in an issue with a 'Bonus Bridal Fashion Lift Out', Murphy described the Bill as an attempt to 'raise' women's 'status' by establishing marriage as 'a relationship between two mature, responsible and equal people', while addressing the 'realities of women's difficulties' in a 'transitional stage of society'. He said that women had a right to legal information about divorce, and promised to make it available at the 'local supermarket' and 'notices in the butchers, if they'll let us'.[47] Later, in the Senate, Murphy conceded that the legislation did not go as far as he would have liked, but declared it was 'a realistic attempt to meet some of the most pressing human problems of modern society in a humane way'.[48]

'While I am waving the women's lib banner'

There were just five women in Parliament when the *Family Law Act* was debated. Most of them – including Labor members Joan

Child, Jean Melzer and Ruth Coleman, and Liberal member
Kathy Sullivan – had been elected at the double dissolution
election of May 1974.[49] They brought a different perspective to the
debate, which, as the records of the all-male Senate Committee
eloquently demonstrate, had so far included a startling number of
brutal, unchallenged and chauvinistic assumptions. For example,
the government's own expert, Ray Watson, QC, objected to the
phrasing of certain clauses in the Bill that would allow 'every
difficult female, difficult mother' to 'insist that her 2-year-old
child's brain-washed ideas be passed to the judge',[50] while an
allegedly progressive judge from South Australia opined, 'I do not
know that it matters two hoots that someone has beaten his wife
most violently'.[51]

Melzer spoke from the floor of the Senate during the second
reading debate. She praised the Bill for the way it took the law out
of the hands of geriatric male judges, whose 'whole emphasis is
on sex' at the expense of social welfare concerns such as the care
and wellbeing of children. Melzer described the legal system as
unnecessarily formal, intimidating and complex. She said:

> Ordinary people who do not know anything about the
> law are confused by the formality. They are covered with
> a feeling of guilt. If they have families, there is no place
> to leave the children or have them cared for while their
> parents attend these courts. There is no possible way for one
> to know how long one will be there … People are confused
> … They are overwhelmed … One can walk around those
> dirty, cold, miserable, stone corridors and find people
> literally taking their lives apart bailed up in corners with
> nowhere to sit.[52]

Melzer contrasted this dismal series of legal scenes with what the
government envisaged as a 'helping court'. A court in which legal

information was readily available, in which people who could not afford legal representation could access assistance from legal aid, and where social and emotional support could be obtained from family counselling services specifically designed for the purpose. 'A woman with small children should feel she can go to the local town hall or some such place,' said Melzer, 'and find out factually what happens, what to do, how much it will cost'. The new system was to be underpinned by an idea of genuine equality before the law, rather than a recourse to justice that only served the wealthy. But Melzer also raised criticisms:

> Like other speakers in this debate, I am concerned about the [financial] maintenance provisions. I can imagine people saying: 'Oh, well, she is a woman, so she would be concerned.' ... It is not enough just to say that equality is desirable and is being attained by women. Equality or independence, or call it what you will, is being achieved slowly. In this instance, 'slowly' is the operative word.

She explained:

> Some women, whether they come from the working class or the most affluent, have never had any money of their own. They have had to ask their husband even for their tram fares ... While I am waving the women's lib banner, let me point out that even some of the younger wives are not trained to earn their living ... [but are] actively discouraged from continuing her education after fourth form.

Melzer slammed the increasingly militant Divorce Law Reform Association, quoting from one of its brochures that declared that the equity provisions in the new laws would aid 'the neurotic, the greedy and the vindictive [wife]' and the 'neurotic woman whose own ineptitude or greed caused the breakdown of the marriage' to '[grab] the assets of the marriage' to support her 'lazy, good for nothing' lifestyle. She concluded, 'I ask the Senate to acknowledge that, although our society is changing, the cry of women's lib is not an excuse for bypassing social and economic justice'.[53] Liberal Senator Kathy Sullivan drew on Melzer's words, similarly concluding, 'I suggest to the Senate that for all that many honourable senators have said, women in Australia today are not equal ... If the Government – this Government, or any future government – brings forward legislation which will genuinely enable women to be more independent, particularly economically, then I shall welcome it'.[54]

But this struggle would be long and hard.

'Equality has proved an elusive concept'

The Family Court of Australia opened its doors in 1976. The court's innovations broke with the adversarial model of justice, introducing revolutionary ideas about the role of counselling and social science in meeting families' needs. An air of informality grounded the new court: judges sat on the same level as parties, rather than behind a high bench, and barristers appeared without wigs or robes. The rules of evidence were also relaxed, so the court had greater discretion to accept evidence related to credibility, character and tendency. The traditional bar and judiciary were predictably appalled by the radical overhaul of their profession embodied by the Family Court and threw up fresh obstacles at every turn.[55] After the dismissal of Gough Whitlam as Prime Minister, the court was systematically starved of funds. But the real problem with the new family law system – as WEL had clearly signalled – invariably arose from the wider social and gender inequalities intrinsic to the family.

Over the ensuing decades, successive governments have

legislated against more obvious forms of inequality, finally passing the *Anti-Discrimination Act*, the work of Susan Ryan, during the Hawke years. But less visible forms of gender inequality are yet to be dealt with in law. It is mostly women who are victims of domestic abuse, including coercive control of their finances and their everyday lives. Women also contribute more unpaid labour to the family, through housework and parenting, and a gender pay gap persists, which cannot be accounted for by a simple arithmetic that factors in time off for child care. Law remains a male-dominated profession that has struggled to understand, interpret or act on these gendered social realities. Elizabeth Evatt, looking back on this 'period of optimism', wrote that 'Equality has proved an elusive concept ... [and] family support, the division of property, children's needs, violence, abuse and a myriad of other issues will continue to give rise to controversy – and keep family law high on the agenda for debate'.[56]

The *Family Law Act* brought about a decisive shift in thinking about the institution of the family, and the role that men and women play in maintaining or disrupting it. The impact can be read off the pages of newspapers and magazines from one decade to the next. In 1971, for example, the *Women's Weekly* ran a story under the headline, 'Advice for the Woman on the Verge of ...' followed by the word 'Divorce' in a large black font struck through with a seismic crack. In the article, the bestselling women's magazine advised its readers to 'Think again ... and again' before embarking on a course of action that – according to the writer, at least – would certainly result in 'barren bitterness' and 'emotionally crippled' children. 'How can a divorced woman cope with loneliness and the sense of failure? How can she cope with the guilt ...?'[57]

And yet, by the end of the decade, the same magazine would be offering women a very different kind of advice, marked by a tone of practicality and confidence. In a '5 Part Special' subtitled

'An Easy Guide to Family Law' published in 1979 – alongside articles on 'Easy Summer Cooking' and 'How to Make a Beer Can Hat' – the *Weekly* told its readers that they had legal and economic rights, and that their unpaid domestic labour would have economic value in the eyes of the new Family Court. 'With you running the household and caring for the children, your husband has been able to go to work and earn the money to pay the house off,' the writers explained. 'So you have helped to buy the house, even if it hasn't been with money.' Under the subheading 'Personal Protection', the 'Easy Guide' explained that a woman could apply to the Family Court for an injunction to stop a husband from 'beating you or the children', 'taking the children from you', 'coming into the family home', or 'selling the family home'. It advised, 'If you are afraid that your husband will ignore the injunction, do not hesitate to call the police'. It provided contact details for women's refuges in every state and territory where 'women and children who choose to leave a home where there is continual violence' would find support.[58]

By 1979, the Fraser government had already dismantled crucial aspects of the social programs that had underpinned the 'helping court' idea, but the ideal of genuine social equality that marked the Whitlam years – along with a foundational framework to support that aspiration – had irreducibly entered the mainstream of Australian life. In the pages of the 'Easy Guide', ideas about gender equality that had once been considered radical and controversial are presented as a form of cultural common sense.

PART THREE
HEALTH AND
SOCIAL POLICY

INTRODUCED BY KAREN SOLDATIC

A small group of Australian women made significant and enduring contributions to health and social policy during the Whitlam years. The four chapters here recount the journeys of those women, who were central to Whitlam's gendered equality reforms in those key areas. The authors demonstrate the significance of placing women at the core of policy reforms and the intergenerational outcomes of women's leadership in government. The Whitlam years saw the possibilities of redressing women's health and social policy inequalities galvanised to advance gendered equality and opportunity for women. Fifty years later, Australian women remain the beneficiaries of such incredible foresight. We are able to get a divorce on our own terms, receive payments as mothers of children born outside of marriage, and pursue, to a large extent, our goals for education and professional change. Medical and health care, such as breast screening, pap smears, along with appropriate public maternal health, remain cornerstones of our public health system. As the child of migrants growing up in the working-class suburbs of western Sydney, I too have been directly gifted by the tenacity and persistence of these women, and their continued activism and commitment to gendered equality policies.

The voices of these women contributors provide an important context for the 2022 federal election and the successful electoral results of women candidates. These chapters offer personal narratives of former women leaders in their years working inside the Whitlam government, chairing the Social Welfare Commission (Marie Coleman), agitating for local-level reform with the Women's Electoral Lobby (Margaret Reynolds), firmly establishing femocrats throughout the federal bureaucracy (Eva Cox), or driving reforms to give single mothers the economic security required to properly care for their children (Terese Edwards). The authors eloquently capture the feminist movement's energy and commitment. And importantly, each chapter marks out the struggle to disrupt long-held views about the role of government institutions, policies and programs in addressing women's structural inequality. Rich in narrative and nuanced in analysis, they distil the constraints, barriers and opportunities for reform built upon creativity, imagination and possibility.

Combined, these accounts demonstrate Whitlam's desire for more than the representation of women in leadership roles within the Australian political landscape. The authors identify how Whitlam and his team personally encouraged women to apply for core leadership roles in the very early days of gaining office. As Margaret Reynolds and Eva Cox explain, women were supporting women through their collective activism and sharing of resources to enable women's participation. Each of the authors articulates the ways in which Whitlam and his ministry clearly understood the vital importance of women's leadership in promoting women's gendered equality and equality of opportunity. For too long within the Australian historical landscape, women's social policy had been made without the voices of the very women it concerned – poor women, single mothers, women forced to rely on low-waged and often precarious work, and women who were seeking divorce. Whitlam ensured that women made women's policy by actively recruiting women into critical leadership roles. Fifty years later, the central place of women in making the very policies, decisions and institutions that shape their lives has become the norm in Australian social institutions and policy-making practices.[1] While we have not reached the ultimate goal of gendered equality and parity of participation – and as Terese Edwards outlines, have gone backwards substantially on issues of economic rights for single parents – recent activism by a new generation of women leaders, such as Grace Tame and Brittany Higgins, continues to demonstrate the enduring nature of the values and commitments pioneered by the Whitlam government for gender equality. There is no doubt that the 2022 federal election's gendered dynamics expressed these very sentiments.[2]

Whitlam and his team trusted and respected the women leaders installed to reform and drive forward change across the polity and social institutions. These women were trusted to set the agenda for women's policy-making in the health and social policy areas. As much as this was an exciting opportunity, in many ways, it also placed significant pressure on those women. They knew, as the contributors suggest, that getting these new institutions 'right' was critical to ensure long-lasting change.

One of the most important insights offered here is the continued demonstration of the ways that the personal remains political. As an Australian disability scholar, for the first time I began to understand the connection between Whitlam's gendered equality program and the early commitments to disability equality.[3] Marie Coleman recounts the ways that her personal exposure to disability and inappropriate servicing as a professional social worker in the early years of her career influenced and informed her work as Chair of the Social Welfare Commission.

It is only more recently that the Whitlam government has begun to be recognised for its innovations in disability policy, advocacy and equality of opportunity.[4] In the public arena, ongoing debates about the National Disability Insurance Scheme continue to suggest that the NDIS is something new and novel.[5] Yet the health and social policy agendas of the Whitlam years, with the rise of the global disability rights movement, actively took up and embedded emerging ideas of disability justice.[6] Whitlam's commitment to dismantling older systems of disability inequality and practices of institutionalisation is shown in the *Handicapped Program Assistance Act 1974*, the report on disability poverty by the Henderson Inquiry, and the proliferation of support for small, tailored disability services.[7] Policies such as the Regional Assistance Plan incorporated services and opportunities for people with disability. For the first time, the concerns of people with disability for equality, dignity and respect were recognised by government health and social policy departments.[8] Some of these initiatives and programs are now rejected as out of date, but at the time, Whitlam's proposals for personalised and responsive disability services were squarely outside the dominant models then operating.[9] The Whitlam years lay the groundwork for later reforms that both supported people with disability, and made sure that they were at the centre of making their own decisions.[10] Proposals developed by the Social Welfare Commission and supported through the Regional Assistance Plan offered a vast network of disability service provisions more in line with global trends towards independent living and de-institutionalisation, such as those proposed by student protestors at UC-Berkeley in the 1960s and 70s.[11] Disability equality was enshrined in international law only in 2008, when the United Nations Convention on the Rights of Persons with Disabilities came into force. Australia only ratified the Convention with the election of the Rudd Labor government, after continual pressure from the Australian disability rights movement.[12]

Whitlam's commitment to women and gendered equality propelled women into roles in which they developed and implemented new gendered pathways of reform. Through their lived expertise – as professionals working in highly gendered roles such as social workers, feminists who were also migrants, and as single parents of children – the women actively recruited into the centres of power have had a profound impact. Reforms in health and social policy have enabled Australian, migrant and refugee women, alongside people with disability, to forge independent lives, and to continue to challenge policies that undermine their capacities. The Whitlam government's reform efforts in these policy areas were built upon a desire for women's equality and employed a deliberate strategy to centre women in core positions to drive broad-scale social reform. Many of these initiatives remain with us today, but there is an ongoing struggle of solidarity to ensure that the gains made during the Whitlam years are not eroded.

WOMEN'S HEALTH, WOMEN'S WELFARE

MARIE COLEMAN

When the shadow Minister for Health and Welfare Bill Hayden called me before the federal election in late 1972, he told me that Whitlam was planning a combined Health and Welfare Commission, with my friend Dr Sydney Sax as the Health Commissioner, and myself as the Welfare Commissioner. Would I be up for it?

I was then the Director (CEO) of the Victorian Council of Social Service. I had been recruited by David Scott, of the Brotherhood of St Lawrence, in 1965. Previously I was the initial social worker with the Asthma Foundation of Victoria, and before that, a medical social worker at what was then Preston and Northcote Hospital. In those positions I had become very familiar with the deficiencies in the national health insurance scheme, with its high cost and failure to cover people with chronic debilitating conditions, not least those requiring ongoing nursing home care. In those positions I had worked with both the Australian Association of Social Workers and the Victorian Council of Social Service (VCoSS) to develop policy positions, and to help run advocacy campaigns. Social security policy was greatly in need of rethinking, because there were substantial gaps. Community services were a patchwork, and generally lacking in coordination at the local level. There was no broad focus at national or state level of reform, such as had taken place in the United Kingdom after World War II, and there was little appreciation of the social determinants of health.

The debates over reform of private health insurance, reform of age care and care of people with long-term disability all continued while I was at VCoSS. One outcome was the introduction by the Commonwealth of supplementary Nursing Home Benefits in 1968. I had begun a close association with researchers at the University of Melbourne, associated with Professor Ronald Henderson, on reform of age care, and of health insurance. Helen Ferber, who had links to the West German Embassy, took an interest in my work. In 1966 the West German government invited me to tour that country to learn about social policy there, I believe at Helen Ferber's suggestion. This tour helped me greatly in clarifying thinking about the role of central government in developing overarching strategies on social policy.

VCoSS also developed policy positions and campaigned for reform of child care. We brought together a group of experts to develop a report. The inaugural Director of the Women's Bureau in the Commonwealth Department of Labour and National Service, Lenore Cox, had published a pioneering series of studies of child care in Australia in the late 1960s providing crucial information for those concerned about women's workforce participation.[1] This eventually led to the Minister for Labour and National Service, Billy Snedden, asking to see me, and he went on to republish our report. The report contributed to the debate in Canberra, which led to the passage of the *Child Care Act* of 1969. VCoSS also dipped a toe into regional social planning, and more.

At the same time as I was working for VCoSS, I was also a member of the planning group of what became Family Planning Victoria, the chair of a reform body for an intellectual disability service called Star, and a member of the planning body for the first community health service to be developed by the Alfred Hospital. More significantly, along with Professor Ronald Henderson and David Scott of the Brotherhood of St Lawrence, I had been involved in the 1971–72 consultation with the Social Services

Minister, William Wentworth, in the creation of the Royal Commission of Enquiry into Poverty in Australia, to be chaired by Ronald Henderson.

The concept was attractive: a combined Health and Welfare Commission that could bring together thinking about the social underpinning of better health, along with such issues as better approaches to women's and Indigenous health issues. It is fair to say that the idea of broad social policy working across health, welfare, housing, education and other sectors was not then well advanced in Australia. But in the end, it was not to be.

Chairing the Social Welfare Commission

In 1972 I was a young mother with three daughters aged between 12 and 9 years, and we were all active in our local community. When the invitation to head the Social Welfare Commission was formalised after the 1972 election, we had family conferences. My husband and the children agreed that the opportunity to influence the way Australia might go forward was important. I accepted the position of interim Chair of the Australian Government Social Welfare Commission. We sought someone dependable to manage our household during my absences. The magazine *Woman's Day* did a spread about us, and our eldest daughter was uncooperative, hamming for the photographer. We were unnerved by the general astonishment that a woman had been appointed to such a senior role. My daughters found the publicity uncomfortable.

Once the government had been elected, and Cabinet determined by the process of a Caucus vote, Dr Doug Everingham became the new Minister for Health. Whitlam found himself with a minister he hadn't planned for, a quirky medical practitioner from sugarcane country, and the result was two separate commissions – Social Welfare, and Hospitals and Health Services – although Hayden retained in Social Security (as the department was renamed) responsibility for the introduction of Medibank, and aged care.[2]

Nothing prepared me for the newspaper banner on the day of the announcement of my appointment: '$15,000 a year job for a working mum'.[3] I almost drove off the road as I took the girls to school. Dr Sax's appointment was announced simultaneously but did not attract similar treatment. An ancient family friend of my mother-in-law began a series of letters to the Prime Minister, denouncing the appointment of a woman, a social worker no less, to a position at such a rate of pay.

I flew to Canberra to assume my new career on my 40th birthday (3 March 1973), excited, but full of trepidation, having never worked in the public service. My appointment, the most senior appointment ever of a woman, was a novelty and attracted much attention. The Melbourne *Sun* pursued me, knocking on my motel door at 7.30 am wanting a story on women who earned more than their husbands. I redirected them to my friend Senator Margaret Guilfoyle, while enquiring about the relative marital income of the journalist. My career had risen rapidly, but I can say in complete honesty that not until I reached Canberra was the issue of my being a woman ever raised to attack me. Critical and sometimes snide attacks began from the first day, when the young person who drove me from the airport to my motel told me how the department was joking about how the title of Chairlady sounded so like Charlady.

The department was welcoming, but cool. There was no office for me. Hayden directed that I should establish the Commission from his ministerial suite in Juliana House, the head office of the Department of Social Security. The department provided me with a secretary, and after a few days a personal assistant, Zrinka Moran. Hayden had also appointed the commissioners, none of whom were personally known to me, and the first task was to organise the first meeting of the Interim Committee for the

Commission, which in due course was formally opened by the Prime Minister, accompanied by his wife Margaret.

Margaret had been a social worker in Sydney and was also treading an innovative path for the wife of a Prime Minister, writing a column for *Woman's Day*. She was receiving voluminous public correspondence about social issues, which was initially sent on to me, until I was forced to insist the Prime Minister's Office find a means of managing them.

The commissioners debated on working processes, agreeing that some projects would be headed by individual commissioners where relevant. Policy would be determined by agreement. When the Interim Committee considered the draft legislation to legally establish the Commission, it insisted on a clause making the Chair the head of the statutory agency with powers equivalent to those of a permanent head of a department. When royal assent was given later in 1973, I became the first woman in Australia to hold a position equivalent to the Secretary of a department. We recruited staff, among them Andrew Podger from the Australian Bureau of Statistics, later Secretary of several departments, and Mary Scott from the Department of the Interior as Secretary to the Commission. Later, Mary was one of the core officials in the Hawke administration working on the management of Australia's response to the HIV epidemic.

The pace of work was unrelenting, and I visited many parts of the Commonwealth to consult locally and gain wider understanding of issues and concerns. I flew from Melbourne to Canberra each Monday morning, returning each Friday afternoon – often to find my husband had organised a barbeque for 40 or so guests for the Sunday. There would be other domestic tasks, and school-related matters. I was unimpressed to hear that my daughters' (private) school held prayers for working mothers at assembly and was pleased to help my eldest daughter form a school Women's Liberation Club. The second daughter, to her father's distress, insisted on liberating the local volunteer bushfire brigade, becoming a radio operator, proud of her boiler suit embroidered with 'Firewoman Coleman'.

Reforming social welfare

Whitlam, the son of a former Commonwealth Solicitor General, had a clear understanding of the nature, role and limitations of the Commonwealth Public Service, and came to office with an established plan for reform of public administration. He rapidly established various statutory commissions (similar to the Universities Commission) in areas where he thought the existing policy and administration was too narrowly focused or lacked understanding of his policy agenda. He commissioned a wide range of inquiries, such as that of Mr Justice Woodward into a national Compensation and Rehabilitation Scheme; Woodward had conducted a similar inquiry in his native New Zealand.[4] The Henderson Commission of Inquiry into Poverty in Australia was expanded to cover additional areas, with new commissioners for each appointed. Dr HC Coombs was appointed to conduct an inquiry into Commonwealth public administration. The Social Welfare Commission was to make submissions to all of these, in addition to its self-determined work program, and references from the Minister.

It is useful to bear in mind that in 1972, beyond the role of the Universities Commission in higher education, which had taken over the funding of universities from states, the Commonwealth had little involvement in many of the policy areas prominent in Whitlam's proposed program. Moreover, Whitlam was actively pushing in areas where he thought states had been dilatory. No Commonwealth funding went to states' public hospitals, nor government schools. Aged care funding was a mishmash, with the Commonwealth funding not-for-profits (NFPs) to build aged care homes, and both NFPs and for-profits to run nursing homes, while states were responsible for acute hospital care and geriatric rehabilitation.

The Commonwealth had begun limited funding for child day care, and for training for pre-school teachers, while states were responsible for early childhood education (kindergartens). The states were responsible for programs for Indigenous Australians. States provided such residential, rehabilitation and therapeutic programs as existed for people with disability – although younger people with disability were beginning to find their way into nursing homes for aged people. Alongside that, the Commonwealth ran a major residential and ambulatory program of vocational rehabilitation for individuals otherwise eligible for invalidity pensions, as well as subsidising sheltered workshops and hostels for people with disability.

The Commonwealth, from Federation, had full responsibilities for aged pensions, and a gradually widening range of payments for widows, sickness and unemployment payments and the like. A constitutional referendum in 1949 had confirmed the scope of the Social Services power, including the introduction of medical insurance and pharmaceutical benefits, with the caveat of not involving medical practitioner compulsion along the lines of the post-war National Health Service in the United Kingdom. Registration of health professionals was entirely state based, so that a nurse attending a patient on aerial transfer from Alice Springs to Adelaide would need at least two separate registrations. The Commonwealth had no role in general state welfare responsibilities, such as child welfare, juvenile corrections and adoptions.

During the second half of the 1960s, in New South Wales and Victoria, there had been an expansion of local government in provision of various community services, notably child care, and aged care services such as home help and meals on wheels.

Whitlam, and Hayden, were seeking some overarching reform of welfare to give the Commonwealth a lead role, developing new initiatives, as had briefly happened under Chifley during the post-war reconstruction period.

Whitlam was initially determined to promote local government, passing over the states, as a local service provider or coordinator, including for air transport, housing and community services. Over the months he became somewhat disillusioned by some conservative councillors' resistance to these plans, and much more anxious to promote regionalism, and regional structures, again as an alternative to states. The states resisted all of this, as did some Commonwealth agencies: universities, airports, hospitals did not usually fit tidily into either local or regional government. States were hostile to proposals for the radical reform of health insurance (Medibank), but rather more receptive to proposals to renew and expand states' hospitals and community health programs, with money going through more traditional state grants routes.

The Department of Social Security (DSS), alongside which the Social Welfare Commission sat as an independent body answering to the Minister, was uncertain as to how much it welcomed the new policy body. Early referrals to the Commission by the Minister trod on departmental toes, notably a reference from the Minister to review aged care policy, and separately, to review the proposal to establish a payment for unmarried mothers, in addition to the existing Class A and Class B Widow's Pensions.[5] There were, of course, no payments for widowers.

In Melbourne, at VCoSS, I had been a strong proponent of a Commonwealth pension for unmarried mothers, which was introduced in 1973. An effective group of women, who subsequently formalised as the Council for Single Mothers and their Children, had worked assiduously to promote their cause. They were able to recruit the services of Peter Cullen, a Melbourne consultant who had previously worked for both Whitlam and Senator Patrick

Kennelly. Peter volunteered his time, having had a family member in rural Victoria with experience of single parenthood. I sat in on departmental meetings on the matter, since the commissioners all supported the proposal. I separately advised the Minister of the Commission's view that it ought to proceed. Peter Cullen did valuable lobbying with Caucus members, and Hayden was able to win support in Caucus and Cabinet. Payments for sole male supporting parents were introduced in 1978: old assumptions about widowers easily remarrying to find another child carer were still strong. The introduction of the payment for unmarried mothers underwent several iterations. Subsequently, it was folded along with the Class A and Class B Widow's Pensions into the Sole Parent Pension – a move intended to remove any remaining stigma. However, the Howard government ultimately destroyed this approach, forcing new applicants onto unemployment payments once the youngest child turned eight years old. The Gillard government completed this destruction, moving the 'grandfathered' women onto unemployment payments. I will not attempt a full review of the Hayden initiatives in income security here, but Professor Peter Whiteford has published a range of important papers.[6]

Around the same time, work began within the Commission on the development of a tool for allocating government grants to local government authorities, based on need, rather than political advantage ('pork-barrelling'). This was led by Andrew Podger, using statistical methods developed by Dr Tony Vinson (then Senior Lecturer in the Department of Social Work at the University of Sydney). It was in those very early months of 1973 when the Minister asked me to advise on the development of the Australian Assistance Plan. He provided me with a Minute from the Department, which consisted of a proposal to provide an annual grant of $2 per head of population to each local government authority for general welfare purposes. Some have speculated on Hayden's interest in emulating the similarly titled Canada

Assistance Plan. There was never any intention by Whitlam or Hayden of seeking to cost-share the funding and administration of Commonwealth income support payments with the states. Equally unlikely would be the willingness of states to share the financial costs. In Australia, the colonies had made national government takeover of their age and other payments schemes a condition of Federation. Social services is a Commonwealth power set out in the Australian constitution. Moreover, the Commonwealth programs funding aged care homes, disability services and homeless services were all directly funded, not paid through nor cost-shared with states. After due deliberation, the Commission recommended to the Minister an experimental pilot program, based on community development principles, and on regional structures, to parallel the Regional Organisations of Councils then being developed by the Department of Urban and Regional Development, on a direct to local body payment basis, not via, nor cost-shared, with the states (which were becoming increasingly inflamed and uncooperative with most of the Whitlam initiatives).

The scheme developed by the Commission, the Australian Assistance Plan (AAP), was to encourage the development of regional councils of social development (RCSD), which would be provided with funds to employ a social planner, and community development officers, and to have as seed money the original proposal of an annual grant of $2 per head of population. The councils should incorporate representatives of local government, relevant state government agencies, and the local community. The RCSD should map local communities, identify unmet needs and facilitate applications for financial support to appropriate funding bodies. The entire initial pilot program would be externally evaluated, and the evaluation published, before the AAP took final ongoing form.

The proposal to the Minister drew on my experience at VCoSS, which had been approached in the late 1960s by the

Geelong Community Chest, an original initiative of the Ford Motor Company executives. They asked VCoSS to develop a proposal to assist in the distribution of the funds they raised. I appointed a staff member, Hayden Raysmith, to the task, and he developed the original structure. Subsequently, Hayden worked with me in the Social Welfare Commission to develop the AAP. While the Commission retained its own staff to develop and monitor the pilot program, DSS regional offices were most enthusiastic to work on the AAP, with leads taken by regional social work staff. Some states were cooperative, others not. Several academics at different universities were contracted to evaluate the pilot projects in their states – a total of 35 pilots in all.

Grace Vaughan of the Western Australian Department of Community Services was seconded to work full time for the Commission developing the Western Australian pilots. Many local women became very engaged, sometimes as volunteers, some as community development workers or social planners. In her memoir *Gough and Me*, Christine Sykes describes her life in Cabramatta, Whitlam's involvement as local member in community issues, and her recruitment through the AAP to a position with the local council, and eventually to a full-time career with the Department of Urban and Regional Development.[7] Local activities very commonly involved playgrounds, after-school projects, social programs for isolated people and other small-scale but valuable initiatives. Many of these projects were community-led, and of particular benefit to women within their own communities.

The Australian Assistance Plan (AAP) was eventually defunded by the Fraser government, but several RCSDs continued after the cessation of the federal program. Evaluations of the pilots were published after the AAP was defunded. In the mid-2010s, Professor Melanie Oppenheimer conducted a study of the AAP, funded by the Australian Research Council, which involved the only consultation directly with people who had worked at the community level in the AAP, and provides the only current description of it.[8] This study found that the AAP had encouraged volunteerism, empowered grassroots activity and encouraged people to become more involved with their local communities, especially in regional Australia.

These new programs and approaches required new workforce skills, such as community development and social planning. I recruited Eva Lerner to assist the Commission in addressing this.[9] Eva, an Australian social worker, was then Social Work Education Adviser to the UK's Central Council for Education and Training in Social Work. She subsequently had a distinguished career in Australia in education as well as law reform before returning to the UK.

Reforming child care

Early childhood day care (as it was then called, differentiating it from residential child care) was the subject of interdepartmental rivalry: the former Department of Labour and National Service lost the *Child Care Act 1972* to the new Interim Committee for the Pre-schools Commission in the Education portfolio. The Department of Social Security considered it a welfare program, the Department of Health considered it to be child development. In late 1973, as the Interim Committee for the Pre-Schools Commission was working on the brief given it by Whitlam, the Women's Electoral Lobby began agitating with Elizabeth Reid, the PM's Women's Adviser, complaining that there was insufficient priority given to child day care.[10] The women were also successful in reaching Whitlam, including through his principal adviser Dr Peter Wilenski, whose wife Gail was highly active in WEL.[11] The Committee brief was to enact the election commitment of a year's free pre-school. Once the report of the Interim Committee was presented to the Cabinet, the interdepartmental rivalry over early childhood resumed, but the matter being most strongly pressed, especially by the Women's Electoral Lobby, was the need for child care, because pre-school, with its shorter hours of care, was insufficient to meet the needs of many working parents.

I was summoned to The Lodge one Saturday in 1974 to a meeting at which the PM expressed his dissatisfaction with the lack of emphasis on child care in the report of the Interim Committee for the Pre-Schools Commission. There was an unpleasant scene. I was asked to provide an alternative report, and the Priorities Review Team was tasked to keep a watching brief. I recruited Lenore Cox, the former Director of the Women's Bureau, to lead a team to work on the task. In late 1974 the report was ready and as Lenore and I entered Parliament House with the report in my briefcase, we passed an election poster: 'Vote Whitlam, He's the One with a Child Care Plan'. At that point, no one in the ministry had seen so much as a draft.[12]

Shortly after delivery of the report, I was admitted to hospital in Melbourne for major surgery, but I returned to Canberra as soon as possible. Issues were developing with some of the AAP's regional councils straying into local politics, and clashing with local Labor politicians, who were making their displeasure known to the Minister. It was a tricky time, with Hayden publicly stating his intention to disestablish the Social Welfare Commission, then retracting. Charles Perkins in the Department of Aboriginal Affairs was against the RCSD having any engagement in Aboriginal matters, arguing reasonably that the degree of racism in many regions made effective Aboriginal participation difficult. The Department of Social Security was opposed to RCSDs having any role in the administration of aged or disability services.

After the election, disputes continued as to who should be the lead department on child care. This led to the Children's Services Program, and the new Children's Commission Interim Committee being created in the Prime Minister's Department with Tony Ayers appointed as Chair, and the former Interim Committee Chair Joan Fry as Assistant Secretary, with responsibility for workforce.[13] This ongoing dispute over child care was never resolved satisfactorily. After the election of the Fraser government, the Interim Committee for the Children's Commission was disbanded, the Office of Child Care was created, and I was appointed Director of the Office of Child Care, reporting to the Minister for Social Security, Senator Margaret Guilfoyle. The Fraser government promoted child care and withdrew from funding pre-schools. Yet the policy did not promote or encourage child care to be associated with the primary school system, or the pre-school system, so that each ran separately. The Hawke Labor government reintroduced pre-school funding that the Coalition Howard government then sought to withdraw. Regular ongoing Commonwealth funding for pre-schools appeared to stabilise under the Morrison Coalition government. Child care was an important election issue in the 2022 campaign. The new Albanese government is planning a substantial increase in Commonwealth investment in child care, and both the News South Wales and Victorian governments have announced their own investments in pre-school and child care.

The lack of integration between child care and early education/pre-schools remains a policy issue. Early childhood is such an important period for child development, and programs need to be culturally appropriate, provide stimulation for those children who are experiencing disadvantage, and prepare children for primary school. At the same time, the rapid return of women to the workforce, and the social changes which effectively demand two-income households, mean that affordable and accessible early childhood care services are a critical element in workforce participation and productivity. Even with the new government's expansion of child care, training, expanding and retaining the child-care workforce will be crucial. Workforce shortages will not be resolved solely by improving wages and conditions: training and education have a vital role to play. Integrated policy which recognises all factors is important. In 2022 we still seem to find this hard to achieve.

Reforming health

After the double dissolution election of 1974, a joint sitting enabled the passage of legislation to establish the Scotton–Deeble plan for Medibank, a compulsory national health insurance scheme. This brought access to affordable health care within the reach of many low-income families, especially women and children who may have previously been solely reliant on attendance at the Emergency Departments of public hospitals. The Australian Medical Association was bitterly opposed to this plan, the states less so since they were now in receipt of generous support from the Hospitals and Health Services Commission for both new and renovated hospitals, and for community health programs. The Victorian Health Department was virulent in attacking Medibank – I remember seeing a poster in their office depicting Hayden as Hitler, with a big 'SS' over his head. Fee-for-service dentistry was not included in Medibank, although states did get some assistance for publicly provided school-based dental services.

There were many initiatives beneficial to women in the broader health field: the first National Women's Health Conference in 1973, the development of national women's health policies, placing oral contraceptives on the Pharmaceutical Benefits Scheme and funding Family Planning associations – all energetically promoted by WEL. Other initiatives included the funding of Women's Health Centres through the Community Health Program, and of course the funding of the first women's refuges in 1975. These were incorporated into the Community Health Program because the Department of Social Security ruled them ineligible under the *Homeless Person's Assistance Act 1973* – itself another Hayden initiative.

Much of the Whitlam government's program derived from and built on the policy ideas being developed prior to its election in universities, the community sector, the health sector and beyond, which had been frustrated by the torpor of conservative governments nationally and at state level. The new urban and regional development departmental policies, for example, had been largely developed by people such as Pat Troy, of the Australian National University, who was immediately recruited to the public sector.

It is important to understand the importance of the women's movement in driving the changes in sectors such as child care, the development of women's health policies, and the introduction of services such as women's refuges. These had not been central to the initial Whitlam program, but were a response by Whitlam and his ministers (albeit sometimes reluctantly) to the growing importance of women's views. There were no women in the Whitlam ministry, but there were increasingly strong voices in the resurgent second-wave women's movement speaking to the ministers. Women were becoming influential in numbers in local government, and there were women in important roles in broadcasting.

Reforming the public sector for women

While employment conditions for women were not good in the private sector, the Public Service Board at the Commonwealth level had been working pre-Whitlam on improving conditions for women. Women had been employed in the Australian Public Service since its establishment, and certain types of work were reserved for women. However, their employment opportunities were severely restricted. A major change occurred in 1966 when the *Public Service Act* was amended to permit married women to be appointed as permanent officers and to allow female officers to retain their permanent status in the Service after marriage.

A provision was also included in the Act to allow women to take (unpaid) maternity leave for a maximum of 26 weeks and to resume duty afterwards without loss of any rights.[14] The legislation bringing the new provisions into effect came into operation on 18 November 1966.[15] In June 1967, there were 2027 married women employed as permanent officers in the Service. By June 1968, there were 4832 permanent married women officers, an increase of 139 per cent. These developments were not so significant for me personally as they were for the women beginning to enter and progress in the Australian Public Service. Paid maternity leave was an enormous boon for young women. Permanent part-time positions enabled many young mothers to continue working.

On 19 June 1969 the Commonwealth Conciliation and Arbitration Commission handed down the Equal Pay case decision, an event of great industrial significance. In its decision, the Commission declared that they were prepared to implement the principle of equal pay for equal work to the extent and on a basis which was similar to those provided in the various state statutes. Each determination and award was required to be separately examined on the basis of nine principles, with implementation phased over a period from 1 October 1969, with 100 per cent of the male rate being achieved by 1 January 1972.[16] A further decision handed down by the Commission in December 1972 introduced a new principle based on equal pay for work of equal value. The main Australian Public Service groups affected by this decision were the keyboard, telephonist, cafeteria, cleaner and hospital staff groups, in which men were generally not employed.[17]

The Board's 1972 annual report indicated that conditions of employment for women were under examination, including provisions relating to maternity leave.[18] In response to government initiatives and as a result of these studies, the Board took several important steps taken to further improve women's conditions of employment.[19] In November 1972 a memorandum was widely distributed seeking views on the Board's initial conclusions. As a result, all remaining restrictions on men or women in those employment groups where restrictions still applied were removed. The Board also began to examine the whole question of part-time employment.[20] On 3 April 1973 the Prime Minister announced that all women Australian public servants, whether married or not, would be eligible for 12 weeks' paid maternity leave from 1 January 1973. Also granted was an additional 40 weeks' leave without pay, or (by converting sick leave, recreation leave or furlough) paid leave. Men were also provided with a week's paid leave at the time of the birth of a child.[21] In May 1973 upper age limits for appointments to designations such as Clerk, Clerical Assistant and Typist were removed, a reform particularly relevant to women as it enabled them to return to work after a period out of the workforce.[22]

In December 1973 a sub-committee of Joint Council (a statutory employer/union consultative body chaired by the Public Service Board) was established to consider a number of aspects of the employment of women in the Service, including equality of opportunity, specific accommodation difficulties and the application of the married rates of allowance to women.[23] The Chairman of the Board wrote to permanent heads in April 1974 about the employment of women in the Service. The letter affirmed the Board's belief that the principle of equality for men and women should be applied to every aspect of employment and that every effort should be made to ensure that women were given the training and experience to prepare them for advancement to senior positions. Particular mention was made of the importance of ensuring that women were included as members of selection and other committees, and as departmental representatives on promotion appeal committees, interdepartmental committees and training courses conducted by the Board and other institutions.[24]

A section was established in the Public Service Board in 1975 to provide a focal point for the further development of policies and activities related to equal employment opportunity. The Board also advised departments of the need to designate positions to provide assistance to management in developing departmental equal employment opportunity policies.[25] Over this period, the Board also participated in the design of flexible working hours in a large number of departments[26] and examined the issue of part-time employment.[27]

In summary, much of the legislative framework removing discrimination against women in the Australian Public Service was in place or had been considered by the Public Service Board prior to the change of government in 1972. As indicated above, other important changes continued to be made which were strongly supported by the incoming government.

Of course, Edna Ryan, the ground-breaking trade unionist and feminist who had known Whitlam from his electorate in which she had been a local government councillor, was successful immediately after the election in persuading Whitlam to reopen the Equal Pay case before the Commonwealth Conciliation and Arbitration Commission for private sector employees – as Mary Gaudron used to say, we won equal pay for the first time, but we had to win it again and again. In 2022 it still proves elusive.

Looking back over the period, and subsequent decades, it is my view that while the Whitlam government did introduce many policies and programs of considerable benefit to women (see, for example, free tertiary education), it was not consciously pursuing a feminist agenda, nor did it focus on related structural reform. That came with the Hawke government, and Senator Susan Ryan's work on the *Sex Discrimination Act*, and the promotion of a range of measures to develop a gendered lens on the Budget process. I would characterise Whitlam's reformist agenda as driven by a powerful sense of social justice, a need to modernise public administration, and a deep commitment to humanity. Women were but one of the groups that benefited from this vision.

A final personal note. By the time of the tumultuous events of 11 November 1975, my two youngest daughters were living with me in Canberra, the eldest would follow in another couple of years, my marriage was over, and I had begun helping my new partner, Mary Scott, build a mudbrick house on a rural property she owned outside Canberra. Our daughter lives there today, renovating and restoring the building with her partner. My personal revolution.

WOMEN FOR WHITLAM EVERYWHERE: THE WHITLAM GOVERNMENT AND REGIONAL AUSTRALIA

MARGARET REYNOLDS

It's time

When I heard Gough Whitlam's 1972 election speech, with its famous opening line 'Men and Women of Australia', his words resonated with me personally in distant Townsville, North Queensland, where I believed there was an urgent need for change. As a young married woman with two small children, I was very aware of the sexism and double standards applied to men and women in my community. In the deep north, men were always the decision-makers and women rarely became involved in public life, so an aspiring Prime Minister who actually addressed the women of Australia directly was highly significant. There was also an 'It's time' theme to his speech which appealed to many of us who were demanding equality at home, in the workforce and in the community. The second wave of feminism had broken onto Australian shores in the late 1960s with fresh debates led by feminist writers like Germaine Greer and Gloria Steinem.

The Women's Electoral Lobby

The Women's Electoral Lobby (WEL) emerged out of the 1960s Women's Liberation Movement, which saw a range of protests demanding equality for women. WEL Australia was established in 1972 as a national organisation with autonomous branches in each state and territory as well as in a number of regional areas. This organisation was a catalyst for many Australian women, encouraging them to mobilise and demand action on women's policy implementation that for so long had been ignored by previous governments.

One of its objectives was 'to involve women and the community generally in processes which will achieve a society based on gender equity and justice'.[1] I was a founding member of WEL Townsville, which we started early in 1972, and we began our lobbying locally, demanding our city council establish a Women's Advisory Committee to change its preoccupation with roads, rates and rubbish. We wanted council-sponsored child care, well-equipped playgrounds, a women's refuge and public transport: all of which seemed distant goals in 1970s Queensland.

However, in the lead-up to the 1972 election, we knew it was our responsibility to energise debate around the national agenda, which we imagined might also lead to local reform. We organised interviews with the all-male candidates for Herbert, the federal seat based in Townsville. We used the WEL questionnaire and rated candidates according to the responses that we considered best reflected a commitment to reform and women's issues.

John Rockett, a young teacher and Queensland Teachers Union organiser, was the Labor candidate and easily scored well to gain the support of many local women. We promoted his posters around the city and fronted a Liberal Party function to ask questions about their women's policy. The reply was all too typical of that era because we were advised that Prime Minister McMahon had passed the WEL questionnaire to his wife! I was also part of a local political advertising campaign, which incorporated individual photos of (mainly) young people indicating why they were voting Labor, with the key issues identified being education, employment and health.

Whitlam and some of his younger advisers were very familiar

with the demands of women and indeed of a new generation wanting to discard the remnants of the 1950s and project new ideas which were more in touch with modern Australia. This influence had been increasing during Whitlam's time as Opposition leader, so it helped shape the policies he took to the 1972 election. In that landmark speech in Blacktown on 13 November 1972, the alternative Prime Minister announced he was leaving the old ways behind and outlining an exciting program of change. I had never heard a politician talk with such conviction about social reform and it was certainly a revelation to hear one whose commitment was:

- to promote equality
- to involve the people of Australia in the decision-making processes of our land
- and to liberate the talents and uplift the horizons of the Australian people.[2]

It was a wide-ranging speech that reached out to all Australians, but for many women it was a speech that not only included them but also responded to their priorities.

A federal Labor government

The election of the Whitlam government on 2 December 1972 created a national mood of expectation among women of my generation. Was it even possible that Australia could undergo such a transformation as Whitlam had outlined during the election campaign, and would women see practical steps that changed their lives and place in the community? One of Whitlam's first decisions as Prime Minister was to announce the end of conscription and the release of seven men jailed for resisting the draft. In 1964 the government had introduced compulsory national service based on a twice-yearly random ballot which selected the birthdate of those who would be obliged to register for two years full-time service in the army. During the 80 years of conscription, more than 15 000 national servicemen served in Vietnam and 200 lost their lives.[3]

In Townsville in 1966, I had established a branch of Save our Sons, the anti-conscription women's organisation, aligned with all those who opposed Menzies' decision to follow the United States into the Vietnam War. The Vietnam Moratorium against this war saw many protests and marches, but it was conscription that angered many women who reacted against this government policy, which so intruded on their families. In his Blacktown speech, Whitlam had signalled that

> The war of intervention in Vietnam is ending. The great powers are rethinking and remoulding their relationships and their obligations. Australia cannot stand still at such a time. We cannot afford to limp along with men whose attitudes are rooted in the slogans of the 1950s, the slogans of fear and hate.[4]

The official declaration ending conscription within days of Whitlam becoming Prime Minister was a symbol of hope for a generation that had seen government take control of young lives. It was this pledge which galvanised many families, politicised by the Vietnam War, to vote for change.

As a new leader, Whitlam could have been seen as an unlikely advocate for social reform that began to change the lives of Australian women wherever they lived. He was urbane, intellectual and totally focused on his vision to modernise the nation. He was often impatient with the minutiae of government processes, so he could have easily overlooked the day-to-day lives of women, especially those in regional Australia. However, he had already managed to introduce new ideas to the very traditional

Labor Party as Opposition Leader from 1967. These included not only a major domestic reform agenda but also political and economic participation for women.

When Whitlam spoke of the attitudes of old men in the McMahon government, he could also have been referring to some of the old guard within his own ranks. While the ALP is a party of reform, it was slow to offer women the equality on which it was based. Senator Dorothy Tangney (Western Australia) was the first Labor woman to be elected to the national Parliament, in 1943, and there was a 30-year gap before the next Labor woman, Joan Child (Member for Henty, Victoria), was elected to the House of Representatives in 1974. This followed her great performance as a candidate in 1972 when she achieved a swing of 9 per cent and only missed election by 308 votes.[5]

After his election victory, Whitlam wasted no time: he and his deputy, Lance Barnard, were sworn in as the two-person ministry to begin implementing the government's national agenda. It was early December and Whitlam knew the traditional Australian summer close-down would limit introduction of the new government's program until mid-January if he was not creative in starting the promised reform process. He considered it urgent to reopen the Equal Pay case which had seen the McMahon government intervene against the ACTU's claim for equal pay, and he wanted to immediately register his government's support. Mary Gaudron was briefed to present a fresh case based on the principle of equal pay for work of equal value.[6] In 1973 a ruling by the Australian Conciliation and Arbitration Commission finally granted an equal minimum wage to all Australians, regardless of their sex, and in 1974 the 'breadwinner' component of the male wage was removed in recognition that more Australian women were providing for their families.[7]

In April 1973 Whitlam appointed Elizabeth Reid as special Adviser to the Prime Minister on Women's Affairs, demonstrating he was serious about change to benefit Australian women. A woman leader would promote legal and administrative reform as well as practical programs that reached women around the country.[8]

This unprecedented commitment to a women's reform agenda was a tremendous boost to women's confidence in the Whitlam government. Whitlam's vision for women was to be overseen by a woman based in his office! However, in the early 1970s, the macho media was not ready to accept a professional woman taking on such an unknown role. The role must have seemed quite overwhelming, with negative sniping from all directions. Critics both male and female were convinced that women's aspirations for a fair go were a threat to the family and the world as we knew it! However, the women's movement itself, while very supportive of Liz Reid, was impatient for reform, so some women's organisations became critical of both the pace and scope of change. Australia's first Women's Adviser had to advocate for immediate reform within a political and bureaucratic structure that was locked into preserving the status quo where women knew their place. However, Reid was a skilled negotiator able to prioritise her immediate and longer-term public policy goals and strategically advocate from the centre of the new government. The seismic shift to introduce policy recognising Australian women is attributed to the Whitlam government, but we should remember the essential influence of Liz Reid.

Whitlam was committed to equal pay and an end to discrimination in the workplace, but it was the specific campaigning of the Women's Electoral Lobby which broadened his understanding of women's issues that had never been included on the political agenda. In determining that change was overdue, he considered women in his commitment to recognise both the Universal Declaration of Human Rights 1948 and the United Nations Convention on Political Rights of Women 1962.

During her first meeting with Whitlam, Reid was impressed with his 'tremendous awareness of women's issues'.[9] Coinciding with Reid's appointment, Whitlam introduced a review of the employment of women in the Australian Public Service, announcing that government would be a pacesetter in promoting the status of women.[10]

How Whitlam's reforms affected women in regional Australia

In documenting the impact of Whitlam government reforms on Australian women, it is important to also identify generic changes in education, health, employment, social security, and urban and regional development. Whitlam reflected on his vision of creating equal opportunity throughout Australia when he looked back on his first 12 months in office:

> When I speak of equality of opportunity I am not thinking simply of the removal of poverty or the redress of obvious injustices such as those in education and health. The evidence of unequal opportunity is to be found at all [...] we are pledged for example to give greater equality of opportunity to women, who have long been disadvantaged – often in subtle and hidden ways – in a male oriented society.[11]

Education

The Whitlam government's national education reform, introduced in 1973, was wide-ranging. His government doubled education spending in its first Budget, established the Schools Commission as an independent statutory body to give aid to all schools on a needs basis, and started the process by which the federal government assumed responsibility for Australian universities. Most significantly for women and people from lower socio-economic backgrounds, university fees were abolished.

An area of special importance to women in remote areas of Australia was the focus of benefits for isolated children. A standard boarding allowance was paid for children deemed to be living too far away to attend a local school. In addition, there was an allowance for clothing and books as well as a further means-tested allowance.

The Australian Pre-School Committee was established to make recommendations to government on developing pre-schools and child-care centres throughout Australia. The Child Care Standards Committee advised on the payment of grants for child care and to establish appropriate standards for child-care facilities financially assisted by the government. In Townsville a voluntary pre-school program called Kindergarten Headstart, established in 1967, received recognition and funding and was visited by Margaret Whitlam in 1974.

As a young teacher, I started to notice change within my local school, especially as I was working in a new special education unit. In 1969 I had been introduced to the Queensland Education Department, which was quite a shock after my training and experience in Tasmania and London. Classrooms were poorly equipped, and the desks screwed to the floor, so every child faced the blackboard. Rote learning was the norm and my experience of individual and group teaching unfamiliar. However, over the next few years, Queensland schools underwent major reform with new ideas influencing a modern curriculum. Much of that change can be attributed to the Whitlam transformation in putting education at the centre of his reform agenda.

Employment and training

In June 1973 Australia ratified the International Labour Organization (ILO) Convention on Discrimination in Employment
and Occupation (C111, 1958) and in December 1974 the ILO
Convention on Equal Remuneration (C100, 1951).[12] The 1973
Budget increased funding for women's training and retraining
schemes, and of course the abolition of university fees was a
major incentive for women to aspire to a tertiary education that
led to more professional job opportunities. The review of Public
Service Employment had opened all positions to men and women,
and employment advertising had been changed to avoid the
apparent favouring of men over women. Age limits for permanent
positions were removed, allowing older women to return to their
careers, and married women were no longer disadvantaged in
the Commonwealth Public Service. Discussion was underway to
introduce permanent part-time work as well as a scheme of flexible
working hours. Maternity leave was extended to 12 weeks on full
pay with the option of a further 40 weeks unpaid leave without
loss of continuity or status. Teacher training scholarships trebled
in 1973 with new book and equipment allowances introduced at
the beginning of the academic year.

There was a particular impact for North Queensland
Aboriginal and Torres Strait Island women, because the Townsville
College of Advanced Education was able to introduce an important
in-service training program for teaching monitors from remote
communities where Aboriginal and Torres Strait Islanders were
employed in schools, but few had standard qualifications because
of the difficulty of accessing tertiary institutions.

Health

Eligibility limits for low-income families receiving subsidised health benefits were revised in 1973 after the national wage case decision, but it was a complicated system of assisting low-income families, a situation that was to be addressed by the creation of Medibank, a universal health insurance scheme which was designed to provide health coverage for all Australians, especially those who could not afford private health insurance. However, Medibank was opposed by the medical profession and private health funds, as well as being blocked by the conservative Senate. It led to the 1974 double dissolution and was finally passed at a joint sitting of the Parliament in July of that year but did not begin operating until October 1975. The Fraser government repealed elements of Medibank, but it was restored as Medicare in 1983 by the Hawke government.

An early decision of the Whitlam government was the removal of sales tax on the contraceptive pill and its inclusion on the Pharmaceutical Benefits Scheme. In addition, family planning was extended with grants available to establish clinics, and as a result the voluntary Townsville clinic was able to expand and employ permanent professional staff. This was despite the hostility of the conservative Queensland government, which opposed sex education and adopted a moralistic view of any aspect of women's reproductive rights.

Social security

Whitlam launched a range of initiatives to implement priorities in social reform. His government established the Australian Social Welfare Commission as a source of advice. The Commission developed an Australian Assistance Plan that worked with local government and non-government agencies to share the cost of providing welfare services throughout the country. After the decisive 1967 referendum to change the Australian Constitution to give the federal government power to take control and fund Aboriginal policy, I helped organise the Townsville Inter-Racial Seminar 'We the Australians: What is to follow the Referendum?' This two-day event brought together the local community, including large numbers of Aborigines and Torres Strait Islanders. We heard from prominent guest speakers like Faith Bandler, Joe McGinness, Charles Rowley and Colin Tatz, who inspired us to push for specialist health, housing and legal services. Townsville community leaders like Palm Islanders Iris Clay, Eva Geia and Thelma McAvoy were determined advocates for these services, which were established in the city from 1974.

Reform of social security policy was marked by the introduction of the Supporting Mother's Benefit in 1973. The Benefit recognised unmarried mothers, deserted de facto wives, and de facto wives of prisoners. It also included women separated from their husbands providing they had custody and care of children. The discrimination between widows was removed so that all widows received a common rate.

Pensions were increased in the first Whitlam Budget and a common benefit rate applied on all pensions, unemployment and sickness benefits. There was recognition of benefits for student children over 16 and payment of additional pension for full-time students, together with mother's or guardian's allowance. There was also recognition of children and adults living with disability and new opportunities offered to local government to establish sheltered employment. Additional support was given to home care programs and hostel care for the aged as well as subsidies for meals on wheels.

Employment of women in regional areas in the 1970s was difficult unless in the traditional nursing and teaching professions. Women in Townsville were mainly employed in retail, the local meatworks or in low-skilled jobs where wages were very poor. Indigenous women were particularly disadvantaged. Encouraged by the Whitlam mood of optimism, a few WEL women organised to drive a large group of Aboriginal and Islander women into the city for interviews at a new major retailer opening in central Townsville. About 30 women filled in application forms and were given a cursory 'interview', but sadly not one of them was employed as a result of our efforts. I spoke to a local journalist accusing that company of racism but was advised this was libellous, so my statement couldn't be published!

Urban and regional development

The Whitlam government created the Department of Urban and Regional Development in December 1972. Together with the Cities Commission, it was the first national initiative committed to restoring cities and planning new growth centres and new towns. In focusing on local government and town planning, the Whitlam government was demonstrating its commitment to improving the quality of all Australians wherever they lived. In addition, there was special focus on the role of local government, which was included in a reconstituted Grants Commission to ensure all councils and municipalities received a share of national revenue. A major focus was on funding sewerage treatment works in the outer suburbs of major cities and local area planning programs to upgrade a range of local services in the western suburbs of Sydney and Melbourne. Albury-Wodonga was launched as a centre of accelerated growth with plans to develop a new city between New South Wales and Victoria.[13] This increased focus on local communities inspired many women to get involved in their councils; getting elected at local government level was much easier for many women interested in taking part in decision-making than at a state or federal level.

International Women's Year

International Women's Year (1975) seemed to many of us to have been particularly scheduled to celebrate the reform era we were experiencing at that time. In city suburbs and country towns around Australia, women responded to the new mood for change. In Townsville we had a number of plans to ensure that there were opportunities for women to share ideas and learn more about how women were working in other communities. Women's Electoral Lobby Townsville received an International Women's Year grant to run a special speakers program throughout the year. It included Brisbane lawyer Quentin Bryce and Dorothy McRae-McMahon, an early advocate for women's equality in the Uniting Church. In addition to this lecture series, we engaged with the editor of the local daily newspaper, the *Townsville Bulletin*, to run a regular column reporting on events and debates that were central to International Women's Year. We also organised the first International Women's Day march in the city, obtaining an official permit and encouraging women who had never marched in the streets before to join us. We probably seemed a rag-tag collection of hippies, children and well-dressed workers when over 100 of us marched with police escort down the main street of Townsville, past jeering blokes and surprised bystanders. We chanted slogans like 'Free Safe Abortion Now' and 'A Woman's Place is in the House – and in the Senate too'.

However, the highlight of that year was the Women and Politics Conference in Canberra. Led by the Townsville Deputy Mayor and hospital social worker, Joan Innes Reid, six local women travelled to the national capital where we joined hundreds of women from many different backgrounds and regions. Many of us had never been to Canberra and few to Parliament House, so the first night's reception at the centre of Australian politics was very exciting and memorable. A very crowded King's Hall was overtaken by old and young, radical and conservative, urban and rural women all determined to find ways to transform national reform into their own lives.

Throughout the conference we were challenged to remember that 'the personal is political', and we needed to keep progressing long overdue change that gave women equal opportunity to participate in all areas of working and community life. We were also reminded that Australian women's struggle was part of the global campaign for women's human rights.

Media reporting of the conference was condescending, inaccurate and extremely critical of a number of international speakers. In response to the way reporting had trivialised such a major national event, a large group of us occupied the office of the *Canberra Times* to demand professional journalistic standards. Like many women who attended that historic conference, I found the speeches and debate most stimulating, and those few days reinforced my personal commitment to feminism and my determination to work for change in North Queensland.[14]

In 1976 I was persuaded to nominate for the safe state seat of Townsville, standing against the popular male candidate, who went on to be elected. However, the upset I created by daring to nominate for a safe seat for the ALP taught me that I would meet considerable resistance in aiming for a political career. I learned that I had to be both patient and strategic in building support in my community. Three years later, I was elected as a member of the Labor team to lead the Townsville City Council.

The Dismissal

I remember the afternoon of the Dismissal very clearly because I was at Central School in Townsville and we had just finished interviewing candidates for the position of After School Care Coordinator, a position made possible with a grant we received from the Australian Social Welfare Commission. I was interrupted by a colleague reporting the radio news from Canberra. 'Gough's been sacked by Kerr,' she declared with alarm, and the news spread quickly around the school. In my son's class of 11-year-olds, his teacher gave an impromptu speech on the implications for Australian democracy, an impassioned speech my son John still remembers. In schools around Australia many teachers were stunned by the news, but one in particular earned a place in history and was recorded years later by a former primary school student:

> Sister Margaret glided into the classroom her usual serene
> appearance replaced by a concerned expression. Please kneel
> for the restoration of the Socialist Government … the prayer
> that followed would have called upon several religious
> heavies to assist Gough Whitlam and forgive John Kerr. I
> will always be grateful to Sister Margaret for etching in my
> memory the sacking of the Whitlam Labor Government
> and the injustice.[15]

As the country absorbed the implications of 11 November 1975, a number of women's groups rallied to set up 'Women for Whitlam'. In Townsville we found ourselves thrust into a highly charged election campaign with a great deal of hostility demonstrated towards anyone prepared to publicly support the Whitlam government. Our family home displayed a Labor election poster, so we had to deal with threatening phone calls and rocks thrown on our roof as the election drew closer. The southern-based Women for Whitlam headquarters sent me a box of red poppies for women to wear to signal their support for the Prime Minister removed from office on Remembrance Day. While this message may have been understood in some parts of the country, it seemed unlikely to be welcomed in the military city of Townsville. Instead, I donated the box to the local RSL and found more direct ways of rallying women to Whitlam's defence. 'We want Gough' was the chant of that campaign and we shouted it loudly whenever a group of us confronted visiting politicians on the election trail.

A Brisbane Women for Whitlam group produced radio advertisements, but I was unable to persuade a local station to play them, even though I offered to pay the standard fee for a not-for-profit organisation. The messages were in jingle form reminding women to support the Prime Minister who had introduced reform to benefit them. Of course, not all women could be persuaded to vote for a leader whose very enthusiasm for reform was seen as threatening the status quo and the traditional roles of men and women. The electorate of Herbert remained in Liberal hands, as it had throughout the Whitlam era, but it was finally won by Labor in 1983.

The Whitlam legacy

Many of the Whitlam generation were of course deeply troubled by his dismissal and its aftermath. Yet Australia had been changed during his time in government and some reforms had a lasting impact in so many areas of public policy. It was hard to turn back the clock, particularly when so many Australian women had glimpsed what was possible for them and their families. While we ranted and raged against Fraser's Razor Gang – which slashed funding to important policy areas like Medibank, the Australian Assistance Plan and local government – nevertheless, in seven years, another progressive Labor government was elected. Bob Hawke became Prime Minister in 1983, and many of those elected were from the Whitlam generation so were able to revisit social reform. Both the Hawke and Keating governments greatly benefited from the election of younger men and women who had been strongly influenced by the Whitlam years.

Labor women had started to break through the traditional

male-only ranks of federal parliamentarians to help refocus on policy directions initiated by the Whitlam government. Ros Kelly (ACT), Elaine Darling (Queensland), Joan Child (Victoria) and Senators Susan Ryan (ACT), Pat Giles (Western Australia), Jean Hearn (Tasmania) and Ruth Coleman (Western Australia) commenced their parliamentary terms in the 1970s and early 1980s. Susan Ryan, elected in 1975, was determined to increase the number of women preselected, and to convince senior Labor strategists to re-engage in building the women's vote. In 1983 Helen Mayer (Victoria), Jeanette McHugh (NSW) and Senator Rose Crowley (South Australia) joined the new Hawke government to renew the reforms inspired by Liz Reid ten years earlier. I, too, was part of that group of women who entered Parliament in 1983, as a senator for Queensland.

My opportunity to become the first Labor woman to represent Queensland in the Senate owed much to being part of the Whitlam generation. Living on the frontier in North Queensland, my three priorities were an end to sexism, racism and conscription, so obviously I was drawn to Gough Whitlam's agenda. During the period 1966–82, I worked locally to challenge old ways and introduce reform. As a relatively apolitical youngster, I was forced by my environment to take a stand, learning my politics from so many old Labor families and trade unionists. I arrived in Canberra quite clear that I was there to continue promoting equality and social justice. Susan Ryan became the first Labor woman Cabinet minister and the Minister Assisting the Prime Minister on the Status of Women. With 12 Labor women colleagues forming the first women's caucus, Susan was able to introduce sex discrimination and affirmative action legislation and restore some of the initiatives introduced by the Whitlam government.

Whitlam's speech to the Opening of the Women and Politics Conference in Canberra on 31 August 1975 remains a rare tribute given by an Australian Prime Minister to the women of Australia, and as such it should be included in our schools' curriculum as a reminder of his vision and commitment:

> It is often said, and truly, that the home limits women's exposure to political experience and information. But one of the most enlightening changes that has recently occurred is that women are insisting more and more that concerns of the home be the concerns of politics, that the personal be the political. Child care, family planning, housework and so on are now becoming issues for the political arena. To this extent women are in the process of trying to re-define and to re-describe, the political. I am not here however to lecture women about the responsibilities of citizenship or the need to join political movements or to be politically active. Women are in politics. They know how to organise. They recognise their needs. But now is the time to define and formulate their demands and to seek a full share in political power and leadership. It is my deep belief that what is good for women will in turn be good for the entire society.[16]

JUST ADD WOMEN AND STIR: REVISITING THE FEMOCRAT REVOLUTION

EVA COX

It is somewhat significant that I am starting this account of the effects of Whitlam's reign as PM almost exactly 50 years after I started my political activism. It was March 1972 and my small market research firm had just suffered a recession collapse, so I enrolled in a degree in Sociology at UNSW. I was a sole parent returning to full-time study to complete my abandoned BA when the professor's secretary asked me if I'd liked to come to a meeting of a new feminist lobby group that was planning a survey. It seemed like a great idea. I joined the then newly forming Women's Electoral Lobby (WEL).

Research and feminism seemed a good mix and I was looking for some activism. The meeting was at the Sydney home of Wendy McCarthy and had a scattering of other mothers. This was a better fit for me than the Women's Lib meeting I'd recently attended, which was all younger radicals and students with no kids! They wanted consciousness-raising, I wanted political action.

The Women's Electoral Lobby was just what I was looking for: a feminist lobby on the model of the American National Organization for Women (NOW). NOW was running surveys of candidates' attitudes in the lead-up to the US presidential election. WEL was working on a local version for our federal election late that year, designed to influence political policies and inform voters.

Women's political issues were not easy to promote, but feminism was making ground. So too was the anger at the results of over 20 years of Menzies and the Coalition's conservative controls. A shift to the ALP looked likely and we hoped its policies would propose changes that acknowledged the disadvantages women were facing.

The introduction of the contraceptive pill in 1961 had changed women's lives completely, allowing us to plan pregnancies and thus our lives. Betty Friedan's *The Feminine Mystique* in 1963 and Germaine Greer's *The Female Eunuch* in 1970 were part of a cultural shift that was instrumental in getting women to demand political change. And there was a rise in fiction and critiques that dealt with feminist issues. It was time to become more politically practical and change the political agenda so that it focused on fixing gender biases and inequities. Australian women were ready for political action.

Post-war reconstruction had seen some social welfare and health reforms and expanded tertiary education. But women's needs were overlooked politically despite – or perhaps because of – our capacity to work during the war. It's not surprising that in this atmosphere WEL and other groups were formed to work for gender equity.

Our first project was to survey politicians and candidates to test their views on women. We made sure to use our contacts to set up media interest in publishing the data. As I had considerable experience in running a market research company, I became involved. Research data can be a powerful influence on change when well promoted and convincing! Many of the men's answers to the survey questions were pathetically awful, so that we had a lot of publicity. Ultimately, this affected the number of votes that went to those bad candidates.

WEL grew rapidly in the early years, publicised by the survey responses which showed serious, often ludicrous deficiencies of views on women's needs and rights. By the end of our first year, there was a change-focused ALP government in power. Whitlam became Prime Minister and his first action was to ensure that equal pay for women was still on the agenda. This feminist movement was seeing that our views and actions could change the inequities we faced if they were effectively addressed. The brief personal account is included to show that we had, for the first time in living memory, many more possibilities of being both heard and successful.

Why this personal account of personal experiences in the formation of an active feminist change organisation in the '70s? As a sociologist, I feel it is necessary to understand that the 1960s and '70s bred particular social movements that had then, and still now, offered basic optimism and success. We were creating positive social changes to laws and funding that still are sometimes in effect.

This time came to be known as the second wave of feminism. The first wave had laboured in the late 19th century for women's suffrage. Australia was an early adopter, with white women enfranchised and voting in federal elections in 1902. The following decade saw other reforms: a basic wage for men was adopted in 1908, aged pensions around the same time. We led internationally in the fair go, but not when it came to women.

Other inequalities continued, including pay rates at around two-thirds of male wages because we were not 'breadwinners'. The movement slowly diminished, so by the 1960s there remained only a few older adherents who encouraged our desire for change. The public services and political parties were very male in senior ranks, and few women were either seen as public advocates or elected to power.

This meant that WEL and other advocacy groups had a blank slate and a long list of changes we wanted to see. Some WEL groups had a mix of political party members, mainly ALP, and others who were familiar with political processes, particularly in Canberra. There were those who worked in the public services or the universities, and some had family ties with active men. An example, Gail Radford (then Wilenski) was involved from WEL's start. She was then married to Peter Wilenski, a senior public servant who later became Whitlam's Principal Private Secretary.

With these contacts we were well briefed on how the political system worked and the importance of having links on the inside. We realised that we needed more women in influential positions to best change the political agenda. It wasn't easy because there were very few women in senior positions and male support was rare.

At the time there was only one specific unit for women's needs, the Women's Bureau in the Department for Labour, which dealt with the workforce. It was established in the 1960s by Dame Ada Norris, who was Gail's aunt and an active feminist Liberal. The Bureau provided us with lots of useful material and skills.

Using this as a model we came up with an idea – why not a establish a full-time Women's Adviser to assist the Prime Minister with the feminist changes we needed? WEL lobbied for a position to support and assist the PM and Cabinet members to see the value of our proposals for change. We needed to make sure we had someone on the inside if our efforts were to be successful.

In 1973 just such a position was created and advertised. Scandal in the newspapers as the pay was $10 000 per annum, which was declared to be too much! I was an applicant and made the short list. We went to Canberra for the interviews and the local Women's Liberation group gave us each a purple T-shirt ironically labelling us as Superwomen. The creation of this role was a big win, with Elizabeth Reid ultimately getting the job.

Shortly afterwards, we lobbied for a unit to support them both, and Sara Dowse was selected to head up an Office of the Status of Women (now the Office for Women) in the Department of the Prime Minister and Cabinet. WEL, having invented and invested in the first Women's Adviser for a leader, continued our lobbying for more senior positions for 'femocrats' – that is, relatively senior women with specific responsibilities for delivery of reforms for women. We were very aware that the success of our early lobbying was at least partly achieved by informal help from many sympathetic women in the system.

We had something new for women, a network to promote and establish services to meet women's needs. While this was a novelty for us, access to networks was the established male model for seeking support internally for required changes to be implemented. And it worked!

Gail Radford was prominent in establishing equal employment opportunity programs for public servants in the federal public service. These were successful in increasing the proportion of senior women, which saw the states follow suit and implement their own programs. Feminists also started joining the public service. Others started working for elected members or became members of other outside relevant lobby groups. Now there were plenty of recruits and supporters of the new feminised positions. However, there were conservatives and career public servants who were concerned at this apparently favoured inflow.

Hester Eisenstein, an American feminist academic who moved to Australia and gained a senior feminist job, has written on the femocrats.[1] She records the very strong critique by Professor Leonie Kramer, an influential conservative and critic of feminism. At a conference in 1985, Kramer attacked femocrat viewpoints, claiming they distorted public services by applying radical feminist analyses. Hester defended the use of equal employment opportunity legislation and affirmative action models, which Kramer saw as wrong.

While many feminists saw EEO and affirmative action as necessary, others objected, seeing it as reformist and not radical enough to create serious changes to women's status.[2] These objections from right and left, as well as from male MPs, showed the prejudices and deep flaws in broad acceptance of the model implemented by femocrats. However, both EEO and affirmative action created many useful changes in the 1970s and '80s before many jobs were lost in the following years.

In my 1996 book *Leading Women* (a deliberately ambiguous title), I made some comments when the femocracy had started losing ground in their public role.[3] There were embedded difficulties that were created by major changes inside the public service. The earlier objections to gender changes were indications of the ongoing pressures on the 'women's units' that were to come. They were seen as problematic per se, and the difficulties they still face require major gender acceptance that we still don't have!

Shredding the femocrats

In *Leading Women,* I wrote about femocrats working in 'women's units':

> These positions and units tend to be far less secure than other parts of the system and are often watched and disliked by power brokers opposed to equity outcomes. The managers of these units are often in difficult positions, experiencing unrealistic expectations from the community on one hand and suspicion from professional public service mandarins on the other.
>
> Success in such a setting would require superhuman skills, and even a good performer would be at risk of failure. Sometimes incumbents have been short of a halo or two and do not do very well. Many have had the experience of being publicly bagged by the media and most have met

with hostility from some angry organised and disorganised women's groups.

This is inevitable, given the peculiar status and roles of these units. A point of concern, however, is the way the attacks come. I note that when the flak flies it is rarely, if ever, based on effectiveness or otherwise in achieving the often limited, possible gains. Rather, it tends to be on the basis that the woman in charge is not a good manager or she has a bad 'style'. There are stories about shouting, about unreasonable demands and about injustices done. The criticisms are almost always of the people-based competencies of the woman in charge. In some cases the criticisms are probably accurate. There are incompetent and mediocre women in senior positions, just as there are men. Not all women can be exemplary, and this expectation is in itself a problem for equity.

Again, we need to remember that there are many appalling male managers in the public and private sector and, in general, they survive without being publicly pilloried. We must examine whether we should, and when we should, expect women to conform to different and more narrow prescriptions than those demanded of men. As part of a reform agenda we obviously want to validate better management and behaviour by managers. However, we need to question whether it is fair or even useful to apply our criteria so tightly to women and not equivalently to men.[4]

This quote from my book is still as relevant today as when I wrote it in 1996. It can be seen in current arguments about the power of 'infiltration' of hostile institutions to affect serious policy changes.

Sadly, few of these units have survived, though most states, the Northern Territory and the Feds still have women's units that are involved in policies and budgets. However, many of these are more likely to be told to 'sell' government policies to women than the reverse.

Part of a continuous women's movement?

Although WEL and other groups lobbied to get issues relevant to women onto the political agenda, ultimately making a real difference in women's lives, much of our progress stopped when the Coalition government of John Howard came into power in 1996. The neoliberal shift to a market-based paradigm had no way to take into account the social agenda. This fixed a macho version of monetised GDP as the only measure of a good society. We lost our citizen status and were redefined as customers with so-called choices but fewer rights.

I believe it is important to revisit the years before the economy was the only metric, and record what was done by feminist advocates, so we can work out how to close the remaining equity gaps. In a time of bad political actions and the growth of undemocratic macho rulers, women need to consider how we return to valuing the feminised social roles and care skills of social democracy.

There have been accusations that our concerns back then were only those of white middle-class women. However, from early days we were very aware of the need for serious reform for Indigenous women, and Pat O'Shane was part of the advocacy in this area. We also became aware of the neglect of the needs of immigrant women after I undertook a survey, funded as jobs for women from non-English-speaking backgrounds, after contact with Sara Dowse asking about an employment project. On the basis of the data, we lobbied for English lessons that recognised the lack of literacy in many female migrants. WEL also supported the abolition of university fees, giving many older and disadvantaged women the chance to upgrade their education levels.

Contacts at senior ranks proved to be very useful. For example, children's services were one of my interests, and, as a sole parent I had started a rare after-school care service at my daughter's school and was lobbying for funding. Before the 1974 election, I was contacted by a senior woman in the Prime Minister's Department, asking me for data on costs and staff ratios. My model was adopted and after Labor won the election it became policy and was funded. Other WEL members took on the issue of equal pay, and funding for women's refuges and women's health centres was also high on our agenda, as were contraception and access to abortions.

WEL can also claim to have achieved changes to legal status with equal pay, as well as sex discrimination changes, and there are now more women in senior positions and sometimes leadership, which should be celebrated. However, there still remain huge issues about the low-paid, underpaid and unpaid work that is, in the main, carried out by women. Aged care workers, nurses, community workers – the list goes on – receive very low pay. The contribution of this feminised unpaid work is not included in the algorithms used in the dominant monetised market values. The flaws are showing in a falling trust in democracy, pandemics, environmental damage and a lack of public support for social, communal and citizen rights and needs.

That's why it's worthwhile recording how WEL was so effective at using the contemporary political system by creating useful networks and offering clear options for needed changes. In the 1970s and '80s, we achieved a lot. As WEL was reformist in its actions, we needed to establish the types of networks and links that allowed us to have our ideas adopted. There were some downsides, nonetheless, to this model as Marian Sawer points out in her 2008 history of WEL.[5]

WEL members did seize opportunities to influence policy from the inside, which meant that fewer women with political and policy skills were available for community-based politics. While women within government were able to direct resources to women in the community and enable more diverse groups to organise, dependence on public resources rendered these groups vulnerable to political change. The ebbing of the community-based women's movement in turn deprived feminists within government of their political base, for there was no longer a visible presence in the community for politicians to appease. Beyond women's services, whose policy advocacy and community education became increasingly constrained by competitive tendering and under-resourcing, there was little ongoing community activity to enlist support for change.

The lessons we need to learn

The times were changing. In 1995 I scored an AO for my contribution to feminist changes, but the decades since the late '90s have seen feminism and social interests being less successful politically. The enthusiastic adoption of the neoliberal model of cutting State spending and reduced public interest in funding social reforms have certainly helped hinder progress.

An account by Marian Sawer in Linda Hancock's collection, *Women, Public Policy and the State*, outlined the demise of much of the system. [6] She states clearly that the ambitious model no longer existed by the late 1990s. Using the example of a Women's Advisers' Workshop in February 1998, we saw signals were clear that standards were lost. First item was no central location and access to the leader, the next was lack of access to intergovernmental links with budgets and policies. She lists many examples of less access and governments relinquishing the action groups that assisted in making changes.

My own involvement since the mid-1980s has been as an outsider contributor, not working within the government structures. I am still actively involved in seeking changes to the status of women, including our uncounted and unpaid contribution to society. The grip of the market models, that has deleted the value of the social, is obviously failing to attract voter trust. The privatising of children's services, care for the aged and for those with disabilities, shows flaws in public policy as governments have moved these services away from public and community controls.

As the focus on GDP as the monetised measure of wellbeing ignores unpaid contributions, women have 'progressed' by filling more male-defined roles and being 'acceptable'. We still have a major deficit in the lack of recognition of unpaid contributions and a big gender pay gap, exacerbated by low wages growth.

The lessons we need to learn from the time of progress in the 1970s and '80s are about creating networks and infiltrating structures. If we do this successfully, then serious change, on our terms, will be valued. The continuing prejudices against women per se make it difficult to 'just add women and stir'. We need an action plan to radically change the still dominant macho attitudes and discontinue the valuing of masculine criteria. We need to shift macho values so we all become citizens with rights rather than badly monetised customers.

The critiques and aims of WEL were effective in starting the change in social values in those early decades. Infiltration of change agents into the decision-making areas worked for a while, but it was too easy to return to macho dominance via the market-based models. For change to be successful now, these models need to be replaced by social wellbeing goals rather than just financial individualism. The next feminist revolution will need to promote our leadership to ensure societal fair goals to manage coming technology shifts and environmental crises and to impose serious social changes.

And it will have to come from women as leaders, together with really supportive men!

Aux armes citoyennes! NB: Our arms are not lethal weapons.

OUT OF WEDLOCK, OUT OF LUCK: SINGLE MOTHERS AND EX-NUPTIAL BABIES

TERESE EDWARDS

The Whitlam government brought a wave of reform after three decades of political inaction and discrimination against single parents. Remarkably, eliminating State-sanctioned harm for single mothers and their children was achieved in less than 18 months. Understanding the magnitude of the Supporting Mother's Benefit offers us a way to shine a light to understand the darkness of our political policy system. While some matters find the spotlight, others must forever compete for the attention of policy-makers and the public.[1]

Single mothers before the 1970s

For much of the 20th century, women were not viewed as requiring financial autonomy, and their citizenship was defined through marriage and reproduction. The severity of these rigid constructs meant that single mothers with ex-nuptial children were treated especially harshly. They were not recognised as 'proper' families and characterised as a social problem, which hampered their ability to make direct claims on government assistance.[2]

The Widow's Pension was introduced during World War II (1942) for women not able to access paid employment due to age or parenting. Class A, the superior payment, granted due to the death of a husband or de facto (defined as three years of cohabitation immediately prior to the death), extended to deserted or divorced women if they had 'just cause' for their separation and attempted to retrieve maintenance.[3] All had to prove that they were of 'good character'. Class B and C were for women without dependent children. Single mothers with ex-nuptial children could not claim the Widow's Pension.

If a woman found herself pregnant and unmarried at this time, she may have received the Special Benefit. This payment was a pitiful amount with a short time span: paid 12 weeks prior to the birth and six weeks post-birth. This was the situation experienced by Brenda Richards, who was pregnant in 1962:

> If you had not married, you could get a small 'special
> benefit' which was only for a few months. The Welfare
> Department man told me this was because 'Unmarried
> mothers are a dirty word.' 'Show me where it says that,'
> I demanded. He pointed to a book. 'That will have to
> change,' I yelled, with more bravado than knowledge about
> how this could occur. I walked out of the office with my
> head high. I didn't cry till I was out of his sight.[4]

The only real option for many women who were single and pregnant was to relinquish their baby for adoption. There could be no stronger statement of a more unjust and inequitable belief in the predominance of the nuclear family than the forced adoption policies and practices that occurred in the 20th century.[5] Unmarried women were expected to relinquish and then forget. As Brenda Richards later recalled of her experience of giving birth:

> I looked at this miracle, stunned by her beauty. Then they
> whipped her away into the intensive care ward, not letting
> me touch her. They stated that as she weighed just under the

regulation six pounds, she needed 'special care.' I was not
allowed to hold her at any stage, or to breast feed her. They
dried up my milk.

Daily I would go down to the 'prem' ward and look at my
precious baby through the window. My discharge was a
week later, after signing a form, headed 'Registration of
an Illegitimate Birth.' Wendy had to stay in hospital. I
came in every day and gazed in wonder through the glass.
Eventually they got the idea that I was not going to give
her up.[6]

Reflecting on experiences like these, the Commonwealth committee inquiring into the practice of forced adoptions concluded
in 2012 that 'there was not appropriate government funding
available to mothers prior to 1973 that would have provided the
ongoing financial support necessary for mothers to keep their
babies'.[7]

Agitating for change

A harsh story unfolded if women stepped beyond the boundaries
of respectability with an out-of-wedlock baby. This is the backdrop
to the formation in Melbourne in 1969 of the Council of Single
Mother and her Child (CSMC), the forerunner of the national
body, the National Council of Single Mothers and their Children
(NCSMC).[8] Rosemary West, one of CSMC's co-founders,
explained the 'assistance' provided by the social worker based at
her birth hospital:

I was told that if I really love my baby – I would give it
up. Given a copy of a book by an American social worker,
Leontyne Young, which justified pressuring single mothers

to give up their babies, [which argued] that ex-nuptial pregnancy was caused by personal pathology that made single mothers unfit mothers.[9]

Years later, in an interview, Rosemary heard the same social worker say she 'had never met a single mother who wanted to give up her child'. Defying the social worker's advice, Rosemary kept her child, and determined to help single women keep their babies.

In 1969 Rosemary was elected the organisation's inaugural Convenor, and Brenda Richards the Treasurer. Some other early members of the CSMC included Sandy Fitts, Anne Mathisen, Jo Clancy, Jill Millthorpe, Jo Murray and Tricia Harper.[10] These women decided that as well as providing support for single mothers by single mothers, they also needed to overcome and erase the discrimination and injustice single mothers faced. They knew that the stigma attached to single motherhood created anxiety and stress and could result in poverty or forced relinquishment of their children. West described the ever-present stress and anxiety of her position:

> I shared a house with another single mother. I worked at
> The Melbourne *Herald*. What would happen if I lost my
> job, or my place in one of only eight child-care centres then
> operating in Melbourne, or the housemate without whom
> I could not have paid the rent? I would lose my child.[11]

One of the group's first actions was to ensure that children born out of wedlock had a fair start in life, and this meant a level of financial certainty, as provided through the Widow's Pension. The CSMC produced a briefing statement, *Request for co-operation and support in approaching the Commonwealth Government,* in which they called upon

The Commonwealth government to amend the social
services act 1947 so that it includes all unsupported mothers
and their children. When the CSMC was formed, out of
wedlock children and their mothers were not eligible for
the commonwealth social services entitlements available to
other unsupported mothers and children (example prisoners'
wives, deserted wives, and widows).[12]

At the same time, the CSMC was garnering the support of
a reputable panel of advisers to advance their campaign for
economic justice. Advisers consisted of representatives from the
Royal Women's Hospital, employees within babies' homes, and
academics from a number of universities. There were legal experts
such as Ron Sackville, while the commitment from Eric Benjamin,
a psychologist and social worker, was unwavering.[13] Altogether,
the CSMC brought together 16 panel advisers to advance 'social
services justice' and abolish 'illegitimacy' from laws.[14]

The activists continued to work to build momentum for
change in the early 1970s. In 1972 the CSMC's advisers wrote to
the Prime Minister, William McMahon:

We, the undersigned, act as advisers to the council for the
single mother and her child in Victoria. We work in areas of
medicine, religion, law, social welfare, childcare and other
social fields. In our professional capacities we see the very
difficult and frequently distressing circumstances in which
the child of the single mother is placed and for this reason
we are seeking Commonwealth assistance to alleviate these
conditions.[15]

While the letter's ink has faded, its strength, purpose and tone
remain. The letter elaborated on the 'most common causes of
difficulties' for single mothers, which they summarised as:

1. Vulnerability to evictions due to an inability to maintain rent payments on restricted income.
2. Delays in processing payments, delays, or unknown ineligibility if a mother moves to another State where payments are not available or at a reduced level.
3. Loss of allowances due to arbitrary decisions by staff officers of the Victorian Social Welfare Department.
4. Difficulty with obtaining maintenance payments from recalcitrant fathers (men treating court order child maintenance [now known as child support] as a voluntary payment, knowing that the court process was both ineffective and costly).

The McMahon government refused to act on the CSMC's suggestions for reform on the grounds of cost: the Minister for Social Services claimed that 'the States asked that the Commonwealth should bear the whole cost, but this was obviously out of the question'.[16] However, in further correspondence between the Head of the Department of Social Services and the responsible minister, WC Wentworth, the ideological basis of the government's objections was made clearer:

> A few other old bogies reared their unlovely heads,
> 'undermining family life', 'threatening marriage' etc.
> Mr Wentworth also mentioned that he had representation
> from certain widows who do not wish to see the Act
> altered.[17]

With progress through the McMahon government stymied, the matter was nevertheless gaining traction through a more receptive Labor Party, which was developing policies for implementation should it win the next election. Peter Cullen, a political lobbyist, was working with the CSMC within the political system, while the CSMC itself was focusing on gaining a receptive response from various religious leaders and raising community empathy. Single mothers attended meetings, shared their personal stories, wrote correspondence, and spoke to the media. Their goal was to personalise the issue, and to make single mothers more visible in the community. Rosemary West, a journalist, recalls, with a laugh, that there were great debates at the *Herald* as to 'how much we should crop or show a pregnant belly' in photos accompanying her articles.[18] Tricia Harper, a teacher by day, became an activist in the evening: 'once [my daughter] Ruth went to bed I would start typing. Carbon paper and the typewriter on my kitchen table'.[19]

Progress, or the lack of it, was documented in correspondence and meetings. Peter Cullen reported a positive development in March 1972, noting that he had 'been to see Bill Hayden [shadow Minister for Health and Welfare]. He is already on record as saying that the single mother should be treated in the same way as a deserted wife'.[20] At this time, the Labor Party was on the brink of winning government. Led by Gough Whitlam, the Labor Party carried the expectations and hopes of single mothers and their children. While Whitlam did not explicitly mention single mothers in the campaign, welfare, women and equity were all on his agenda, and hope resonated from his election speeches:

> Australians should no longer tolerate the view that, once governments have decided the level of cash payments, the community has discharged its obligations to those who depend upon the community for their sole or main income and sustenance.[21]

The Whitlam government, elected on 2 December 1972, complemented its new political ideology with system-wide social welfare initiatives. The Commission of Inquiry into Poverty, established by McMahon in 1972, took on a more expansive role under

Whitlam, and found an over-representation of financial hardship within single-mother families.[22] The Whitlam government created the National Social Welfare Commission in 1972, chaired by Marie Coleman. The Commission provided an alternative source of advice to the Department of Social Security. Coleman stated that:

> The Department [Head] was very negative, utterly negative to the idea of having any kind of benefits introduced for never-married women. To that extent, the resounding recommendation that the Social Welfare Commission gave to Bill Hayden was what he took to cabinet, to assist him in gaining the relevant approval of Whitlam.[23]

Similarly, Andrew Podger, who had worked on the Henderson Inquiry and then with the Social Welfare Commission, experienced a similar attitude, recalling that the 'Deputy Secretary of Social Security was totally against extending support for unmarried mothers'.[24]

Introducing the Supporting Mother's Benefit

The new Labor government was swift to act on social welfare reform: two social security bills were introduced in March and April 1973. A third Bill, containing the Supporting Mother's Benefit, was introduced on 22 May 1973. Hayden, now Minister for Social Security, described the Bill 'as a further step along the road to realising the Australian Labor Party's objective of removing anomalies and discriminatory practices imposed by past governments', and that it was the 'Government's determination to bring an end as quickly as it can to the discrimination'.[25]

The Supporting Mother's Benefit came into effect on 3 July 1973.[26] It was a watershed moment in the history of Australian social welfare as it directly responded to the needs of women with ex-nuptial births.[27] It was both unique and provocative, providing an alternative to a problem (birth outside of wedlock).[28] With a level of legitimacy granted by the Whitlam government, the benefit challenged religious institutions and moral conservatives. Most importantly, it gave single mothers greater autonomy over their lives.

The introduction of the benefit coincided with a significant reduction in the practice of forced adoption (at least for white women) because it offered a level of economic certainty until the youngest child was 18 years or, if dependent and studying, 24.[29] The payment made no distinction between the circumstances of the pathway into single motherhood, and was set at the same level as the Widow Pension Class A, albeit with a six-month waiting period.[30] Tricia Harper, one of the members of CSMC who worked towards this new payment, recalled:

> I was present at the Committee meeting in CSMC's Wesley Church office in 1973 when we learned that the Supporting Mother's Benefit had been passed. It resulted in quiet exhilaration and celebration, but not much more than that, as there was always so much more to do![31]

Economic justice became a reality: single mothers could now gain workplace qualifications, making it possible to juggle paid work and single mothering; parenting was protected and enabled, ensuring children a decent start in life. No longer would an interruption to paid work bring the fear of losing children, and there were opportunities for the mother to be active outside the domestic sphere. The stubborn moral compass moved, and stigma reduced. Women who wanted to leave violent relationships, but who had felt trapped by financial dependence, could now leave because they had financial support.

Brian Howe, Minister for Social Security and then Health in Bob Hawke's government, once remarked that 'the Whitlam Government was amazing on women given no women were then in Cabinet'.[32] As Marie Coleman noted, the benefits of Whitlam's social change agenda flowed to women.[33] The presence of ministers like Bill Hayden was crucial to this improvement in social welfare for women. Hayden later commented that the Supporting Mother's Benefit was 'an overdue matter of social justice for a group of women whose essential social and economic needs were being denied by the indifference to this issue of our national parliament'.[34] A number of factors converged to produce the Supporting Mother's Benefit: the 1973 Commonwealth Commission into Poverty, Labor's expansive social policy expertise and an enthusiasm for gender equity, while the CSMC and Hayden were shining constants. This powerful blend helped to combat deprivation, coerced adoption and stigma.

Lessons for today's activists

Public policy has a degree of fluidity. Notwithstanding this, it is plausible to expect, in a country as rich in intellect and resources as Australia, that various governments might continue to advance policies to enhance women's and children's financial safety while actively reducing entrenched hardship. Sadly, this was not to be, and single motherhood has continued to be a political football in today's policy debates. My involvement with the National Council of Single Mothers and their Children Inc. began 15 years ago, and I was the organisation's CEO for 12 years. In 2017 a journalist asked me, 'What are you hoping for in the budget?' My immediate reply was, 'I hope we don't feature as single mums, as each year we seem to be the panacea for budget savings'.[35]

More recent policy changes continue to shape the lives of

single-mother families. Unfortunately, it is not a positive story. Ugly ideas that have long influenced our social security system – such as 'deserving' versus 'undeserving' welfare recipients, the undervaluing of unpaid care and an acceptance of gender inequality – have re-emerged.

The Howard government reversed over 30 years of progress for single-mother families from June 2006, when single mothers were no longer eligible to apply for parenting assistance if their youngest child was eight years or older.[36] In 2012 the Gillard Labor government took Howard's reforms a step further, revoking the only 'saving grace' retained by Howard (the Parenting Payment Single for current recipients). When this change came into effect on 1 January 2013, more than 85 000 single mothers were transferred from Parenting Payment Single to the unemployment payment (Newstart, now known as the JobSeeker payment). With this shift, single mothers were characterised as 'unemployed', and suffered a loss of income, the Newstart payment at that time being $160 per fortnight lower than the Parenting Payment. The biggest and unreciprocated losses were experienced by women who had some paid work.[37] A single mother in paid work now had her Newstart payment reduced once she reached a meagre $50 of income per week, compared to the Parenting Payment at the time, where the equivalent income was $111 for a family with three children. The unemployment payment was never designed for sole parents.

When the changes were announced in 2012, the NCSMC responded by appearing before the Joint Parliamentary Human Rights Committee, where our testimony contributed to the Committee's supportive and favourable findings. We made many media appearances and lobbied key Members of Parliament. I maintained a 'sit-in' at the office of Bill Shorten, the Minister for Employment and Workplace Relations, until he could attend a pre-arranged meeting. Yet in the meeting, neither exposing spin nor sharing real stories of women's hardship worked to shift the government's position.

Since the legislation was passed, various members of the Labor Party have made belated public apologies, with the notable exception of Julia Gillard herself.[38] Her famous misogyny speech occurred while Cassandra Goldie (CEO of the Australian Council of Social Services) and I were leading a protest on the lawns of Parliament House. I watched the passing of the legislation, stunned by the betrayal of women who did not have a platform, autonomy, or any such cachet, but now had many masters. Our efforts culminated in the premiere in Parliament House of *10 Stories of Single Mothers*, a documentary. The audience included representatives from every political party, who committed in unison to make the necessary changes to the lives of the women who starred in the documentary, but their political will and fortitude soon evaporated.[39]

The cut in payments to single mothers raised a fundamental question: Had Australia violated the human rights of single mothers and their children? A complaint to the United Nations about human rights violations has to follow a particular template. Having long since turned to Facebook as a channel for widespread communication, the NCSMC posted a call for a 'victim' – a woman affected by the perverse ending of Parenting Payments Single when her youngest child turned eight years – and found Juanita McLaren. As prescribed by the United Nations, I was the 'author' of the complaint and Juanita the 'victim', while Beth Goldblatt provided expert advice on human rights law.[40]

In 2019, fortuitously, the priority theme of the UN Commission on the Status of Women was social protection systems. Our team was granted a prominent position and consisted of Philip Alston, who was then UN Special Rapporteur on Extreme Poverty and Human Rights, Juanita McLaren, Cassandra Goldie and myself. Nudged into action, Australia responded to the

United Nations. In a live ABC media interview, we learned that the Attorney-General at the time, Christian Porter, had put out a media release refuting our position – an indication that placing the matter on the political agenda was working. The complaint is still under investigation.

Media stories are peppered with women's voices – but restoration of social justice and financial security has yet to be achieved for single mothers. Single mothers and their children live with a depth of hardship that is completely out of step with the wealth of Australia. We are hoping for the next Gough Whitlam, but until this happens our advocacy and determination for our government to 'do the right thing' for *all* Australian families will continue.

PART FOUR
MEDIA, ARTS AND EDUCATION

INTRODUCED BY JULIE McLEOD

Equality of opportunity and the responsibility of governments to turn that aspiration into reality was a defining theme of the Whitlam years and a recurring focus in Whitlam's own writings and speeches.[1] The three chapters here explore what these ambitions looked like for women and girls in the domains of education, media and the arts – sites of reform, especially education and the arts, that have become axiomatically associated with Whitlam's term and the legacy of his government.[2] Whitlam often brought the arts and education together in his own commentaries, highlighting them as areas of significant achievement, ones that perhaps most tellingly distinguished his government from its predecessors. While taking different approaches to their subject matter, each chapter considers the priorities for reform in the respective areas and the different pathways to translating these into programs and policies. The authors acknowledge the pioneering work of key people and their role in bringing these ideas to life, drawing attention not simply to the biographical dimensions of large-scale social reform. Rather, the chapters bring to the fore the rich details and contexts of personal lives, in the case of the arts and media, as supporters and beneficiaries of particular reforms, and in the example from education, as allies driving reform agendas, working to make the vision possible through the pragmatic machinations of committees and compromise.

Craig Campbell and Deb Hayes' chapter is attentive to processes of educational policy reform, and to the dynamics of intersecting personal and political histories with the nuts and bolts of building the case and evidence for change, in this case, to help drive agendas to remedy the educational disadvantages faced by girls. Patricia Amphlett adopts a more autobiographical approach, recalling what the elevation of the arts as worthy of government advocacy and funding meant for artists, and especially women artists at the time – herself included. Equality applied as much to greater recognition of the contribution of women artists as it did to giving greater recognition to the inherent value of the arts itself and its role in nourishing the life of the nation. She documents some of the many changes and new initiatives established during this heady era for the arts, such as the Australia Council, the Australian Film Commission and the National Gallery of Australia, and active support for Aboriginal and Torres Strait Islander art. And she provides personal cameos of select women artists. The choice of figures is infused with Amphlett's own personal insights, giving an intimate sense of how transformative these initiatives were for women, and offering a glimpse into the world of women artists at the time that takes us beyond an official discourse.

Of particular note is how Amphlett tells the story of the growing confidence in Australia's own creative and arts sector. In part this reflects the cultural nationalism evident in Whitlam's pronouncements at the time – culture was to be found at home in Australia, and not only elsewhere – but she adds to this familiar theme by drawing out the profound effect this had on the felt sense of opportunity and openings for women artists. Amphlett also writes from the vantage point of a young adult growing up in a Labor household. She deftly evokes the sense of frustration with the double standard facing young women at that time, along with a strong sense of excitement and new possibility, suggesting how the 'It's time' message spoke to her personally and professionally as a musician – she went on to perform as Little Pattie.

Whitlam saw his government's encouragement for the arts as a driving concern and major legacy, one that grew from a sense that other social and economic 'objectives are all means to an end', whereas 'enjoyment of the arts is an end in itself ... [A] society that cares about education and social reform will be a society that cares about literature and the arts. It will be well supplied with the qualities of understanding, discrimination and compassion that are the basis of artistic creativity'.[3] This formulation of the special qualities of 'the arts' echoes longstanding defences of the uplifting and morally enhancing character of 'high culture' and perhaps feels somewhat at odds with the more egalitarian direction of social and education reform. But it also reflects Whitlam's persistent advocacy for the arts in Australia to be recognised and taken more seriously, as much by Australians themselves as by international audiences. Amphlett reminds us of the widely held belief that 'living in Australia before Whitlam was akin to living in a cultural desert', and her candid essay shows how this summation of a sense of profound change across the arts sector was felt by artists.

Gillian Appleton considers the impact of Whitlam's agenda in a related area: the mass media. She vividly paints a picture of a deeply sexist mass media, which addressed female readers as 'girls' or 'housewives', and which portrayed members of the women's movement as 'man-haters' and 'bra-burners'; Elizabeth Reid was dubbed Gough's 'supergirl' by a curious and baffled press gallery. It will come as no surprise that the Australian media was dominated by men in the early 1970s, or that expanding women's roles within the media became the goal of women journalists, producers and reporters. The male-dominated media would go on to shape the Australian public's reception of International Women's Year in 1975.

Recalling her own role as media liaison for the International Women's Year secretariat in 1975, Appleton had direct experience of the ease with which the media could ridicule government-sponsored activities and spending that focused on women's experiences. Yet she also argues, rightly, that many of the events staged for International Women's Year were transformative. The mass media is no longer as male-dominated as it was in the Whitlam era, though as Appleton reminds us, it remains deeply gendered, and men continue to hold most of the leadership positions in the industry.

The chapter by Campbell and Hayes offers an illustration of one important aspect of Whitlam's reforming agenda in education, one defined by the language of equality of opportunity and outcomes, and remedying structural and place-based disadvantage. The education of women and girls was high on the list of priorities, exposed as a form of inequality that cut across class or differences in socio-economic status, even if the consequences and expressions of that disadvantage looked different depending on family background or social class. In the preceding decades, sociological attention to educational inequality had largely – not exclusively – been driven by the extensively documented and highly visible ways in which schools tended to reproduce, to normalise and cement, social inequality rather than deliver on meritocratic promises, a failure accentuated in Australia with its so-called 'fair go for all' ethos.

For Whitlam, remedying the structural and economic aspects of educational inequality was intertwined with a quest to improve the quality of education for all, such that educational provision itself – at the school or tertiary level – was a site for uplift, not for reproducing structurally differentiated and determined experiences and pathways. Reflecting on these matters in 1974, Whitlam saw that much of the government's important work in education lay ahead: 'to ensure that the money and the institutions that Government has provided will be effectively used to implement our goal and produce the results we desire – higher standards and greater equality of opportunity'.[4] Similar to the approach to supporting and raising the profile of the arts, Whitlam emphasised the importance of raising 'community standards of expectation about the Government's role in education and the quality of our children's future'.[5] Consequently, the goal was 'to bring all schools up to the standard of the best schools',[6] which involved tackling privilege head-on. Leaning on the British social reformer RH Tawney for support, Whitlam called out the resistance of conservatives to improve the quality of education for all so as 'to safeguard their privilege at the expense of the majority'.[7] Destabilising the status quo to expose how educational inequality was sustained was also a feature of attempts to improve the educational experiences and post-school lives of girls and young women.

Campbell and Hayes outline the key themes of the 1975 landmark Schools Commission report *Girls, School and Society* and the social and political context surrounding its development.[8] This includes the establishment of the Schools Commission under Whitlam, and the roles of Peter Karmel, Director of the Schools Commission, and Jean Blackburn, effectively the primary author of *Girls, School and Society*. In the language of the day, the educational inequalities facing women and girls were framed as arising from differences in sex roles and associated patterns – in curriculum, careers and post-school life – that systematically disadvantaged them, restricting their opportunities and deepening the authority of sex-role stereotypes. An earlier report from the Schools Commission, *Schools in Australia*, had found that 'to be a girl is an educational disadvantage' – with the important caveat – 'except when it is associated with high socio-economic status'.[9] Attention to the intersection between class and gender disadvantage continued in *Girls, School and Society*, with the connection between differentiated schooling experiences and post-school opportunities a key consideration. The focus and recommendations of this report crystallised the characteristic features of political engagements with the potential of schooling to either entrench or transform educational inequalities.

According to Campbell and Hayes, Jean Blackburn navigated this sensibly and pragmatically, holding on to the idea that no matter the harsh criticism of schooling as part of the social apparatus reproducing inequalities, it only made sense for governments to intervene in those processes if there was a kernel of hope that reforms might make a difference. Navigating how schooling might be harnessed towards transformative ends, away from the determinism of past inequalities and injustices, was a strong focus for feminist educators and teacher activism more broadly. The early 1970s was an era of considerable radical activity in schooling, with initiatives to establish alternative, community or open-plan schools, and calls for new ways of organising curriculum, of breaking down hierarchies and barriers between schools and community and of making schooling and curriculum more democratic: Blackburn herself went on to make significant contributions to these discussions.[10]

The second strand in this rich chapter is the parallel account of Blackburn herself, outlining her intellectual, political and even bureaucratic biography, given her immersion in the machinery of government during a period of massive social reform. Indeed, in light of her early political years as a communist and member of the Fabian Society, it seems likely it was only under a deliberately reforming government that Blackburn's evident prowess as a policy adviser, educational commentator and pragmatic reformer could come to the fore. Campbell and Hayes then point to important elements of Australian feminism during the 1970s and the rise of a distinctly femocratic politics, well documented in Australian feminist scholarship. As the insights into Jean Blackburn's life suggest, this form of politics intersected with the biographies and lived experience of women reformers who were themselves experiencing some of the openings up and new avenues that feminism, no matter how fraught or attenuated, was making possible for women in this era.

WHITLAM, WOMEN AND THE MEDIA

GILLIAN APPLETON

It *was* time!

In the polarised, often poisonous, political environment of the 2020s, it is difficult to convey the surge of hope and excitement that greeted the election of the Whitlam Labor government on 2 December 1972 – an unforgettable date to my generation of Australians. The prospect of a Whitlam Labor government energised us after 23 years of conservative rule. Expatriates returned, full of optimism. Whitlam's extensive policy program, developed over years as opposition leader, potentially reached into every aspect of our lives, with its focus on promoting equality, involving all Australians in decision-making processes, and lifting our horizons.

The election catchcry was 'It's Time' – and we were ready for change.

A hostile media

'Media' in the early 1970s meant print newspapers and magazines, broadcast radio, and depending on where you lived, up to three television services. Between them, three commercial organisations controlled metropolitan and regional newspapers and popular magazines, and had significant holdings in TV and radio.[1] The sole alternative was the government-funded ABC. There was no FM radio, internet, pay TV, streaming services or social media.

Radio and television stations relied heavily on imported program material. There was minimal Australian-made entertainment or drama.

Whitlam proposed to reform the media. He initiated a Department of the Media to encourage more Australian program content and foreshadowed a possible independent newspaper commission – an idea which provoked 'outrage and derision' among media proprietors, and the most controversial policies were quietly dropped.[2]

Whitlam later wrote that the media had been 'uniformly and implacably hostile' to his government. His special adviser Graham Freudenberg argued that an editorial in May 1975 in the influential *Sydney Morning Herald*, implying the Whitlam government was totally unfit to govern on grounds of personal immorality and corruption, set the government on a path to destruction.[3] Journalists at *The Australian* took unprecedented action by striking in protest at their own paper's hostile stance.[4]

The women of Australia had high expectations of the new government, and Whitlam was quick to move in areas of special importance to women, such as the removal of the tax on oral contraceptives, payment of the adult minimum wage to women, and equal pay for 70 000 female workers in the public service. The conservative, male-dominated media's response to these moves only intensified their negativity towards Whitlam.

Newspaper language and reporting practices reflected deeply embedded sexism. Simplistic and demeaning stereotypes – 'girls', 'ladies' or 'housewives' – were common descriptors for women. No report on a woman appointed to a responsible position – a school principal, a department head, a judge or a winner of a major award – would fail to describe her motherhood status or comment on her appearance and dress. The advent of the women's movement and visible feminist activism gave rise to a whole new range of offensive stereotypes ('bra-burners', 'libbers', 'man-haters') in editorials, cartoons and carefully curated photographs, which helped foster negative attitudes to the women's movement among the wider public. As Evan Williams, Gough Whitlam's press secretary, wrote in his reflections on the media coverage of International Women's Year, the media stereotype of the

> female activist [is] an intellectual, she's unfeminine in a particular sense, she's probably morally lax, she's shrill, intolerant, slovenly, noisy and of course she hates men. [T]he media are more likely to give prominence to women who reinforce this image than those who don't fit the pattern.[5]

In April 1973 Whitlam confirmed his commitment to women by appointing Elizabeth Reid, ANU philosophy tutor and committed feminist, as his special Adviser on Women – a first for Australia, indeed, for the world. The headline writers coined the patronising term 'Supergirl' to describe Reid and other shortlisted women who applied for the adviser job.[6] Male journalists were blindsided by Reid's frankness when questioned on topics like marriage, abortion, masturbation. In a 1976 interview with celebrated American feminist Gloria Steinem, Reid stated that almost every article about her mentioned her age; or that she was wearing no makeup, no bra, and jeans; or that she was separated from her husband, with whom her daughter lived.[7]

Women were almost totally absent from the media workforce in key production, presentation, reporting, editorial and managerial roles.[8] It was not surprising that there was meagre coverage of women and our interests. Women's sport was not reported at all. Nor were policy issues central to women's lives like child care, equal pay, abortion and women's refuges; 'women's pages', with few exceptions, carried fashion and society gossip. In the early '70s, there were no women newsreaders or reporters on television; no women editors of any major newspapers; no women in positions of editorial or programming power within major broadcasting networks.[9] Media companies exercised powerful influence over the way we viewed our own society, and gender roles particularly.

Change through activism

In 1969 I joined the ABC as a trainee publicist/journalist. At that time ABC women were clustered in service areas as personal assistants, typists and switchboard operators. By 1974, we had established the Australian Women's Broadcasting Co-operative (AWBC) to help develop career paths in program production and administration and to counteract the effect of a heavily masculine workforce. After considerable pressure, ABC management allocated the AWBC air time for our own weekly radio program, *The Coming Out Show*.[10]

ABC women were not alone in battling sexist media practices. The Media Women's Action Group gathered feminist women from all forms of media, including broadsheet and popular press, women's magazines, and ABC and commercial radio and TV.[11] With discrimination and workplace harassment rife across the industry (for example, women journalists were excluded from membership of the Journalists' Club on the grounds that there were insufficient women's toilets), this mixed group found many issues in common.

Group consciousness-raising was central to second-wave feminism. We experienced the excitement of meeting with other women, sharing common experiences and being able to speak uninhibited by a male presence. We found our voices in heated discussion on workplace issues, the need for women's refuges and work-based child care, the gender balance of work in the home. We realised that sexism permeated all aspects of our everyday lives: relationships, education, employment, the arts, health and welfare, and advertising. Women working in the media brought this new awareness to their workplaces, and set about changing the roles open to women and offering new perspectives on the ways women's issues were reported.

A voice for women at the seat of power

On her appointment as Whitlam's adviser, Elizabeth Reid launched into an Australia-wide process of consultation with women, travelling widely. She invited women to write to her in an effort to identify their issues of greatest concern. Reid's office received more mail than anyone except the Prime Minister, and Reid remembered later that 'the creation of my job unleashed a flood of feelings from women all over Australia. And so many letters began: "At last there is somebody who will understand what I am talking about"'.[12] Reid's privileged access to the Prime Minister caused some resentment, with intermittent rumblings of discontent from many groups that felt entitled to speak for women. By any standard, Elizabeth Reid was an outstanding appointment, but as I was soon to observe, it was a job that no one woman – not even a 'Supergirl' – could have done.

International Women's Year

When 1975 was designated as International Women's Year (IWY), Reid successfully encouraged Whitlam to back an Australian response, and on 8 March 1974, the government announced an allocation for 1974–76 of $3.3 million (equivalent to about $24 million in 2021) to Australia's IWY celebrations. The media saw this as unwarranted and excessive largesse dished out to Australia's women. *The Age* headlined their story '$2M for the Sheilas – Surprisingly it's Not a Joke'.[13]

Any hint of conflict between women, or criticism of Reid and IWY from women across the political spectrum, became a recurrent motif in media coverage of the International Women's Year. Radical feminist organisations felt that the independence of the women's movement might be compromised by taking government money, and some groups refused to participate at all.[14] Many long-established women's interest groups saw a chance for recognition and a funding boost to their activities. Australia's aims and objectives for the Year were announced in late 1974. The desire to change attitudes ('... not only the way men see women but also how women see themselves'[15]) was prominent among them. It was clear that the media had a crucial role to play in any attitudinal changes.

A personal experience

The media reaction to IWY presented something of a microcosm of the negative media coverage suffered by the Whitlam government in general. In early 1975 I was offered a position involving media liaison at the IWY Secretariat, based in Canberra. As well as media liaison, the job would involve assessing funding applications in my main areas of interest – the arts, film and theatre. I was 33 and had five years' experience in ABC radio and TV and daytime commercial TV. The prospect of working with women better versed in feminist theory than I was, and with strong credentials in the women's liberation movement, was daunting. I was under no illusion about the difficulties ahead, particularly in view of my lack of experience, with national political media, the Canberra press gallery in particular. But the appeal of working for the Whitlam government and helping implement its program for women was decisive.

I arrived in a frigid Canberra in early June 1975. The offices of the IWY Secretariat were in a shabby group of buildings on the edge of the ANU campus. There were few people around. I was to share an office with Susan Ryan, who like me was one of a number of project officers appointed to oversee particular areas for the year – in her case, education. Susan (soon to be a Labor senator for the ACT and a distinguished minister in the Hawke government) was absent along with other staff who were attending the United Nations IWY Conference in Mexico City as part of Australia's delegation. I spent the time before the travellers returned sifting through a pile of funding applications for IWY-related cultural projects. To my alarm, there was also a fat file of press cuttings with comments about the year, overwhelmingly negative.[16]

In response to a media release about my appointment, I soon received calls from (male) journalists inviting me to meet for lunch or a drink. I opted for the former as being safer, but I found that many journalists thought nothing of consuming two bottles of wine over a lengthy lunch. The intake of alcohol in Canberra in those days was prodigious. They obviously saw me as a useful future contact. They were already pumping me about Elizabeth Reid and her close working relationship with the Prime Minister; and about relations between Reid, the Women's Office in the Department of the Prime Minister and Cabinet, and the bureaucracy generally. I soon learned to make frequent use of 'off the record' to avoid saying anything I would later regret.

The IWY workplace

In 1974 the government appointed an Australian National Advisory Committee (ANAC) for IWY of 12 people (ten women and two men) chaired by Elizabeth Reid, which would make decisions about the direction of the Year and the kinds of projects that would be supported. ANAC members included veteran Western Australian feminist Irene Greenwood, broadcaster Caroline Jones, Indigenous activist Ruby Hammond, migrant worker Maria Pozos – and the Prime Minister's wife, Margaret Whitlam. The media had already lambasted Margaret Whitlam for agreeing to write a regular diary for *Woman's Day* magazine, and to front a television program (though it was made clear she was donating any payments to charity). But she was more than equal to adverse media comment, always ready with a quick and witty retort in response.[17]

The first set of IWY grants had been announced in December 1974. The Committee's policy was to refer projects which required ongoing funding to relevant government departments and agencies, a strategic way of turning the attention of the public service to their responsibilities to women. It wasn't always easy to get their support. For example, the Department of Foreign Affairs objected to a photographic exhibition on the lives of Australian women, to be shown in embassies abroad, which included shots of remote Aboriginal communities and migrant workers in factories, as being 'too negative'. The show went ahead, however, thanks to the Office of Women's Affairs under Sara Dowse.

Nearly 700 grant applications in total came from all over Australia, and 80 projects were supported with as little as a couple of hundred dollars and up to more than $50 000. Funded projects included publications on women and employment, women's studies, feminist journals, seminars and forums, films, writing, arts and theatre. Applicants sought funding for projects which – regrettably – are just as relevant today, including research into domestic violence, women as carers for aged parents, abortion, single parenting and menopause.[18]

The very diversity of women and women's organisations meant that distribution of the funds was likely to be controversial. Despite our best efforts, media coverage was sparse and often ill-informed. By far the most favourable coverage of IWY funding (and indeed the year generally) came from country newspapers covering projects in their region and interviewing recipients;

and from women's magazines and a few women journalists from metropolitan dailies who gave thoughtful coverage to IWY initiatives ignored elsewhere. The most outraged media reaction of the year followed the allocation of $100 000 as part-funding for a major television series on human reproduction. The involvement of Germaine Greer, a favourite media target, as writer and producer, intensified the outrage. 'No More Sex Please, Ms Greer' was a typical headline.[19] This documentary was never made and the money was diverted to become the Australian Film Commission's Women's Film Fund, established in 1976. Despite its modest budget, the Fund had a decisive influence on the development of Australian women's filmmaking and supported much innovative work, mainly in short films.[20] Filmmakers funded included Tracey Moffatt and Helen Grace, and women were able to work in technical roles unavailable to them elsewhere.

International Women's Year conferences

On the international stage, the UN World Conference of IWY held in Mexico from 19 June to 2 July 1975 was the major event of the Year. In total, 133 countries attended. Elizabeth Reid led Australia's delegation of 14, which included Margaret Whitlam, other members of the ANAC, IWY Secretariat staff, and diplomats. The Sydney tabloid *Daily Telegraph* farewelled the delegation with a story headed 'Mum's the Word as the Big Yak Yak Begins'.[21] Only the ABC and the *Australian Women's Weekly* sent reporters to cover the Conference.

Divisions were clear from the start between US feminists and Third World women rejecting a Western-determined feminist path, and there was heated debate on the relationship between politics and women's issues – and whether they were inseparable. Some saw a focus on the patriarchy and women's exploitation as simply distractions from the class struggle and national liberation.

Elizabeth Reid and other feminists had pointed out during IWY planning that UN economic data did not count enormous amounts of uncommodified labour by women. In her account of the year, Jocelyn Olcott comments that 'journalists attended mostly to the spectacular and with few exceptions paid little attention to the day-to-day efforts by thousands of participants'.[22] Reid's brilliant, challenging plenary speech in which she highlighted sexism, and linked it to racism as reflecting the same need for power over other human beings, thrust her into international recognition; but it was virtually ignored at home, despite the release of a full transcript.[23]

Concurrently with the World Conference, several thousand women from many cultures and countries, representatives of non-government organisations, and private individuals, attended the less formal Tribune. The government sponsored ten people to attend, among whom were two Aboriginal women, activist Pat Eatock and welfare worker Vi Stanton. Media coverage primarily highlighted differences between Western feminists and women from the Third World, and the meagre Australian coverage only picked up wire service releases with this focus. Despite this, the Australian participants found it an unforgettable experience. Although the Tribune was widely reported at the time as disorganised and chaotic, in the longer term its very informality and the diversity of its participants proved more productive than the main conference in identifying the issues that would come to the fore in ensuing decades.

Back in Australia, the Women and Politics Conference, held in Canberra from 31 August to 6 September, was designed to emphasise the stark under-representation of women in local, state and federal politics and in the public service, the judiciary and trade unions. More than 700 women from different political, religious, ethnic and social backgrounds attended. As well as individual women, there were representatives from the political parties, many women's organisations, ministerial staff, lobby groups, trade unions, the churches, academia, local government and the public service, along with notable international guest feminists. Commissioned conference papers explored the history of political involvement by individual women and women's non-government organisations, and discussed strategies for engagement in the decision-making processes that excluded women.

I had the task, with a team of experienced journalists, of putting together the conference daily paper/updated program, *New Dawn* (a reference to feminist Louisa Lawson's newspaper *The Dawn*).[24] We hoped that a paper written specifically for conference participants would provide a balance to other media coverage (or lack of it). The team spread out every day to cover as many sessions as possible, and returned to type their reports late in the afternoon. One hasty headline 'Flo Gets the Women Together' – a reference to US visitor Flo Kennedy attending a speakout of Aboriginal women – was taken to imply that they had not convened their own meeting, and we printed a contrite apology. Aboriginal women spoke of racism as a far more important issue for them, and for all First Nations people, than sexism. A similar theme had emerged at the Tribune in Mexico, a foretaste of developments in the next wave of feminism.

The conference itself provided plenty of headline fodder. The sight of women wearing men's suits to a reception to open the conference in King's Hall that specified 'lounge suits', was reported as an insult to the dignity of Parliament; interrupting the Prime Minister's welcome speech was deemed disrespectful by the very media that regularly pilloried him. The same media sought out critical participants for comment. The *SA News* reported an Adelaide mother of three describing the Conference as being run by 'a feminist rabble'.[25] But among both male and female reporters who actually attended, coverage was generally favourable. One press gallery reporter told me that the week had been, for him, an incredible experience in consciousness-raising. A scathing editorial in the *Canberra Times* on 2 September 1975 became the focus for women's rage at the media coverage. A crowd of over 300 Conference participants marched on the offices of the newspaper and successfully sought permission to publish a response.[26] A commercial TV current affairs program offered a night to highlight women's concerns – only to sneer at the female production team's efforts the following night.

In terms of consciousness-raising, the Women and Politics Conference was the most influential initiative of the IWY National Committee. Many participants returned home determined to stand for political office, join or form lobby groups, and implement strategies for pressuring the media and the advertising industry. The two-volume Conference report is a valuable record of a remarkable moment in time for Australian women. A further IWY gathering, a UN Media Seminar planned for November–December 1975 in Sydney, was cancelled shortly after the Women and Politics Conference. The official reason for cancellation was a government expenditure review.[27]

Reid quits, Whitlam dismissed

On 2 October, Elizabeth Reid resigned. Secretariat staff were not surprised. We had seen her total exhaustion after trying to fulfil an impossible overload of work and meet constant competing demands for her attention. She later said that she was left with an all-pervasive feeling of incompleteness. She had no doubt 'that the Australian press is partially responsible for the government's backtracking on women and hence, for my resignation. The schoolboy immaturity of the press led to constant sensationalism, and distorted reporting of our issues and activities'.[28] Paradoxically, most of the media managed to report her departure without adverse comment, even acknowledging her significant contribution.

On 11 November, barely a month after Reid's departure, there was an even greater shock when the Governor-General dismissed the Whitlam government, dashing the hopes of a generation of women.

Women and media, then and now

There is little doubt that overreach in the media of the 1970s contributed to a lingering impression that the Whitlam government was a failed experiment. Since that time, however, many writers, analysts and historians have acknowledged Whitlam's reformist legislative record and remarkable achievements.

The importance of Australia's role in the International Women's Year was barely recognised here at the time – unsurprising in a year of high political drama. But in hindsight, in Australia and internationally, IWY emphasised the role of the media in prevailing attitudes to women, and the need for action. The media were firmly on the agenda for the first UN Decade for Women 1975–85.

To anyone for whom newspapers are relics of a distant past, the sexism and entrenched bias of 1970s media might seem positively quaint. But the outrageous treatment of our first female Prime Minister, Julia Gillard, 35 years later reminded us how little had fundamentally changed, as did revelations in 2021 about reprehensible behaviour towards women at the heart of the Australian political and legal establishment.

Over the past 50 years, developments in information and communications technologies have generated a massive upheaval of the media landscape. Print media is now just one of many sources of news and information, and its readers are ageing. Many younger people have turned to electronic sources. In 2022 independent online (and print) publications featuring evidence-based reporting and sophisticated commentary offer readers a variety of choices.

The Australian mainstream media today routinely report many issues important to women that they once ignored, and women journalists fill prominent roles in all forms of media. Rare examples of sexist language and stereotyping are called out and lampooned. It would be a mistake, however, to think there is no longer a problem, or that change cannot be insidiously reversed.

Key objectives for the media in the UN's Platform for the Decade for Women (1975–85) were to increase the participation and access of women to expression and decision-making in and through the media; and to promote a balanced and non-stereotyped portrayal of women.[29] The UN-supported Global Media Monitoring Project – the world's largest and longest-running research and advocacy initiative – has conducted ongoing research since 1995 into gender balance in and through the news media. Its 2020 report concluded that on current indications, it will take 67 years to close the average gender gap in traditional news media (that is, in the numbers and status of women working in the media and the way women and their concerns are reported – or ignored).[30]

The Project also reported that stories on gender-based violence are very rarely the major news of the day. Girls and women are under-represented as subjects and sources for stories about sexual harassment, rape and sexual assault, even during the COVID period when such acts have reached epidemic proportions. In media reporting of the pandemic itself, the Project found that women comprise only 27 per cent of the health specialists appearing in coronavirus stories, far fewer than the 46 per cent world average given in labour force statistics.

A 2021 report on print media by the Women's Leadership Institute Australia found that male journalists wrote 65 per cent of all opinion pieces, and topics were gendered: for women journalists, health and entertainment; for men, politics and sport. Women were interviewed or quoted significantly less than men.[31] An earlier (2011) study of women in the media covering 500 companies in 59 countries found that in Australia, women made up only 20 per cent of boards of directors, and 10 per cent of top-level management.[32] Men made considerably more than women in the average high salary range in all of the occupational levels.

Another study of 200 major news outlets across four continents revealed that only 23 per cent of the top editors across the sample were women, despite an average 40 per cent female journalists in those markets.[33] Every market had a majority of men among top editors, even in countries where women outnumbered men as working journalists.

Changes will be at the margins until enough women hold positions of real power in media and information and communications technology organisations, filling top management positions or as board members where they can influence policies on gender and appointments at all levels of these organisations. In my working life, I have seen irrefutable evidence of the positive differences women in power can make, both in opening opportunities for other women and in influencing the fundamental culture of an organisation and its standing with the public.

Where to from here?

Large-scale national protests like 2021's Women's March4Justice undoubtedly influence public perceptions of the disadvantages women still face.[34] Decades after the second feminist wave, many women experience the same daily humiliations at home and in the workplace as their mothers and grandmothers: harassment, sexual innuendo, racism and outright abuse. How can we maintain momentum towards real, women-defined change? Are there lessons for activist women of the 21st century in the experiences of the 20th?

The first step is to acknowledge that the battle is far from won. In today's political environment, Australian women need to be constantly alert to developments that threaten to further diminish or even sweep away the gains that began with Whitlam. The following initiatives suggest themselves:

- **Join or form groups:** In an era of technology-induced social isolation, the value of *groups* joined together by common interests is even more vital to the continuing fight for women's rights and for speaking truth to power. Politicians respond best to numbers and perceived voting power.

- **Use social media** and other new forms of communication that can serve as weapons for good and spread positive messages to counteract vilification, stereotyping, and material that promotes negative body imaging among girls and young women. Humour is an effective way to draw attention to ludicrous sexism.

- **Lobby:** Legislation and regulation are important tools for reform, and we need to monitor existing structures and identify where change is needed. We must also be alert to incursions on hard-won previous changes and take care to avoid over-reliance on government.

- **Identify women with media skills** and qualifications in particular subject areas and circulate lists to all media outlets as sources for comment and on-air/online appearances.

- **Stage major events:** Forums, protests, etc. remain key to keeping the issues at the forefront of the public agenda, and generating wider support

- **Get involved in politics** to understand the workings of government at all levels, and use this knowledge for the benefit of women. Make submissions to government inquiries involving ICTs and media, and any other areas touching on women's interests.

- **Know feminist history:** Without knowing our history, we run the of risk reinvention, stasis or outright failure.

Final considerations

The COVID-19 pandemic foregrounded the continued gender imbalance in domestic responsibilities; the unforgivable incidence of homelessness in this affluent country, and in particular its effect on older and single women; and the persistent massive disadvantages suffered by First Nations people.

At this point in humanity's history, the looming catastrophe of climate change overrides every consideration of the future of the planet, the natural environment and all humanity. Male-dominated neoliberal societies built on self-interest and profit at all costs have been at the root of the failure to protect our planet. A possible solution seems obvious. If unlikely.

WHITLAM, WOMEN AND THE ARTS
PATRICIA AMPHLETT

We had conservative governments all my life until Gough Whitlam became our Prime Minister in 1972. It's often said that living in Australia before Whitlam was akin to living in a cultural desert. It felt like we'd been suppressing our discontent for so long, the balloon was about to burst.

We wanted change, real change. As performers we were as keen as our audiences to embrace our own culture, whether it was a David Williamson play or a Billy Thorpe concert.

Without doubt, one of the most important achievements of the Whitlam government was its support of the arts. In his book *The Whitlam Government*, Whitlam declared:

> In any civilised community the arts and associated
> amenities must occupy a central place. Their enjoyment
> should not be seen as something remote from everyday life.
> Of all the objectives of my Government none had a higher
> priority than the encouragement of the arts, the preservation
> and enrichment of our cultural and intellectual heritage.
> Indeed I would argue that all the other objectives of a Labor
> Government – social reform, justice and equity in the
> provision of welfare services and educational opportunities
> – have as their goal the creation of a society in which the
> arts and the appreciation of spiritual and intellectual values
> can flourish. Our other objectives are all means to an end;
> the enjoyment of the arts is an end in itself. Education and
> social reform may not be cures for all our ills, but a society
> that cares about education and social reform will be a

society that cares about literature and the arts. It will be well
supplied with the qualities of understanding, sensitivity,
discrimination and compassion that are the basis of artistic
creativity.[1]

'We want Gough! We want Gough!' we shouted. I'll never forget
that night. It was 13 November 1972. The Bowman Hall in
the Blacktown Civic Centre was packed to capacity and there
were thousands more outside. From those first words of Gough
Whitlam's speech, 'Men and women of Australia', to the last,
'I do not for a moment believe that we should set limits on what
we can achieve, together, for our country, our people, our future',
I was captivated. He outlined Labor's election policies, including
a coherent policy for the arts which stressed their value and
contribution to society. He promised support for the development
of professional standards of work and the development of cultural
activity throughout the whole community. He would encourage
our national identity through the arts and promote Australia's
image overseas with the work of our artists.

Without question, before 1972 the arts in Australia were badly
in need of encouragement and support. Many of our finest artists
were working overseas. There were several government advisory
agencies for the arts, all of which offered very little assistance to
artists. Our national cultural institutions were almost non-existent.
Each state had an art gallery, a library and a museum, but many of
them were run down and understaffed. Valuable collections were
in dire need of care and restoration. There were a few small but
dedicated theatre companies and there were symphony orchestras
in the capital cities, but the basis of a national arts and cultural
policy did not exist. There were no major performing arts centres.
The fledgling Australian Opera and Australian Ballet companies
were underfunded. There were no regional theatre companies
or galleries; there was no film industry; there were no state arts

ministries. Recognition and support for Aboriginal arts and the crafts in general was virtually non-existent; support for writers and artists was also virtually non-existent. It is hardly surprising that artists in Australia felt despondent and neglected.

Gough Whitlam's understanding and support of the arts epitomised his great vision for Australia. In government he established the Australian Council for the Arts in 1973; it became a statutory authority in 1975 under the name Australia Council. The Council advises governments and industry on arts-related issues, but primarily it funds arts projects, on an arm's-length basis, and formulates and implements policies to foster and promote the arts. It comprises seven boards: Aboriginal and Torres Strait Islander Arts, Dance, Literature, Major Performing Arts, Music, Theatre, Visual Arts. Up until 2014 the Council provided more than 1700 grants each year to artists and arts organisations.[2] Then, in 2015, the Abbott government's Arts Minister, George Brandis, cut the Council's budget by $100 million, leading to the loss of a whopping 65 arts companies and 70 per cent of grants to individual artists.[3]

When Whitlam opened the Film and Television School in August 1975, he gave credit to one of his predecessors, Prime Minister John Gorton, for recognising the needs of the Australian film and television industry. They both agreed that Australia needed to develop an industry of world standard, a thriving industry with expertise in all areas of production, from trained technicians to scriptwriters and directors. To this day the Film and Television School, now known as AFTRS, the Australian Film Television and Radio School, continues to flourish and contribute to the success and sustainability of Australia's screen and broadcast industries by developing the skills and knowledge of talented people and undertaking cutting-edge research.

The Australian Film Commission was established by the Whitlam government in July 1975 as the successor to the Film

Development Corporation set up by the Gorton government. In the first year of its existence, its budget was $6.5 million. The Australian Film Commission acted as a funding and development agency for the Australian film industry. This support contributed to the renaissance of Australian cinema that took place in the 1970s and 1980s, reviving an industry that had stagnated for decades. This support allowed the expression of a new and confident cultural identity through film. Iconic and critically acclaimed films such as *Picnic at Hanging Rock, Gallipoli* and *The Last Wave* were also produced with funding from the new Commission.

Whitlam also established the National Gallery of Australia, whose purchase of *Blue Poles* in 1973 was symbolic of the bold cultural shift. Never had such a picture moved and disturbed the Australian public. Whitlam personally endorsed the Australia Council's proposal that the Australian government would indemnify priceless art that toured the country, instead of cultural institutions paying insurance premiums. This endorsement brought us magnificent works of art we otherwise could never have seen. His support of Aboriginal and Torres Strait Islander art led to the awareness of art forms that now internationally define our country. The former Director of the Art Gallery of New South Wales, Edmund Capon, remembered watching Gough Whitlam from the United Kingdom before he moved to Australia. 'You could really feel him pulling and dragging Australia into a different, independent world,' he said. Most of all, Capon remembers Whitlam's deep appreciation for the arts. 'To have the leader of the nation believing in the arts is very important. It's about credibility. The thing about Gough is that he believed cultural welfare was as important as aspects of social, political and economic welfare.[34]

Others in Australia's arts scene also remembered the role that Whitlam played in fostering Australian culture. Playwright David Williamson said:

When he came to office, Gough Whitlam made it clear,
unlike those who went before him, that the arts was an
integral and vital part of this flourishing country. He
was very generous to the arts and for years and years
after every time he turned up at an arts event, he got
a standing ovation as a debt of gratitude from the arts
community.[5]

Writer Tom Keneally remembered the Whitlam campaign in 1972:
'The Whitlam campaign captured a nation's desire for change, be
it in the arts, Aboriginal rights or feminism. Labor's first 100 days
of office was an extraordinary time to be alive, like being in the
middle of the French Revolution, without Robespierre.'[6]

The Whitlam government saw the production of local
television as an important part of the expression of a mature,
independent Australian cultural identity. Accordingly, it provided
significant support to Australian television industries. Whitlam's
government sought to provide increased support for local actors,
filmmakers and producers by increasing the minimum Australian
content requirements for commercial television networks. The
ABC also conformed to these minimum content requirements,
and was given a major boost in government funding to assist in
the production of local television content.

The Whitlam government supported Australian music by
introducing minimum Australian music content for commercial
radio stations. Ten per cent of music broadcast by commercial
stations was to be the work of Australian musicians. The Whitlam
government established 2JJ, now known as Triple J, as a station
specifically designed to support Australian music and connect
with young Australians. It began broadcasting in January 1975.
The government also introduced FM radio in 1974, allowing much
improved sound quality and the licensing of more radio stations.
Multicultural radio services – 2EA Sydney and 3EA Melbourne

– were established, and licences were issued to community radio stations for the first time.

The Whitlam government provided unprecedented support to Australia's arts sectors, helping a generation of creative Australians to give voice to a new, independent, confident and distinctly Australian cultural identity. For example, the Australian Council for the Arts received $14 million in the 1973–74 Budget, more than double the funding which its precursor bodies had received the year before. The Council's funding was increased by a further 50 per cent in the 1974–75 Budget.[7]

Women and the arts

Gough Whitlam strongly believed, personally and politically, that women were equal to men. He wanted governments to remove unfair barriers to women's achievement of equal opportunities and full participation in our society. The composition of today's workforce – in the professions, most trades, most occupations, universities, the public sector, corporate sector, the media, local government, state government, federal government – clearly shows that Whitlam's vision for the women of Australia has come to fruition. Women have held the posts of Prime Minister and Governor-General. Women now often lead state and territory governments and have held the posts of state Governors. Several women sit on the High Court of Australia.

Susan Ryan, who served as Minister Assisting the Prime Minister on the Status of Women from 1983 to 1988, said:

> The difference between this contemporary picture of
> Australian women and what that picture showed in 1972
> constitutes nothing short of a social revolution. While
> a range of cultural, economic and global factors have
> contributed to the transformation, I find I must source

much of it to the fearless, creative and entirely genuine
pursuit by Whitlam of a fair go for Australian women.[8]

This 'fair go' extended to women in the arts. To illustrate, I want to
share some stories of the ways in which the Whitlam government's
reforms allowed women in the arts to flourish in Australia.

Margret RoadKnight

Undoubtedly one of Australia's finest interpretive singers, Margret
is internationally renowned and one of the most respected artists in
her homeland. Although she had given lectures to music educators
in Australia about black American music, she always knew that
'you had to be there'. In 1974 she applied to the Australia Council
Music Board for a music study grant and was granted $4500.

Margret's trip to the United States was extremely beneficial.
She performed and undertook study of the music she loved, music
relatively unknown in Australia. She 'felt the breadth and depth –
a one-ness' with the music that fed into her distinct repertoire in
performances, live and recorded. The experience and knowledge
Margret gained while in the United States gave her the confidence
to give more lectures to music educators and students, on her
return to Australia.

During subsequent trips to the United States, she studied
and recorded gospel music with 2000-voice massed choirs at the
famous Gospel Music Workshop of America in New Orleans. In
1993 Margret recorded another highly acclaimed album, thanks
to a further grant from the Music Board. Her lifelong love and
understanding of blues, jazz and gospel music led to her performing
in West Africa, the birthplace of so much of this music. Margret
says this trip was a life-changing experience.

Margret has received many awards for her performances, the
most recent in 2018 – the Lifetime Achievement Award from the

Australian Women in Music Awards. Rightly proud of her career, Margret still says she couldn't have done it without Gough!

Judy Jacques

From the start of her career, Judy Jacques has successfully avoided the path of the pop diva. Her extraordinary talent enabled her to explore, improvise, experiment and develop her potential as one of the most unique artists in Australia.

So many Australian artists were very happy when Gough Whitlam became Prime Minister. Full of optimism and possibilities – their feelings were palpable. Judy Jacques said it felt like 'the stodgy old stage curtains had been lifted', opening up to bright and often experimental work in many areas. She said that as artists from all disciplines, not just mainstream, they now felt loved and able to present new ideas to their audiences.

Around 1970 Judy made a personal decision to leave the more accessible music behind and further develop her interest in poetry, spoken word, songwriting and vocal improvisation. This brave decision proved to be both a challenging and rewarding time for her. Non-commercial, non-mainstream artistic work very rarely attracted sponsorship, nor the understanding of the majority of the population. It was hoped that when Gough Whitlam came to power, and with the creation of the Australian Council for the Arts in 1973 followed by the Australia Council in 1975, all areas of the arts would be acknowledged and supported by his government.

Judy's experimental music and improvisation attracted small but enthusiastic audiences. She successfully applied to the Music Board for a grant, which enabled her to undertake a short tour to regional Victoria. Called 'Songs, Poems and Improvisations by the Judy Jacques Quintet', the rather ambitious program played at arts centres to audiences in Shepparton, Echuca and Castlemaine. The program was received with varying degrees of enthusiasm.

When delivering the report of their tour to the Music Board in Sydney, Judy's imagination and creativity came to the fore. She organised a Singing Telegram person, dressed as Alice in Wonderland, holding a life-size doll she'd made. She was The Singer with real hair and a beautiful, painted face. Alice read a poem introduction, then continuing in rhyme, instructed the Board that they would need to cut along the dotted line, then open The Singer's diaphragm to retrieve everything that was needed for the acquittal of the grant: 'Here is The Singer I am Alice I found her in the Queen of Hearts Palace She did not please the court with her atonal rort So they cut out her heart … sadly callous.'

There was also a painted cut-out rabbit involved in the delivery of the report. So the story continued while Judy sat at home, biting her nails and waiting for a call. To her surprise, this unusual acquittal was accepted!

In the early '90s, Judy's Wild Dog Ensemble received a grant to record new original music at the ABC studios in Melbourne. The grant enabled Judy to invite Paul Schütze, an Australian artist, composer and guru of electronic improvisation, who was visiting from London, to produce and mix the recordings. These fabulous recordings became legend.

In 2000, after living alone in an isolated shack on Flinders Island, Judy successfully applied for a development grant for songs she had written during that time. This led to recording the collection of songs as *Making Wings*, which received the inaugural Bell Jazz Award for Best Vocal CD in 2003.

Judy proudly sang 'It's Time' during the Melbourne campaign for the 1972 election campaign.

Today she remains a much admired artist. She believes that the development of her work would not have happened without the hope and spirit that Gough Whitlam brought to the arts in Australia.[9]

Cate Blanchett

In her eulogy for Gough Whitlam at his memorial service on Wednesday, 5 November 2014, Cate spoke of the many policies of Whitlam's government that had changed her life.

She received free tertiary education, where, at university, she explored different courses and engaged with the student union in extracurricular activity, where she discovered acting.

Cate is the beneficiary of a foreign policy that put us on the world stage; an Australia that not only wanted, but was encouraged, to explore its voice, culturally.

In 2004, having worked overseas for a few years, Cate came back home and appeared in an Australian film called *Little Fish*. It also starred Hugo Weaving, Noni Hazlehurst and Sam Neill, all of whom were direct beneficiaries of the wave of Australian cinematic and theatrical creativity unleashed by Gough Whitlam's time in government.

Little Fish told the story of a young woman living in a culturally diverse suburb of western Sydney. Her relationship with an Asian-Australian man is a troubled one, with a history of drugs and personal ghosts. A story like *Little Fish* would not have been told without the enormous changes to the Australian cultural conversation, initiated and shaped by the legacy of Gough Whitlam. This story of Asia and multiculturalism in Australia is unromantic, brutal and sharp. The wonderful production team included Australian director Rowan Woods and Australian writer, now producer, Jacquelin Perske, both of whom graduated from AFTRS. It was produced by Porchlight Pictures, with the assistance of government film bodies that all found their voice and experience under and out of initiatives made in Gough Whitlam's time in government.

Cate Blanchett is a working mother of three. She had just had her second child when she took on the role of *Little Fish*. No one passed judgment, no one batted an eyelid. No one thought she was incapable. The culture around women and their right to work as equals in Australia had already been addressed considerably by Whitlam. Equal pay for equal work began with the 1972 Equal Pay case at the Commonwealth Conciliation and Arbitration Commission and was extended in 1974 when the Commission included women workers in the adult minimum wage for the very first time.

In her eulogy for Whitlam, Cate said:

> Women were probably the main beneficiaries of free tertiary education. So here today I may stand as an exemplar, but if you combine the modernising and enabling capacity afforded women by his legislations, you can begin to see that the nation was truly changed by him through the arts and through gender, thereby leading us towards an inclusive, compassionate maturity. So much of this achievement is directly attributable to policy initiatives Gough Whitlam began, with a series of reforms to extend the degree and quality of social opportunities to women in Australia.[10]

My story

I am professionally known as Little Pattie, performer. Growing up in a Labor family was not without its challenges. My parents, particularly my father, had strong opinions about most things, especially 'those greedy Tories'. He thought the inaction and conservatism of the Liberals was unfair, and bad for Australia. I remember as a young girl accompanying my father to The Domain in Sydney, where we would listen to speakers. Sometimes I didn't like being there, but sometimes I felt proud. On the way home, Dad would talk about politics. That's probably when I began to understand what it meant to be a Labor person. Terms such as equal rights, equal pay were rarely used when I was growing up. However, I innately knew what they meant. At my high school in the early '60s, much emphasis was placed on the assumption that we were as smart and clever as any boy, but the reality of society's expectations was very different. When I became a professional performer, I was not at all surprised to experience what it was like to be a female pop star. It was a given that only males could headline and be the stars of the shows. Even the most successful and popular female performers 'knew their place', and were the support performers for the men.

When Gough came to power, those terms – equal rights and equal pay – were not only commonly used but we women were living them! Thanks to Gough, women gained the courage and confidence to live and enjoy being 'headliners' every day!

JEAN BLACKBURN, GIRLS, AND THEIR SCHOOL EDUCATION

CRAIG CAMPBELL AND DEBRA HAYES

The 1975 Schools Commission report *Girls, School and Society* was a remarkable intervention into thinking about the education of girls and young women in Australia.[1] It was internationally significant as it explored the effects of sexism, self-esteem and equal opportunity issues arising from dominant ideas about masculinity and femininity in relation to schooling and beyond. It changed the way schools operated in Australia. Daniela Torsh and Jean Blackburn were key figures in its writing, although Blackburn's influence prevailed in the final report.

If the report was to be accepted by governments, it needed to be framed, argued and written carefully. The effort was successful: the federal government, and many state ones, mined its contents as an inspiration for action. It was not only governments that did this. The report was distributed widely, and its influence reached teacher unions and teachers in schools. It also contributed to the growing field of scholarship concerning girls and education. What was the influence of Jean Blackburn, not only on the final draft of *Girls, School and Society*, but on the social justice agenda in education that she brought to the Whitlam Labor government? And how is her work relevant for education policy today?

Peter Karmel and Jean Blackburn had been aware of one another as students at the University of Melbourne in the 1940s. Jean was born in 1919, and by the late 1930s was a communist, a fierce critic of fascism and capitalism. She left the Communist Party in 1956 as the truth of Stalinism was incontrovertibly revealed, taking work as a school teacher, and writing a remarkable feminist tract, *Australian Wives Today*, in 1963.[2] A little later, she caught up with Peter Karmel. By 1969, he was Vice Chancellor of Flinders University of South Australia. Asked by the Liberal Country League state government to conduct an enquiry into South Australian education and its reform, Karmel listened to economists at the University of Adelaide who recommended Jean as a researcher and writer for the project.[3] Jean had conflicting thoughts about the efficacy of the report that resulted. By the time it was published in 1971, the Labor government of Don Dunstan had come to power and its reforming Minister of Education, Hugh Hudson, had already begun the transformation of public schooling in South Australia.[4] Nevertheless, at least two people were impressed by the report and its progressive, social justice orientation. One was Karmel himself, who had relied on Jean for much of its writing. The other was Gough Whitlam, leader of the federal Labor Party, and about to lead the first Labor government in Australia since 1949.

Soon after becoming Prime Minister in November 1972, Whitlam asked Karmel to lead the committee that would establish a national Schools Commission and its reform agenda. Karmel agreed to do so, but he wanted Blackburn, not as a researcher this time, but as Deputy Chair of the enquiry, which consequently produced the government's manifesto for reform, *Schools in Australia*.[5]

For many feminists, *Schools in Australia* was a disappointment. There seemed to be little awareness of the deep cultural and structural difficulties that women and girls had in participating equally, let alone powerfully, in society. The best that the report could do was argue that:

> Except at the highest socio-economic level, girls left school
> earlier than boys. Being a girl is an educational disadvantage
> except when it is also associated with high socio-economic

status. The varying expectations which families of differing socio-economic level hold in relation to the likely futures of girls are brought into the school; but the extent to which the school either reinforces the low expectations of some groups or positively sets out to counter them is not as yet well documented.[6]

There is little doubt that this was roughly the position held by Jean at the time as the principal writer of the report. For Jean, there could be no analysis of the consequences of sex difference without social class analysis. Nevertheless, there was enough in the report to have the newly established Schools Commission take up the issue. No doubt there was pressure on the government from Labor women and women's organisations such as the Women's Electoral Lobby as well.

Ken McKinnon was appointed Chair of the Schools Commission when it was finally established in late 1973, and Jean Blackburn, one of its two full-time commissioners. There would be but two years for the Commission to work on the Labor government's goals for social justice through education before that government's demise in November 1975. Perhaps surprisingly, the agendas of the Schools Commission continued to be pursued into the Fraser government years. By 1975, there was considerable support for the Commission from the Country Party and the Roman Catholic Church, and funding for the Commission was secured as the Senate passed the Labor government's supply bills immediately following its fall in late 1975.

The re-emergent feminist and broader women's movement from the late 1960s were always going to have an impact on education policy and schools. The disparities and inequalities between males and females were widely recognised and deeply embedded. Commonly, girls and boys experienced different curricula, women teachers were usually confined to less well-paid positions, fewer girls than boys completed secondary school and graduated from universities and colleges in the tertiary sector; fewer girls than boys were accepted into apprenticeships. Much of the labour market was segmented by sex, with women tending to occupy more precarious and less well-paid 'women's jobs'.

These structural disparities and inequalities were supported by a culture that routinely advocated the confinement of women to a limited number of roles and occupations in families and broader society. Women were expected to enter the labour force but only briefly before marriage. After marriage their major work was to bear children and to be 'housewives', looking after children, and relieving their husbands of domestic labour in the home. These social expectations and roles were sustained by prevailing views about the most acceptable forms of femininity and masculinity.

This gender order had been subject to criticism and disruption for more than a century, including in education, as histories by Marjorie Theobald and Marilyn Lake among others have traced.[7] From the late 1960s, however, the pressures dramatically intensified, and governments, state and Commonwealth, responded.

The main task of the Schools Commission from 1973 was to advise the federal government on the spending of substantially increased federal funds to improve Australian schools. Schools in government and non-government sectors would receive grants to assist with capital works and recurrent expenditure. More important for our discussion here was the Commission's responsibility for devising special programs whose intent was to assist 'disadvantaged' populations in 'disadvantaged' schools. The Commission would also seek to improve the quality of teaching, and relationships between parents, communities and schools. It is important to note that other than through funding, the influence on schools was oblique. The Commission controlled no schools nor school systems. Its role would be to persuade by its reports and the discretionary funding involved in its special programs.

The decision to address the question of equality of opportunity as it affected girls and women initially involved the establishing of a 'study group'. There never would be a special program that isolated the issue of girls' education from other programs, such as the extraordinarily influential Disadvantaged Schools Program. The study group was charged with devising and recommending policy to the Commission. These were its terms of reference:

- to examine the extent of underachievement by women and girls in education and its contribution to the inferior status of women;
- to examine the reasons for this, including community attitudes and implicit and explicit discrimination against women and girls in schools;
- to examine the ramifications of the increasing participation by women in the labour force on Australian education;
- to recommend any program projects and the necessary funding to assist girls so that they have as many careers and life choices open to them as do boys.[8]

The Commission was remarkably fortunate in the people who agreed to become members of the Committee. They, and the consultants who undertook various tasks for the Committee, included women who were or would become leading feminists in Australia. The Committee included Ken McKinnon as Chair, Jean Blackburn (Schools Commissioner), Cathy Bloch (teacher unionist), Jean Martin (sociologist), Elizabeth Reid (Prime Minister's Women's Adviser), Susan Ryan (officer of the national state schools' parent organisation), Bill Thiele (student counsellor), David Widdup (mathematician and gay activist) and Daniela Torsh (journalist and feminist activist). Torsh was appointed executive officer of the Committee. Consultants and research assistants over the life of the committee included Eva Cox, Anne

Summers, Teresa Brennan, Clare Burton, Wendy McCarthy, Mary Murnane, Lorna Hannan and Helen Townsend.

Daniela (Dany) Torsh was working on a doctorate on women and education when she was recruited to the Commission and the Committee. Her theoretical study and the bibliographic resources she brought to the work, and continued to collect, underpinned the Committee's work.[9]

Initially, neither Ken McKinnon nor Jean Blackburn anticipated close engagement with the work of the Committee, but McKinnon became fearful after its first meeting or two that it would become a talk-fest, unable to achieve much productive policy work. He decided to chair the Committee and asked Jean to join it. This was significant because Jean was able to exert an authority based on clear thinking and argument that helped save the exercise from anticipated difficulty.[10] McKinnon and Blackburn worked as a team; she respected him for his 'political smarts', and he for her 'intellectual and political integrity'.[11] The Committee commissioned research and received submissions relevant to its terms of reference. There were vigorous discussions and drafts that preceded the final publication. The Committee as a whole was responsible for the final report, but the Chairman of the Committee, McKinnon, signed off on the report.

Dany Torsh produced a first draft for the Committee, and elements of that draft survived into the final document, but McKinnon, Blackburn and Jean Martin worried that this draft was not suitable for presentation as a Commission report. Jean Blackburn appears to have been responsible for rewriting much of it. Jean Martin was listened to by Blackburn and McKinnon as arguments took place about what should be in the report and how it should be written. The main conflict occurred between Torsh and David Widdup on one side, and Blackburn, Martin and McKinnon on the other. Torsh was a more radical feminist than Blackburn. She was disappointed that many elements of the first draft were either toned down or disappeared.[12] Widdup had wanted more on sex education and sexuality, including the recognition of same sex issues as they might apply to the school curriculum and wider education.[13]

The report would be reformist, innovative and daring but not radical in the ways that Widdup and Torsh wanted. McKinnon and Blackburn, and the Committee as a whole, eventually settled on a draft that would be acceptable to government, and not antagonise too many groups and school systems that had an interest in its recommendations. McKinnon reflected in an interview on the particular strengths that Blackburn brought to the process of developing the report:

> She added much more of the: 'What backing is there?',
> 'How can you say it in a way that would be intelligible to
> the people who were interested in this sort of thing?', 'How
> far can you interpret the statistics to mean this or that …?'.
> And we would together do things like 'Is this phrase, is it
> the right phrase? Or do we need a stronger one, or a weaker
> one so we don't lose …?'. I mean she was indispensable.[14]

The report contained 14 chapters that ranged over changing sex roles, sex differences in school and post-school participation in education, the reform of schools as organisations, their curriculum offerings, sex roles and socialisation of teachers and students, sexuality and human relationships, vocational guidance, and groups with special needs. The three groups with special needs that received the most attention were migrant, Aboriginal and rural girls and women.

The report preceded the development of theorisations of gender, which rejected binaries. Sex difference and sex role differences were key concepts for the report, but attention was given to the concepts of sexism and different forms of femininity and masculinity. Importantly, the report depended on the view that gender is, in the main, an historical, social and cultural construct. The significance of child-bearing for many women's lives, for example, was not underestimated, but the argument was made that different societies managed and could decide to manage the consequences for women differently. The life-consequences of child-bearing need not be pre-determined. Women's lives were subject to changing cultural, economic and social arrangements. Such arrangements could proceed, in part, from reforms in education.

In the early 1970s, it had become common for many feminists and others of the more radical left to despair of the capacity of schools to be a force for substantial reform. This issue was live for the Committee producing the report. The report decided the opposite: that schools and education systems had to be considered capable of reform, and were in fact essential agents if it was to occur. Because the Schools Commission administered no school systems, it was not in a position to insist on any particular changes in their operation. Instead, it used the report to summarise research, to educate the persons who operated schools and school systems, to advise certain reforms, to advocate further research, and importantly, to insist that the issues associated with sexism and sex inequality be addressed through action at all levels of education: Commonwealth and states, school systems and individual schools.

Chapter 14 of the report outlined its conclusions and recommendations. It argued that as a consequence of the problems in education, girls were much less inclined than boys to 'see themselves as people able to influence the circumstances of their lives'.[15] The term 'low self-esteem' was used and popularised in the report. Biological differences were quite insufficient to explain the great range of differences between the sexes. 'What it means to be female or male in a particular social context is largely learned.'[16]

It listed the ways that schools often exacerbated inequality between the sexes and outlined principles for action that schools might undertake. They included the removal of gender-based curriculum barriers, especially those restricting the pathways to a full range of occupations and careers. A series of recommendations about how schools might be assisted to achieve the aims then followed. They included reference to what Schools Commission-based programs, Disadvantaged Schools and Special Projects might do. The Committee argued that all programs of the Commission should be required to address sex-based inequality.

A further set of recommendations provided for ongoing consideration and action by the Commission. The report concluded with a call for change in Australian society more broadly. Australian schools and education systems could only do so much. The overarching aim was to promote 'a shared humanity and mutuality between the sexes'.[17] That formulation was typical of Jean Blackburn's feminism. In this sense, the report addressed the limitations associated with prevailing forms of masculinity as well as femininity; for example, 'Deep seated fears of homosexuality in our society, and stronger condemnation of it among males, undoubtedly play a part in what appear to be more severe early sex role shaping of boys than girls'.[18] Such a statement was strong enough for the Committee – it shied away from addressing the issue directly through, for example, curriculum reform.

The report was published during International Women's Year (1975) and was an Australian contribution to that event nationally and internationally. Though its analysis and prescriptions may seem rather ordinary in the 21st century, the report was pioneering in Australia and internationally for its time. It advanced reform along the lines it suggested as schools and school systems reacted to it more or less favourably. Several conservative groups resisted the report, including segments of the Catholic Church hierarchy, which thought it was too radical in its reimagining of women and their potential social roles, but at the same time there was plenty of support for it in Catholic schools.

The report needs to be seen as part of an historical process that had already begun. For example, restrictions on the wages, promotion and employment of women, especially married women, in education systems were already being addressed as the report was produced. Moreover, girls were also beginning to equal the retention rates of boys through to the last year of high school. Eventually there would be units led by women's advisers in most departments of education in the Australian states. Most school systems produced policies around non-sexist education and eventually 'gender equity' with some resourcing to give them effect.[19] Not much later, as curriculum reform occurred across the education systems as a response to growing youth unemployment, gender equity became part of policy formulations, including the work Blackburn did in Victoria, for the 'Blackburn Report', which reformed senior secondary education in that state.[20]

Many assessments of the impact of *Girls, School and Society* pointed to its revolutionary character for the time. Lyn Yates, sociologist and professor of education, argued that it was 'probably the best one that was done on this area world-wide in the 70s'.[21] Denise Bradley, Vice Chancellor of the University of South Australia and friend of Jean, recalled her response when coming across it for the first time. She was 'stunned', 'It was such a revolutionary document'.[22] Jean Martin's biographers thought that it was an 'epoch-defining document both for education policy and the emerging feminist movement'.[23] Susan Ryan, part of the Committee, but later a Senator and Minister of Education in the Hawke Labor government, argued that it irrevocably changed the debate around gender and education.[24]

In 2005, Alison Mackinnon, historian of the women's movement and education, also looked back at the report's significance in her Clare Burton memorial lecture:

The report heralded a whirlwind of activity in the education of girls over the next decade – activity in which many of you, many of us, were intimately involved, whether as beneficiaries of the changes or in teaching courses on girls and education and in women's studies, shaping educational curricula and policy and arguing for affirmative action in teacher promotion and in employment. I began teaching the history of education in the Department of Education at the University of Adelaide in 1976 and I well remember the excitement of the *Girls, Schools and Society* report and the sense of outrage at the overt discrimination it revealed.[25]

By the end of the 20th century, for a variety of reasons, but including the report, gender-based participation rates and access to broader curriculum choices were to a fair degree improved and achieved in schools, but underlying cultures and structures that limited women's employment, career opportunities and wealth after their school and university years usually remained substantially in place.

It is often a fruitless task to attempt to identify the most influential authors of any government report. Many hands participate in their making. Jean Blackburn, often identified as the most significant of the authors of *Girls, School and Society*, fought against the identification.[26] It was the work of a committee, for which the Chair took final responsibility. She counselled Dany Torsh against too much disappointment concerning the fate of the first draft: 'It is luxurious to be cast in the role of critic rather than creator! However it is hacked about, all honour goes to the one who first has the courage to enunciate a framework'.[27]

Jean Blackburn's was a 20th-century life, uncommon in many respects, but enriched by possibilities that had not existed in the 19th century. Contemporaries of Jean – men such as Australia's

most influential and long-serving public servant, HC 'Nugget'
Coombs – benefited more easily from these possibilities than
any woman could, but their careers belonged to a similar set of
historical circumstances. Blackburn's career not only depended on
her singular education, intellect and ability, but on the coincidence
that she was there, ready to contribute, at crucial moments in the
history of 20th-century Australia. In South Australia first, then
the nation through the Schools Commission, and then Victoria
in the 1980s, were newly elected Labor governments, long out of
office, decades in some cases. The pressure for reform, including in
education, was overwhelming. Blackburn's history of Communist
Party membership in the 1940s and early 1950s would not be a
barrier to her engagement in policy work.

Dean Ashenden, education activist and journalist, had
thought about her broad approach to government and social
reform:

> On the face of it, she was a social democrat working to
> civilise capitalism etc., but she didn't like having to settle
> for that. She was much more acutely aware of the workings
> of power than most social democrats (Peter K[armel], for
> example), and had a much more acute sense of unfairness
> and exploitation, and really knew that in some fundamental
> way the whole set-up was rigged. But she also knew that no
> one intellectual system could capture that, and that the cure
> could be worse than the disease.[28]

A dominating issue for Jean's feminism was an argument about
'dependence'. Without education, women were more likely to be
dependent on others, usually men, as fathers and husbands. If in
paid work, they would usually be dependent on low-waged, often
so-called 'unskilled', employment. Without a labour movement
committed to equal wages and employment opportunities, they

were likely to be poor. Without commitments by governments to equality, including the establishment of the conditions for genuine equality of opportunity including the use of affirmative action, women would continue to suffer.

When Jean came to her work on the Disadvantaged Schools Program, of which she was the major architect and supervisor on behalf of the Schools Commission, these were the ideas that informed her practice. The Program was about much more than girls and women, of course; it was the major, though always under-funded program, committed to social equality and opportunity. The model it established of rewarding well-planned initiatives at the local level was revolutionary. State and Catholic systems of education would not take the funding and do as they wished with it. Schools and school communities would identify their needs, prepare submissions, and state committees populated by education department, Catholic school and other interests would recommend viable projects and the disbursement of funds. It was a new way of organising education. Centralised, bureaucratic control over schooling, the Australian tradition from the 1870s, especially in areas of 'disadvantage', was radically challenged.

The key word in all of this educational policy work and reform was 'need'. The Karmel-inspired reforms of the 1970s, as expressed at its most articulate by Jean Blackburn, had a vision of social justice behind them. The elevated status of 'needs-based funding' in education policy would not last, especially as neoliberal influences challenged such policy. Then the encouragement of school markets, and the empowerment of parents to 'choose' the schools that they wished, and later again, the significance of national competitiveness in literacy and numeracy, and skills – and 'accountability' – began to dominate, in Labor as well as non-Labor education and youth policy development.[29]

The crucial opportunity for Jean Blackburn to contribute to the national debate, indeed, national policy on social justice through education, was provided by the Whitlam Labor government of 1972–75.

What follows is an attempt to summarise Blackburn's contribution to reforming the ways that Australian governments and other authorities operated their schools and school systems. In doing so we are not arguing that Blackburn did it all by herself – nevertheless, her voice was powerful.

Jean Blackburn helped inspire the first social justice reform program in education of any consequence of any federal government before (and since). She was a significant actor in the production of a report on gender inequalities in education and a program towards their correction. It had a remarkable impact on governments, schools and teachers across Australia. She inspired and organised the philosophical and administrative heart of a Disadvantaged Schools Program, which to this day impresses with its focus on community development rather than narrow skills acquisition. She was a curriculum warrior who believed that the basics, literacy and numeracy development, were too mean as the sole goals of school curricula. Schools needed to teach the world, students' place in it, and how to make the world a better place for all. Blackburn was a powerful advocate of the idea that effective teacher development should occur on a whole-school basis. Whole-school improvement would lead to better teaching and the better education of children.

Blackburn argued for a radical reform of the old centralised, authoritarian and assimilationist approaches of public education in Australia. Schools were not to be outposts of the State managing unruly children, unruly parents and unruly communities. Schools had to work with communities, something that Schools Commission program funding guidelines usually insisted on.

Through the Schools Commission and then a Victorian report, Blackburn became a prime mover for the reform of older approaches to senior secondary curriculum. New curricula and credentials should be expected to give all young people the opportunity to make better lives. At the same time, new curricula had to have intellectual worth – none of the 'keep them quiet and busy' approach, nor mere 'functional literacy', that warehoused youth as youth unemployment grew.[30]

For many years, from the late 1980s, it appeared that the perspectives that Blackburn brought to national education policy-making were out-flanked by neoliberal influences, but they did not go away. The Gonski reports on educational reform gave a number of them new voice.[31] The volatility of education policy-making in Australia, and the advocacy of education as a social justice issue by significant voices on the left in politics, also ensure they will resurface from time to time.

PART FIVE
LEGACIES: WHAT REMAINS TO BE DONE?

INTRODUCED BY HEIDI NORMAN

I was a small child when the Whitlam government was elected, and the next-generation beneficiary of the wide reforms for women and in Aboriginal Affairs. My academic work has examined land rights in New South Wales and, as a Whitlam research fellow, I explored how the land rights laws the Whitlam government developed in the north have been taken up in south-eastern Australia. There, colonial dispossession has been most sustained, in nearly always violent circumstances, and land dealings were most extensive; this is also where my own Aboriginal family have roots. In my immediate family, as I reached school age, my mum returned to school and earned entry to Teachers' College. The abolition of tuition fees by the Whitlam government, together with a raft of other changes, allowed many women to realise greater autonomy and freedom; Aboriginal citizens, in particular, found greater dignity. Those reforms changed Mum's life, and mine. It was her courage and action, to be sure. The policy reforms the Whitlam government ushered in, responding to movements for change long held in abeyance by successive conservative governments, made the choices of individuals possible and offered new recognition of collective Aboriginal lives.

Those reforms are worth revisiting. For working women the government commenced the process to ensure equal pay, extended the minimum wage to women, and introduced paid maternity leave in the public service. In welfare, it established a Supporting Mother's Benefit; and introduced community child care. As well as abolishing university fees, the government made contraception more freely available, and introduced divorce reform. It investigated structural and cultural discrimination against girls in our schools, and pioneered the policy of funding schools on the basis of the needs of students, as well as establishing universal health insurance. They appointed women to key roles in Parliament and the bureaucracy, among them the first female political adviser to a Prime Minister and the head of the

Commonwealth Social Welfare Commission. The government also funded community and grassroots specialist health and welfare services for women, such as women's health centres, refuges and crisis centres. It resourced events and projects to mark the 1975 UN International Women's Year, including a major conference on women and politics, and established programs to support women's contributions to the creative arts.

These initiatives – policy, program funding, legislative reform and appointments – undoubtedly brought about social, economic and cultural change for most women and, combined with other changes, crafted a new Australia. Whitlam's reform agenda heralded a new liberation in the public and private lives of many women.

Yet in 2021, as these chapters remind us, the Commonwealth Parliament – the site of Whitlam's feminist reforms – became the focal point of women marching for justice in numbers not seen for a generation. Fourth-wave feminism mobilised in response to the behaviour of men and the power and privilege they held, both by dint of the institution of government and their complicity in reproducing society in their own image. As both a real and symbolic site of power, Parliament, and our elected representatives who convene there, were damned over the domestic and sexual violence many women experience, making us fearful and vulnerable. That the most powerful institution in our collective lives was implicated within a larger system of sexual violence pointed both to the depth and reach of the problem and the limits to achieving change through the democratic institution of Parliament.

The three chapters in this section are all, in one way or another, centred on the federal Parliament. That they reference Parliament might be explained by the devastating realisation that even for middle-class, educated women, the spectre of violence and sexual abuse at the hands of men limits our choices and freedom.

As the authors show, much remains to be done to advance the lives of women. They are mindful that the second-wave feminisms which the Whitlam government responded to have addressed inequality for some women while others have fared markedly worse. They are also mindful of the ongoing economic disparity in women's lives, and that the issues First Nations women face, then and now, continue to be diverse and cannot be reconciled by a gender lens alone. Public policy decision-making and the predominance of economic values over social needs define the position of women today.

So, what remains to be done? Sara Dowse, Ranuka Tandan and Blair Williams respond to this question with accounts that draw on their own experiences. They offer overlapping accounts of the past, reference the present and identify the strategies needed to address the disadvantage most women continue to face.

Writer Sara Dowse speaks from the site of the federal Parliament. Hers is a rare female view that starts in 1975 as a policy adviser. She writes about the heady optimism and ambitious program to remake society in more just, culturally diverse and equitable terms. Second-wave feminists grappled with big-picture social, cultural and economic reforms, but Dowse reminds us that the Whitlam government, under enormous economic pressures and political scrutiny, was beginning to prosecute the case for fiscal restraint – a reality she contends went unnoticed as the dramatic events of 1975 unfolded. Dowse's reflections are as an outlier public servant uncomfortable with the bifurcation of the economic and the social. She contends that over time, and more markedly with Labor's return to government in 1983, neoliberalism has dominated public policy discourse. Tracing the genealogy of neoliberalism, she laments the dashed hopes of the Whitlam experiment, and the rise of a neoliberal ethos which has fundamentally redrawn the social contract between citizen and government and contributed to a fractured social order. This fracturing, Dowse suggests, is made even more obvious under the strain caused by twin crises: a global pandemic and climate change. But Dowse clings to some optimism that remains from the time of Whitlam: 'the one lasting legacy of the 70s women's movement and its involvement in the Whitlam government has been women's view of ourselves, and the aspirations we have held for our futures'.

Like Dowse, Ranuka Tandan locates women's oppression in the intersection of patriarchy and capitalism. Liberation for working people is necessary in order for women to realise freedom. Like Blair Williams, Tandan argues that the #MeToo movement has reinvigorated the politics for change, but that this momentum for change, drawing on lessons from the Whitlam era, will not be realised by appeals to a reforming Parliament.

Blair Williams focuses on the continued violence against and harassment of women, beginning her account in 2010 when Julia Gillard became Australia's first female Prime Minister. Williams maps out the ways in which, over the ensuing decade, the optimism and excitement that many felt about the possibility of Australian women and girls assuming greater power and influence were mercilessly dashed. It became apparent that the exercise of self-assured gendered power was without precedent, and the cruel and sexist reactions, in the media and Parliament, were difficult to counter. The former PM's 'misogyny speech', as Williams reminds us, was the belated riposte to this political sexism. From the heightened optimism ushered in by the first female Prime Minister, Williams walks us through the escalation of gender-based sexual violence and harassment in which the federal Parliament, the site of national political power, was embroiled. Sexual harassment and violence were not restricted to Australia's political leadership, of course, but it was where these issues were most clearly manifest. In early 2021 more than 100 000 people were inspired to protest outside Parliament House and around Australia.

The three authors reach a similar conclusion: that a new politics and new ways of organising are necessary. Looking to the future, they share the view that movements for change must be about society, rather than the economy.

Against a backdrop of declining levels of trust in the integrity of political leadership and mainstream media, increasing environmental degradation, and ever-expanding patterns of growth and consumption, each author grapples with how to advance the lives of all Australian women seeking a different power-sharing arrangement with government. They contemplate the future through an altered lens of political organisation that is local in character and structured by important values of social responsibility and belonging. Aboriginal people, often led by women, should be an inspiration to movements for change.

Among the Whitlam government's initiatives was a recognition of the rightful place of Australia's Indigenous peoples and of their loss of personal and political autonomy and group sovereignty. The outstanding business of Aboriginal land rights was afforded a Royal Commission, and policy shifted from the prevailing frame of assimilation to self-determination. For Aboriginal women, the opportunities that arose from the Whitlam era were significant, as were debates over the best strategies to advance Indigenous rights. There were countless creative responses to these opportunities. One example is the creation by Aboriginal women in Redfern, Sydney, of Murawina child care. Reluctant to see their initiative as directly aligned with Women's Liberation, those amazing women set up Murawina so that they could care for their children, keeping them safe, secure and culturally sustained, and participate in the political campaign for Aboriginal recognition.

Australia's First Nations people have today gained greater clarity for their long-standing demand to realise political rights and group autonomy by exercising a 'Voice' within the decision-making processes of government. This is necessarily linked to being the original people of this land, with distinct rights and a special place within the life of the nation.

The authors note how women's political representation and influence have undergone a revolution since Whitlam's time: from 1972, when not a single woman was elected to the House of Representatives, to today, when women MPs are a (slim) majority and increasingly culturally diverse; and a record number of Indigenous people sit in Parliament. Yet a more significant shift is required, one that calls for a local, community-based politics for change organised around values that differ from prevailing ones. There is much to be gained by considering Aboriginal approaches to thinking about what counts as important, what is valued, how we manage resources, how we relate to people and places, and concepts of responsibility and reciprocity.

THEN, NOW, AND WHAT MIGHT COME: A WRITER'S TAKE

SARA DOWSE

Picture this. The year is 1975, the setting a conference room in West Block, one of the three original buildings in what was called the parliamentary triangle, 18 years before the present Parliament House would be built. It is the depth of a Canberra winter, the building is heated but not uniformly, and while some parts of the building are cooler than they should be, the conference room is overheated, and the public servants assembled are dressed accordingly. It is the moment when the Prime Minister's departmental secretary is informing his senior officers that a change in approach is necessary, that forthwith the government's focus will be economic, in line with the expenditure review committee's recommendations and the Treasurer's stringent new Budget.

To a man the officers nod or voice their agreement. It is not until the meeting is about to close that the lone woman in the room musters the courage to speak. Her statement comes in the form of a question, the standard gendered inflection of women in her day. 'Isn't the economy supposed to serve society,' she asks, 'rather than the other way around?'

It has been nearly half a century since I drafted a minute, a ministerial or a Cabinet submission, but that single interrogative sentence has been forever imprinted on my brain. Since resigning from the service, I have stood outside the arena, taking another direction in my own life as governance in Australia followed the trajectory outlined in that brief senior officers' meeting. It may surprise some to be told that the meeting took place while

Whitlam was still Prime Minister, and that his government was adopting a tighter approach to fiscal expenditure. This is not the general view of things, but the truth is that, under the extreme pressure it was subjected to during that year, the government accepted it was time to pull up its socks and conform to more stringent fiscal expectations. If the Dismissal had not intervened and the government permitted to continue, the received wisdom about its economic capability would be substantially different.

That said, the Whitlam government, and that of Malcolm Fraser, whose election later that year was so ignobly prosecuted, were both still imbued with a fundamentally Keynesian outlook, the legacy of our post-war reconstruction. While the Coalition under Fraser introduced stringent cost-cutting, the Country Party's influence combined with Fraser's reversion to stimulus measures in the 1982 budget indicate that the government hadn't subscribed to demands for wholesale economic reform. Indeed, in 1977 Fraser took back responsibility for women's refuges previously devolved to the states and doubled the allocation for them. It also continued the funding for child care and resisted subsidising commercial centres. It was the Hawke Labor government elected in 1983 that was wholly committed to the new economics, albeit a tempered version, of what was variously called at the time Reaganomics, Rogernomics or economical rationalism. We know it now as neoliberalism, the basic idea of which is that governments should get out of the way to let the market take over.

Understand that this change, though focused on economics and couched in its language, has been ultimately a cultural one, and it has been profound. It is perfectly acceptable even today for professionals of all stripes to speak of 'the market' in quasi-deistic terms. A spate of articles appearing in the 1980s, in ostensibly progressive media like the *National Times* as well as the business journals, valorised the pursuit of riches and those who pursued them in gushing terms. I used to keep score of the number of times the word 'success' was used, meaning getting ahead in some sort of business. By the time Howard came along, we were all businesses – even freelance writers like me were sending out invoices to our editors, and the more fortunate among us were filing quarterly business statements and charging GST. The practice continues to this day and no one bats an eyelash over the paperwork involved, in what was supposed to be a development to rid us of red tape. And I'm not the first to note that in our dealings with government, suddenly we were 'clients' and 'customers' but never citizens. Gradually, many began to see themselves as lone actors instead of members of communities or collectives. Union membership declined, as did that of political parties. Politics too became a profession, instead of a calling.

How have women fared with these developments? Before addressing the question, let me say a few words about myself. I was born in the United States during the Great Depression, and until I was six, Franklin Delano Roosevelt was President. It's hard to explain how a child that young could absorb the zeitgeist of his New Deal, the relief of knowing that a government was there to help, that people who had been at risk of starvation were given work, even artists and writers and actors like my mother, but I did. And it would be years before I would find myself with a government resembling it. I left the United States when the scourge of McCarthyism had only just begun to subside. We were now in the grip of a Cold War and the repudiation of anything smacking of socialism. Though the Australia I came to in 1958 was also enmeshed in Cold War politics, and I was shocked by the blatant racism and what we would come to know as sexism, the attitude towards government I found here was markedly different. To paraphrase the historian Keith Hancock, Australians expected their governments, state and federal, to be at the service of their citizens.[1] I admit that even for an American scarified by those McCarthy years, the easy Australian attitude towards government took some getting used to, and it wasn't until 1972 that I felt I could let my guard down, and was once again experiencing a government whose progressive flavour and sweeping reforms for improving society resembled those of the war years of my youth. Yet less than three years later, the seeds of neoliberalism had been planted, the hope and excitement of the Whitlam experiment came crashing down, and though it would take another eight years for the seeds to ripen, the tenor of the previous contract between government and its citizens was transformed.

Is the purpose of an economy to serve a society, or is it indeed the other way around? Most particularly, how have women accommodated to this profound change in economic understanding, and its consequent changes in governance? For an answer I have to go back to those Whitlam years again, under which some ground-breaking reforms were initiated. Women's reproductive freedoms were enhanced, financial support for single mothers was introduced, advances in employment were set in train with the government backing equal pay for equal work and the extension of the minimum wage to women. Discrimination committees were established, part-time work encouraged and, most importantly, a wide-ranging, substantially funded child-care program was introduced. Free tertiary education, arguably the most significant reform, was not specifically designed for women but did most to expand our horizons. All this required an expansion of the federal public service and the public sector in general. But under the changed zeitgeist and as time has passed, both have been systematically whittled back, to the point where today we are subjected in every conceivable sphere to the signs of a seriously fractured social order.

Climate change and the COVID-19 pandemic have accentuated these fault lines. The accelerated appearance of extreme weather events predicted by climate scientists decades ago have been met with increasingly woeful federal government policy, with the Gillard government's short-lived emissions trading scheme the sole exception. After more than 20 drought years since the turn of the century, whole towns have been left without water and rivers turned dry. The bushfire season has extended, and resources for fighting the growing number of fires and their increased spread and ferocity have been seriously overstretched. What's more, the very means for fighting them – the planes, the water, the fire retardants – add to the carbon discharged into the atmosphere, itself the cause of the heat enveloping the planet. As the planet struggles to adapt, the weather volatility grows. Floods ruin homes and vital infrastructure, damage crops and spread disease and, again, the tools at our disposal for saving lives and rebuilding the damage escalate their cause. The sad truth is that almost every facet of human existence, as contemporary Australians have known it, contributes to this spiral effect.

One of neoliberalism's central tenets is that by reducing the size of the public sector the more efficient markets will stimulate trade and a concomitant growth in wealth. Beginning with the Whitlam government's 25 per cent across-the-board tariff reduction in 1974, the edifice of tariff protection that characterised our post-war years was dismantled, with serious inroads on our manufacturing sector, which grew substantially out of the import substitution policies adopted after the war. I'm not arguing that freeing up trade has been wholly bad for this country, but we have seen how the neoliberal approach, being more an ideology than sound economics, has seriously distorted our economy, made all the more evident in a crisis like the COVID pandemic when supply of vital imports is disrupted. Moreover, the globalisation of assets and the ceaseless movement of goods and people around the planet have all contributed, along with the effects of climate change, to the emergence of pandemic viruses like SARS, of which COVID-19 is but its latest manifestation.

And where has this led for women? Child care has become

prohibitively expensive; the effective marginal tax rate on married women with children has also acted as a disincentive to their participating in the workforce. The safety nets that formed part of the social contract when the Hawke–Keating government signed up to Reagan and Thatcher's economics have either shrunk or are punitively applied, and with deregulation, the weakening of unions and galloping casualisation, working life is transformed. It's arguable whether these changes were deliberately designed to frustrate women's advancement; some were, most weren't. Despite the general increase in female workplace participation over the past 40 years, its predominance of part-time and casual work has resulted in an associated reduction in women's earning power and superannuation, so much so that women in their 50s today have become the fastest growing group among the homeless.

At the same time, the one lasting legacy of the '70s women's movement and its involvement in the Whitlam government has been women's view of ourselves, and the aspirations we have held for our futures. As Elizabeth Reid once put it, what had been a women's movement had become a movement of women, as women became a visible presence in all walks of life. I marvel that for years after my arrival in Australia in 1958, I never saw or heard a woman reading the news or anchoring a current affairs program, let alone driving a bus or piloting a commercial aircraft. Women then formed a tiny minority of management positions, on the order of 3 per cent, and these were mostly in the public sector, or in gender-segregated occupations. It is salutary to be reminded too that when Whitlam came to office, not a single woman held a seat in the House of Representatives. All that has changed, and dramatically so.

Yet somewhere along the way the egalitarian ethos of the earlier movement was abandoned, with class divisions evident in the '70s substantially deepened today. It's true that we feminists of the second wave were predominantly middle class, with many having benefited from the expanded education and tertiary scholarships initiated under Menzies. Yet not all the women who participated were products of middle-class privilege, and the socialist bent of women's liberationists in particular made us acutely aware of the entrenched inequalities in what was all too often touted as Australia's classless society. So while it can be said that the movement's composition was largely middle class, it would be wrong to characterise it as such. That feminists didn't always succeed in erasing unexamined, often racist assumptions about Aboriginal women, for example, doesn't mean we didn't try.

But it is also true that women did advance even as neoliberalism permeated all aspects of society. There's no denying that many of us did well. Women began to be taken seriously in the media. A fair few became professors, a scarcely imaginable trajectory when the movement began, even if the prospects for young female scholars today are considerably less rosy. Casualisation was well underway with the corporatisation of universities, but the future for current untenured academics, particularly in the humanities, has dimmed altogether with the pandemic. What with the loss of international student 'cash cows' consequent on Australia's strict border closures and the Morrison government's pointedly withholding JobKeeper support for the sector, casual positions have been ruthlessly slashed. Women have succeeded in getting themselves elected in increasing numbers and, despite the setbacks, especially on the Coalition side, many more have been ministers. A woman heading a public service department is nothing to marvel at; that there are women chief executive officers in both public and private sectors is barely worthy of comment, yet a whole generation of women in their 20s and 30s are precariously employed, paying high rents and excluded from the ever-escalating housing market. Their day-to-day struggles to keep afloat financially have made it harder for them to organise politically than it was for us back in the 1970s. Although with #MeToo and the 2021 March4Justice there are signs that this may be changing, social inequality is deepening, and democracy itself is threatened.

It's been 44 years since I left the public service determined to become a writer, and six years later my first novel, based on my experience in the Department of the Prime Minister and Cabinet appeared. *West Block* begins two years after the Dismissal, and opens with the teenage daughter of the central character discovering her mother's diary and reading the last entry, dated 9 December 1977. *'Two years have passed since it happened'*, writes Cassie Armstrong, *'when with a shock the trunk imploded. Leaves withered and dropped. We were dazed, stunned with it, and I found myself a conservative'.*[2] In writing these lines through my alter ego, the wording was to convey not only the sudden, brutally executed change of government when those in the department found themselves serving conservative masters, but also to express my dismay that basic Australian traditions were being dismantled, traditions that had become precious to me, and that my heroine, likewise, hoped to conserve. Although it would take a few more years for the neoliberal revolution to take hold, we were standing on the brink of it in 1975, and looking back, we can see it for the revolution it was. There is no little irony, then, that the truly radical revolutionaries of the Anglosphere have not been those on the left of the spectrum, but those on the right. As Cassie Armstrong, head of the department's Women's Equality Branch or WEB, went on to say, *not all change is good.*[3] It is up to us now to do what we can to restore the democratic traditions of fair play and social equality that have been so comprehensively repudiated. But how?

The radical changes ushered in by the moneyed ascendancy have been so pervasive and entrenched it would be dishonest to suggest they could be undone easily. The new Albanese government is left with a massive deficit and, owing to decades of electorally expedient tax cuts and the regressive nature of recent tax reforms, lacks the revenue to govern as Whitlam or Roosevelt were able to. But it would be equally mistaken not to take heart from some changes for the better since those palmier days. Australians generally are more attuned to feminist aims than they once were, more aware of Indigenous achievement and the appalling racism Indigenous people have endured, and more accepting of differing sexual orientations and gender fluidity. For all that, it's next to impossible for any leader today to argue the simple proposition that taxes are not only needed but beneficial, if the revenue raised is directed towards restoring good government and a fairer, more productive society. Tax and what its purpose is in a democracy remains so far a no-go area in the dominant political discourse.

Having participated in the 2019 campaign to elect an independent in the federal Sydney seat of Warringah, I was acutely aware that there was no chance of Zali Steggall winning it if she didn't openly reject Labor's 2019 policies to remove negative gearing and franking credits. And though I've been heartened by Steggall's re-election in 2022 and the striking success of other independent candidates, the vast majority of whom are women, I've yet to hear them make taxation an issue, though most would seem in favour of reversing the Morrison government's highly regressive stage three tax cuts that the Labor government has insisted on keeping – at least so far.

At this point it's worth recalling that the 1970s women's movement not only involved numbers of tertiary-educated women, but that, owing to the effects of sexism, many of us were out of work at the time. In this we could be said to be repeating the part intelligentsias with grievances have historically played in revolutionary movements. And, given the casualisation and precarity of university teaching today, we might consider organising groups to study the new economics developed by women like Mariana Mazzucato by enlisting redundant or precariously employed academics.[4] This could be influential in gaining greater community understanding of the crucial role governments can and have played, both in directing economic development and providing basic services, and how vital progressive taxation is for this.

Women's policy developed in the Whitlam government was predicated in large part on the need for women to be more strongly represented in all aspects of political life. The government's 1975 Women and Politics Conference was excoriated in the media, but its long-term effect is undeniable. No matter the barriers they continue to face, women politicians are no longer the isolated oddities they were when that conference was held. We've had a female Prime Minister, female premiers, female senators and members of Parliament, many of whom have reached the rank of minister. But not all of them, particularly on the Coalition side, have delivered what the community has needed, or indeed what has been expected of them. The 2019–20 bushfires and the COVID pandemic necessitated growth in government spending, but it was reluctantly and inefficiently delivered, with too many sectors rendered ineligible for the Coalition's largesse, while the waves of new variants disrupted the economy further just as it was tightening its purse strings. That women politicians were enlisted in its retrograde parsimony is regrettable.

While advocacy groups such as the Women's Electoral Lobby and the National Foundation of Women continue to foster excellent research in the growth of inequality and other matters important to women, the Morrison government paid next to no attention, and members of their National Women's Alliance faced being defunded if they proved too critical of government policy and practice. The Women's Office in its various permutations had been effectively sidelined. In a sense, then, our success in making women's concerns mainstream political issues has sown the seeds of our failure. In the old days we called that co-option, and my mission at the time once I'd joined the bureaucracy was trying to explain to hardline radical and social feminists fired by anti-establishment sentiment how necessary working within government was. Today, the positions seem dramatically reversed, even though the nomenclature has changed. We have no shortage of groups addressing specific issues of concern to women or their echoes within the bureaucracies, academia and parliaments. What's missing, for the moment anyway, is a widespread, radical, community-based movement engaged in fundamental questions such as what constitutes social value, how it can be measured, and how a more equal society that best serves its citizens should be funded. Climate change and the pandemic have thrown these questions into high relief, and there are glimmers appearing here and there that such a movement's time may be near.

What I've been suggesting is a conscious effort in developing what was once called a double strategy. Yes, we will always need progressive thinkers in government bureaucracies, on government benches and in local and state governments, but the lesson I took from my experience in government is that without the strong, coordinated pressure from within civil society, such penetration can be redirected to regressive aims (for example, greenwashing) or rendered useless altogether. The neoliberal revolution of the past half-century measures every public service in terms of cost, thus forcing advocates to couch almost every proposal put forward in terms of its economic benefit or detriment rather than its social value. This, indeed, has been a cultural revolution that, while enriching some and impoverishing many, has penetrated our thinking, a mindset that, coupled with deeply reactionary social perspectives, has transformed Australia, impacting on women especially. To reverse these developments, along with meaningful action on climate change, is the challenge of our century. To steer us through it, the basic question to ask remains: Isn't the economy meant to support society? And seeing the result of the opposite all around us, how had we ever been persuaded to switch the two around?

WHY A GRASSROOTS WOMEN'S MOVEMENT IS VITAL

RANUKA TANDAN

Most young women today have very little knowledge about Gough Whitlam's time as Prime Minister, or the transformative reforms he enacted in those three short years. We learn about him alongside every other ex-PM, and his appearance does nothing to help him stand out in a sea of faces, which – apart from Julia Gillard's – all look very much the same. Some of us remember learning about the famous Dismissal, and most people would recognise Mervyn Bishop's iconic photograph, which captured Whitlam pouring red sand into the hands of Vincent Lingiari. Yet, very few young women would connect him to the Women's Liberation Movement or understand the impact he had on women's rights more broadly.

Ironically, my introduction to Gough Whitlam, when I was old enough to properly understand and appreciate the policy platform he enacted, took place in October 2014, at the time of his death. One of my most influential high school teachers, a staunch feminist, rounded up a group of interested students – most of whom just wanted a day off school – and put us on a train from the Blue Mountains to watch Whitlam's state memorial service outside the Sydney Town Hall.

At 16, I understood that Whitlam had been an important, progressive Prime Minister, but I didn't know why his passing was making so many ordinary Australians so emotional, or why there were people tearing up all around me as Noel Pearson delivered a eulogy, and Paul Kelly sang 'From Little Things, Big Things Grow'. I've learned since about the impact of free health care and university education, and there is no doubt that his policies were monumental; they changed opportunities for a generation, and gave people hope that we could have good, democratic governments that cared about ordinary people, fought for their interests, and gave them a shot in life.

And yet, when Malcolm Fraser was elected in 1975, he immediately began stripping back the progress that Whitlam had made, dismantling many of the bodies that had been formed, repealing some of the laws that had been passed, and doing his best to weaken whatever was left.[1] Fraser's election speech did not mention the words 'woman' or 'women' once; he made clear that women's issues were not a priority for his government, and he cut back funding and responsibility for them wherever he could.[2]

This trajectory should worry the young women of today. With a feminist movement that has largely left the streets for the Parliament, is our strategy to simply wait for the next Gough Whitlam to come along? How might any reforms be guaranteed, when history tells us that many of Whitlam's policies, monumental and ground-breaking for their impact on our basic quality of life, were so easily repealed by the next Prime Minister? Fifty years later, the Labor Party's policy platform doesn't have the ambition necessary to tackle the deep roots of patriarchy and sexism in our society, and while their successful election offers women some hope of change, we should not be relying solely on it.

Once set in motion, some social movements cannot be stopped, but waiting in hope that we will one day have another Prime Minister like Gough Whitlam is simply not good enough. We need to organise mass social movements strong enough to force change, because if we've learned anything from the trailblazing women of the Whitlam era, it's that asking nicely won't get you anywhere.

My mum was only little when Whitlam was delivered to power, but she grew up benefiting enormously from the impacts of his government, impacts which echoed across the country for working-class families. She was the first in her family to go to university, essentially for free, and her career led her to being the breadwinner in our family, even while she raised two young children. My dad, an immigrant from Nepal, didn't experience Australia under Whitlam, but it was his background, and the racist struggles he faced here, that helped grow my awareness of social justice and equality.

This upbringing gave me a fire in my belly and a motivation to be involved in the struggle against inequality, but it wasn't until I joined the University of Sydney Women's Collective that my own activism began. At that time, we were campaigning against the endemic sexual assault occurring on university campuses and were heavily involved in the fight for safe exclusion zones around abortion clinics and abortion decriminalisation in New South Wales. The collective was organising rallies and reading groups, and running an escorting service at a Sydney abortion clinic three days a week. The experience I gained from being involved in this grassroots women's collective and learning from the older activists who had been around for many years was invaluable. It gave me the drive, and the skills, which led me to become involved in other groups, and to campaign for climate justice and First Nations rights. It's led me to the point I am at now, where the feminists I respect most are the First Nations women fighting for justice on the streets. In *Another Day in the Colony*, Chelsea Watego writes, 'We occupy a social world that refuses to see our humanity, and not because it has yet to discover it, but precisely because its very existence is founded upon our violent erasure'.[3] I believe that a system and a constitution founded on the erasure of First Nations women cannot be the answer to equality for any woman, and while I acknowledge that women have made change using many different approaches throughout the decades, my perspective on the best way to fight for women's rights comes from where I've seen these campaigns be most effective, genuine and emancipatory – at the grassroots level.

Lessons and legacies from the 1970s

With the benefit of hindsight, we seek to learn from the feminist fight of the 1970s. Their movement achieved some remarkable wins, and we cannot attempt to emulate such success without looking critically at the decisions they made along the way. It is important to draw links between then and now, to figure out what was successful, and what was overlooked, what gained support from the public, and what was questioned. We need to make judgments about what our feminist predecessors should have pushed harder for, what was lost in the fight along the way, and how it led to the critical point we are at now. We're under no illusion that the movement was perfect, and we've grown to be critical of the feminism they left us, a feminism which struggles to properly address questions of race and gender.

Today there is a growing divide between the socialist feminist movement and the mainstream liberal movement for women's rights.[4] We are diverging from the Whitlam era, where these feminists were working together within the Women's Liberation Movement, having arguments about the best strategy in shared organising spaces, and coming to joint conclusions. Socialist feminists seek to dismantle patriarchal structures like the police and the State, which uphold control over women's lives and bodies, and further rates of incarceration and child removal; liberal feminists seek to end sexist discrimination against women through policy change and equal opportunity, and believe that as these reforms occur, sexist attitudes towards women will cease, and that issues such as sexual assault can be meaningfully tackled.[5]

Both are valid approaches; however, the reason women fall in one camp or the other often depends on their own class position.

The issues women believe are worth tackling are the ones which have impacted their lives or which they believe may one day impact their lives. It is this phenomenon which led the Women's Liberation Movement to often ignore loud and impassioned calls from Aboriginal women in the Whitlam era, and to downplay the place of lesbians in the movement.[6] The white feminist emphasis on child care and abortion neglected the fact that Indigenous women wanted the right to retain custody of their children; lesbians often felt the movement's emphasis on heterosexuality excluded their perspectives. The mainstream women's movement's focus in the 1970s, on entering the workforce and fighting for inarguably important demands like equal pay, led the Australian feminist movement to the point we are at now.

Many of today's feminists feel dejected when we realise that we have simply won the ability to contribute to the reproduction of capitalism, which itself sustains patriarchal forms of domination and oppression, rather than undermine it. Did we just forget about the horrific inequalities we are inflicting upon others as soon as we ourselves were earning a wage? Should we ignore the inherently exploitative nature of wage labour, and the alienation it fosters in all working men and women? The COVID-19 pandemic exposed how deeply our society still runs on the unpaid labour of women, and the flow-on effects of this to other aspects of life are tremendous but often unrecognised.

Without remaking the structures that we work under, our value system will still be profit-driven, and the inexcusable amounts of unpaid labour that women do will still be undervalued because it does not produce profit. As the Irish feminist organisation RAG wrote, 'One of the misconceptions of the feminist movement has been that for women to be equal to men, we must be the same. Women joined the rush into the modern workplace to have equal access to exploitation'.[7] This was reflected in the rise of so-called 'corporate feminism' in the 2010s, which pushed for narrow, unambitious goals, like increasing the number of women on boards, and offering more support for women in business, all things that are tying us more intricately to a profit-driven value system. By choosing to fight for change within this system, one which has shown its limitations time and time again, the feminist movement has already given up any real commitment to fight for the rights of migrant workers and First Nations peoples. We need to aim higher, and fight for a society that wants to erase inequality altogether.

The policies of Gough Whitlam's government changed the lives of women not just because they were intended to be feminist, but because they sought to erode class divisions, and implement a program that while not revolutionary, was socialist in nature. The Whitlam government wanted to give equal opportunities not only to women and men, but to all people, regardless of their class or race, regardless of whether they lived in urban, regional or rural areas, and regardless of how little or long they had called Australia home. Free tertiary education and free health care changed the course of women's lives, but they also changed the lives of new migrants and working-class people, many of whom lived below the poverty line. It is a national shame that today, in a country as wealthy as Australia, more than 11 per cent of our population lives below the poverty line, and it's important that we support women striking for better pay and conditions in essential care industries, rather than focusing on women rising to the top of corporations.[8]

Figureheads of social movements

When feminist ideas were becoming more prominent in the 1960s and '70s, as writer and activist Alice Nutter writes, 'the media (as always) looked for leaders and personalities. Rather than talk about the anger, the ideas and the needs that were propelling feminism forward, the emphasis was on individuals'.[9] Instead of strengthening the women's movement, picking out specific people to lead from the front served to undermine it, because individuals don't have the power to change a system alone, but the illusion that they can makes other women complacent.[10] It was Germaine Greer and Gloria Steinem in the 1970s, and it's Grace Tame and Brittany Higgins now.

Tame and Higgins are rightfully commended for their incredible bravery in telling their stories to raise awareness of sexual abuse, and while it's inarguable that they generated the momentum that was able to mobilise thousands of women to join the 2021 March4Justice on Canberra and around Australia, that anger was only held on the streets for a day before the incorporation of March4Justice meant the organisers became bound up in administration.[11] By International Women's Day, the energy from March4Justice had been channelled into the Safety. Respect. Equity. campaign, which has decent aims, but no perceivable strategy to achieve them.[12] Despite the clear impact this movement had on the attitudes of Australian women ahead of the 2022 federal election, collective power is whittled down and lost in such an environment, when a movement becomes about specific people to the detriment of the ideas these people are trying to champion.

Greta Thunberg faces the same struggle. She has been an inspiration for school children around the world, her face has been plastered across the internet, and she has given speeches at every important global climate conference for the last five years. And yet, nobody is acting on the things she is actually saying, and alone, she cannot force them to. It's a more subtle but infuriating kind of sexism than the one that women faced in the 1970s: being given the biggest platform in the world, but still unable to effect change.

In Australia, women have a platform now, and it's assumed that with that platform comes power. After all, #MeToo and 'cancel culture' have supposedly given us the ability to tell our stories, though being believed is another thing altogether. When it comes down to it, these platforms are just a distraction. Powerful men were never planning on listening if what women had to say had the potential to dismantle the systems of power from which they benefit. Side by side with our defamation laws, and the disastrous consequences they can have on the lives of ordinary people who speak out, these platforms have been a spectacularly successful way of making women shut up.[13]

The other clear major issue with the figureheads of Australia's feminist movement is that they are all attractive, wealthy white women. When Brittany Higgins made the allegation that she had been sexually assaulted in Parliament House, there was an outcry that permeated every corner of our nation. In contrast, when Indian-Australian Liberal staffer Dhanya Mani revealed her own alleged assault in 2019 – also by a fellow political staffer, in 2015 – it was barely reported on, and it certainly hasn't permeated conversations about sexual assault in the way that Higgins' alleged rape has, despite Mani's accusations taking place at the height of the #MeToo movement.[14] When Grace Tame received mountains of support for her unfiltered show of anger at the government's lack of action, journalist and author Sisonke Msimang was spot-on in pointing out that 'everywhere you look there are Black women who continue to be punished for loudly wearing their anger … Angry white women herald a new frontier in feminism, while loud black women are considered rude and uncouth'.[15]

At moments like these, it doesn't feel like figurehead feminism is doing anything to make changes for the women in our society who need it most, and that is a problem that cannot be addressed unless the feminist movement in Australia is organised collectively, from the ground up. Gender and sexuality do not exist in a vacuum, and a feminist movement cannot be successful without acknowledging the intersecting struggles faced by others.

A self-organised movement led by a coalition of working women with clear material demands would have the power to make real changes. In the last ten years alone, the New South Wales Teachers Federation has won domestic violence leave, maternity leave flexibility, leave for surrogacy and out-of-home care, and extra paid parental leave for both parents.[16] Higher-than-average union density has given the Federation the ability to run such successful campaigns, and should be a blueprint for other unions across the country. Every workplace and every suburb faces its own issues and knows best how to organise to improve them, and by building structures that allow for grassroots decision-making, our communities are strengthened and empowered to push for the changes we want to see. At a grassroots level, two prominent strategies are currently emerging: the push to elect 'teal independents' in traditional Liberal seats, and the increase in strikes in essential industries like nursing and teaching. While the teal independents, who tend to be successful, middle-class women, have attracted the capital of extremely wealthy men like Simon Holmes à Court and Mike Cannon-Brookes, the campaigns run by working-class women striking to force change are hindered by the same structural barriers that make them so important in the first place. Although union membership is increasingly female, workers are limited by laws which prohibit us striking except for during narrow parts of our enterprise agreement periods. People on low incomes are working far more to support themselves and their families, and often don't have the capital or the leisure time needed to run large-scale campaigns on the side. The record number of female politicians from diverse backgrounds elected in 2022 shows the desire for reform among these groups; however, it's important to recognise the limitations of elections, and pursue other avenues for change with as much force as ever.

Feminism in the workplace

In the 1970s working women in Australia found it next to impossible to achieve positive change for themselves through their unions. Deeply ingrained sexist attitudes prohibited progress in male-dominated industries and unions, and women who attempted to organise social movements through them – if they were even allowed to join – usually became quickly disillusioned and turned their focus to organising with the Women's Liberation Movement instead.[17] Women were fighting for the right to work, and were not necessarily in the workforce already, so organising from home and through community groups made more sense.

Now, more women are in the workforce than ever before, and the centre of feminist struggle must shift from the home to the workplace alongside it. Ironically, at a time when union density is at an all-time low, union organising is becoming more important for women than ever before.[18] Despite now having a seat at the table, women don't have it easy in the workforce. This is not only because there are structural barriers that hinder the ability of women to organise for better pay and conditions, but also because industries that are dominated by women workers are highly casualised and substantially underpaid.[19]

Nurses, teachers, aged care and disability support workers, and early childhood educators were some of the most underpaid and overworked people in our society even before the COVID-19 pandemic. Despite the last few years showing how utterly indispensable they are to every facet of life, they suffered public sector wage freezes, and understaffing so severe that in some parts of the country, schools were forced to close, and hospitals were overwhelmed with patients.

Women work in high numbers in deliberately exploited care work industries, and yet care work, whether paid or unpaid, upholds the structure of our society. According to the Workplace

Gender Equality Agency, 'The monetary value of unpaid care work in Australia has been estimated to be $650.1 billion, the equivalent to 50.6% of GDP', and most of this work is done by women.[20] Women are forced to absorb the burden of it when essential services like early childhood education or aged care do not exist, are held in private hands, or are out of reach because they are too expensive. The plan by the New South Wales and Victorian governments to offer all children a year of free pre-school will go some way to help ease the load on working women, but ultimately the plan means nothing without the infrastructure and educators to actually provide good-quality early childhood education.[21]

What is hopeful, though, is that throughout the pandemic, it has been some of the most feminised industries that have shown the most activity in their unions and the most defiance in their strikes.[22] Realising the power they have in their ability to fight for better pay and conditions through militant industrial action, and then taking to the streets in protest, builds the consciousness of younger generations of feminists. These experiences give us the knowledge and confidence to make sure that our work does not dominate every facet of our lives. It means we can fight for living wages that actually rise with inflation, safe working environments, proper parental leave, menstrual leave, gender transition leave, job security, and structures that help avoid burnout to contribute to our mental health, rather than detract from it. When I look to the future of the feminist movement in Australia, and what remains to be done, it is this that gives me hope.

Gough Whitlam's government valued care work; it put money into public education and hospitals, was committed to providing early childhood education, and raised welfare benefits substantially across the board, both for carers and recipients. His government did everything you could expect a social democratic government to do in three short years – except guarantee the life of his reforms after they were gone. A strong union movement, striking when any of these reforms are under attack, could guarantee them.

Lessons from the women of the Whitlam era

Today, it's easy to be disheartened when looking at the women's movement in Australia. After all, liberal feminism has won out over the radical feminism of the 1970s, which sought to change the very structures which contribute to our oppression. In her book *Talkin' Up to the White Woman*, Aileen Moreton-Robinson wrote: 'by working to improve the conditions of impoverished women in Australia, the status of all women will be enhanced'.[23] These words carry just as much weight today as they did when she wrote them more than 20 years ago, but the biggest tragedy of the traditional women's movement is that we have shifted away from this goal. We're uncomfortable with the idea that 'white middle-class women's privilege is tied to colonisation and the dispossession of Indigenous people', and we're uncomfortable with the idea that the women's movement has pushed First Nations, migrant and transgender women down to lift other women up.[24] If we are to ever be truly liberated from the patriarchy, we must understand that it is capitalism that upholds this system, and that we must fight for the liberation of all working people if women are to be truly free.

But all hope of a better world is not lost. Women are more empowered than ever before and we're tackling things like domestic violence and sexual assault much more seriously than before #MeToo. Highly feminised industries are doing incredible work fighting for better rights through their unions, and they are learning to harness the real power for change which comes with that.

There are so many lessons to take from the Whitlam era. But we would be doing those trailblazing feminists a disservice if in looking to them for inspiration, we simply followed their vision and strategy without learning from their mistakes. Fifty years later, we cannot afford to waste any more time politely asking the Labor Party for support when with every passing minute its policy and strategy gets less ambitious.

The strongest lesson we can take from the women of the Whitlam era is to be bold and brave, to break the restrictions placed on us, and to demand more for all women. More important still is that we create our own movements to win the changes we need, and avoid simply tailing our predecessors, or waiting for a new leader or a new government. We need to build movements with the strength to survive beyond political parties, electoral politics and feminist figureheads, movements that have a grander, more optimistic vision of society as their goal. If we are to achieve liberation, we must build a fighting movement that does not stop halfway when things are good enough for some of us, but which continues to fight until all working people are free from exploitation and oppression.

RE-ENERGISING THE REVOLUTION TODAY

BLAIR WILLIAMS

When Julia Gillard smashed through the glass ceiling to become Australia's first woman Prime Minister in June 2010, she brought hope that the country was finally changing and adapting to the sight of women in the top job. Yet Gillard's achievement was marred by an onslaught of sexism and misogyny from within her own party, the Opposition and the mainstream media. She was attacked for the way she ascended to the top job – challenging a sitting Prime Minister – while her gender, clothes, hair and personal life were routinely and publicly scrutinised. This backlash held a mirror to Australian society, culture and, especially, politics, highlighting an underlying misogyny. A decade later, in the first half of 2021, sexual assault and harassment allegations began spilling from federal Parliament, inspiring over 100 000 people from around Australia to march for action against gender-based violence. Parliament's toxic sexist culture clearly has not changed since Gillard's era, but more women and other advocates for change are now publicly calling it out. How did gender shape our political culture over this period, how did the women's movement respond, and what is the future of feminist political activism?

2010–13: The Gillard era

Gillard soared to the highest office in June 2010 when she successfully ousted her predecessor, Kevin Rudd. Though Rudd did not contest, and Gillard ran unopposed, her challenge was seen as an unprecedented displacement of a popular first-term

Prime Minister. While women around Australia were celebrating this historic moment, it was counterbalanced by an overwhelming backlash from others accusing her of disloyalty, treachery, even 'murder', with Opposition and media alike portraying her as an 'unusually bloodthirsty', 'devious and untrustworthy female'.[1] Yet this was only the beginning of the sexism and misogyny that blanketed the next three years of Gillard's prime ministerial term.

Parliament has long been a masculine institution built by and for elite white men. As such, it upholds a masculine culture which advantages men while creating challenges for those women able to enter this space. Despite anti-discrimination rules and regulations – though a formal Code of Conduct for all parliamentary workers does not yet exist – Parliament is a place of entrenched power hierarchies. Even the building itself 'affirmed men's presence and status as the legitimate holders of office',[2] from the hallway of former (male) Prime Minister portraits to the lack of an onsite child-care facility until 2009. Such masculine norms have unsurprisingly led to the discrimination and harassment of women in politics. Even though the Gillard era saw an increase of women in politics, men still defined the rules of the game.

Gillard was ruthlessly attacked by the Opposition Leader, Tony Abbott, undermined by Rudd, scrutinised and criticised by the mainstream media, and even vilified by the public. She experienced extraordinary amounts of gendered, often highly negative and even defamatory coverage that focused on her gender, appearance, childlessness, sexuality, family life and relationship status.[3] Shock jocks called her a 'lying cow' and proposed that she should be put in a chaff bag and thrown out to sea, political cartoonist Larry Pickering bombarded all members of federal Parliament with daily cartoons that often depicted a naked Gillard wielding a strap-on dildo and, at a Coalition fundraiser, a satirical menu notoriously included a dish titled 'Julia Gillard Kentucky Fried Quail – Small Breasts, Huge Thighs & a Big Red Box'.

Gillard was careful to avoid or downplay gender in the early stages of her term. She knew there would be an initial frenzy when she became Prime Minister but thought this would fizzle out as time passed, so she refrained from calling it out. But, as noted in her memoir *My Story*, her assessment 'was wrong. It actually worsened [and] it seemed like sexism had been normalised'.[4]

After two years of near-constant sexist abuse, Gillard finally stood up and declared that enough was enough. During Parliamentary Question Time on 9 October 2012, Abbott accused the Gillard government of hypocrisy for not acting on misogynistic texts sent by the Speaker of the House, Peter Slipper. Uttering the now-famous words – 'I will not be lectured about sexism and misogyny by this man. I will not. And the Government will not be lectured about sexism and misogyny by this man. Not now, not ever' – Gillard launched into a 15-minute speech calling out the sexism she had endured during her time in Parliament. This speech went viral on social media and was an instant hit with many women in Australia and around the world, receiving praise from world leaders and celebrities.[5]

As a 19-year-old watching that speech later that day on YouTube, I was excited that Gillard had *finally* called out the sexist abuse directed at her from all angles. I also felt solidarity with all the women who had been subjected to demeaning comments from mediocre men who benefit from the patriarchal status quo. I was hopeful that things would change – that Australia would reflect on the way it treats women. I was wrong. It fell flat on the Canberra press gallery, who viewed it as a desperate attempt by Gillard to play the 'gender card' and faced a backlash from anti-feminist online 'trolls'. I remember crying in my mother's arms after reading the media coverage and the toxic commentary on social media. I felt complete and utter despair that despite all the toxic sexism our first woman Prime Minister experienced day in day out, her rallying cry that had resonated with so many women around the country and around the world could be disparaged by the media. What hope was there for those of us with less privilege and power? Yet this speech was a watershed moment in breaking the silence over political sexism, and soon many more women in Australian politics would speak out.

The ferocity of misogynistic criticism directed at our first woman Prime Minister left a deep impression on girls and women around Australia. It revealed that women, and especially women in power, were still perceived in a negative light and it demonstrated the risks we face if we challenge the status quo of (male) politics. Such gendered and misogynistic treatment of women in politics can have what is called a 'bystander effect' on ordinary women, impacting their self-worth and even their leadership and political aspirations.[6] Even though they are not the target of this sexism, girls and women are still negatively affected just by witnessing it and absorbing its messages. For example, a 2017 Plan International Australia survey found that only 2 per cent of girls aged 10–14 and 5 per cent of girls aged 15–17 listed politics as a future career option, which then dropped to zero per cent of young women aged 18–25. We need *more* young and diverse women in politics, not less. It is clear, then, that the hypermasculine 'boys' club' parliamentary culture and gendered media coverage of the Gillard era has had lasting ramifications.

2010s: Reawakening the feminist movement

Though the early 2010s saw the historic ascension of our first woman Prime Minister, sworn in by our first woman Governor-General, this era was still caught in a post-feminist hangover from the 1990s when women's rights were assumed to have been won and the 'F' word was seldom claimed unless you 'hated men'. We have seen a lot of change in the decade since the Gillard era. Feminism has gained mainstream appeal through three key events: the rise of celebrity feminism, the backlash to Trump's 2016 presidential election, and the #MeToo movement.

Feminism has made a dramatic resurgence in popular culture and social media. Even male politicians and leaders, like former US President Barack Obama, claimed the label. The 2016 Australian federal election saw Prime Minister Malcolm Turnbull and Opposition Leader Bill Shorten both declare themselves feminists.[7] The rise of 'celebrity feminism' in the 2010s mainstreamed the movement yet also normalised a 'palatable' variety of feminism calling for empowerment (usually of the self) but ultimately non-threatening, with a neoliberal agenda of individual success over-represented by white, middle-class, heterosexual, able-bodied women.[8] 'Unpalatable' feminists or so-called 'feminist killjoys', on the other hand, are transgressive in their politics rather than seeking mainstream attention, endeavouring to contest the status quo.[9] The 'F' word therefore became more mainstream and less threatening, yet the movement had been refracted through the prism of corporate feminism – prioritising the individual over the collective, focusing on women at the top, and selling a 'girl power' aesthetic.

The 2016 election of Donald Trump – an overt misogynist and alleged sexual predator – was a haunting moment for women around the world. The message was clear: white male supremacy reigned supreme while women's competence, intelligence and ambition were seen as a threat and our safety sidelined. But this was also a tipping point for feminist movements. Immediately following Trump's inauguration, the Women's March on Washington saw more than 470 000 people flood Washington, DC while more than five million marched nationwide, joined by demonstrators around the world. I marched alongside hundreds of others in Canberra, angered by his election. Recognising the parallels in our own country, we marched for longstanding issues like sexual assault and harassment, the gender wage gap, racial and sexual discrimination, and attacks on LGBTQIA+ rights. Though activists had long been fighting these issues, Trump's election sent a jolt through many who were previously politically inactive as it demonstrated the persistence of sexism and patriarchal power and showed that the fight for equality was far from over.

Lastly, the rise of the #MeToo movement mainstreamed a more transgressive and less 'palatable' feminism. The term – *sans* hashtag – had been coined by US survivor and activist Tarana Burke in 2006 to connect young Black women survivors of sexual violence. Twelve years later, this movement went viral in 2017 after the hashtag spread on Twitter and drew global attention to the prevalence of sexual violence in workplaces and personal lives. Expanding beyond its initial aims of calling out sexual harassment and assault in the workplace, it sought to empower all women and survivors of sexual violence, highlighting social norms that allow men in positions of power to assault and harass others. #MeToo did not create an immediate explosion in Australia, but instead came in waves that broke away, piece by piece, the façade of Australian culture while strengthening and amplifying the voices of those who have been harmed by the spectrum of patriarchal violence.

2018: The turning point

The year 2018 marked a watershed in Australian politics. In the wake of the #MeToo movement, two politicians notably spoke out about the sexism they had endured from colleagues. Parliament House's façade of propriety was slowly eroding.

First was Greens Senator Sarah Hanson-Young. During the debate of a motion dealing with violence against women in June 2018, Senator David Leyonhjelm interrupted Hanson-Young's speech by remarking 'you should stop shagging men, Sarah'. Doubling down in subsequent media interviews, unprotected by parliamentary privilege, Leyonhjelm implied that Hanson-Young had numerous romantic relationships for which he labelled her a 'misandrist' and 'hypocrite'. Hanson-Young subsequently accused Leyonhjelm of 'slut-shaming' her and successfully sued him for defamation as she had 'had enough of men in that place using sexism and sexist slurs, sexual innuendo as part of their intimidation and bullying on the floor of the Parliament'.[10]

Second was Liberal MP Julia Banks. After Scott Morrison replaced Malcolm Turnbull as Prime Minister in August 2018, Banks announced she would not contest her seat at the next election due to the bullying and intimidation that many women experienced from the Coalition. Morrison subsequently framed her as emotionally vulnerable and claimed he was worried for her 'welfare and wellbeing'.[11] In November, Banks left the Liberal Party for the crossbench and, in her resignation speech, noted that 'when good women call out, or are subjected to, bad behaviour … the reprisals, backlash and commentary portray them as the bad ones, the liar, the troublemaker, the emotionally unstable or weak, or someone who should be silenced'. Many of her male colleagues walked out.

Yet the media response contrasted starkly with the Gillard era and was generally more supportive.[12] Many journalists commented on the institutionalised sexism rife in Parliament, acknowledged the 'slut-shaming' of Hanson-Young and closely examined the Liberal Party's 'woman problem'. While certain dark corners of the media continued their sexist shaming of both women, many others demonstrated progress. As *Guardian* journalist Katherine Murphy later admitted, the sexist treatment of Gillard was obvious at the time, but it was not the cultural norm to apply a gendered lens when covering politics – she has 'certainly learnt lessons' and is determined 'not to repeat the mistakes of that period'.[13]

2021: The year of reckoning

Women in politics have long endured Parliament's toxic sexist 'boys' club', yet aside from a handful of cases, they often suffered in silence. But 2021 would change all of that, and women journalists, like Samantha Maiden, Louise Milligan, Katherine Murphy and Lisa Wilkinson, would help lead the charge.

In January, Grace Tame, a survivor of child sexual assault, was named Australian of the Year for her advocacy in pushing legal reform and raising public awareness of the impacts of sexual violence. In her acceptance speech on 26 January, Tame detailed her experiences of sexual abuse in harrowing detail and proudly stated that she and other survivors would not be silenced. By way of response, Prime Minister Morrison leant over to her ear and whispered, 'Well, gee, I bet it felt good to get that out'. Tame's courage and Morrison's response set the wheels in motion.

Only weeks later, inspired by Tame's example, former Liberal staffer Brittany Higgins quit her job and publicly disclosed her alleged sexual assault by a colleague in the offices of her boss, Defence Minister Linda Reynolds, in March 2019. What Higgins alleged was sickening, but the government response was truly horrifying: from being summoned by Reynolds for a discussion in the very office in which the assault had occurred, her story being swept under the rug in the lead-up to the election, and then made to feel like her career would be over if she lodged a formal complaint, to the almost universal denial of any knowledge of the assault from senior Coalition members, including Morrison, who claimed they had no idea until Higgins went public despite mounting evidence suggesting otherwise. Both Reynolds and Morrison apologised to Higgins days after her public disclosure, but in March it surfaced that Reynolds had called Higgins a 'lying cow' in front of staff after reading initial media reports.

Only two weeks after Higgins dropped the first bomb on

Parliament, a second exploded when ABC journalist Louise Milligan revealed details of an anonymous letter sent to the Prime Minister, ALP Senator Penny Wong and Greens Senator Sarah Hanson-Young, alleging that a 16-year-old girl had been raped in 1988 by a man who was now a Cabinet minister. Morrison noted that he had seen but not read the letter and seemed unfazed by the prospect that one of his ministers had been accused of such a heinous offence. Days later, Attorney-General Christian Porter outed himself as the anonymous minister in a national press conference, and strenuously denied the allegations and refused to step down from his position. The victim had reported her complaint to the New South Wales Police in 2020, but they suspended the investigation a day before she took her own life in June of that year. The police dropped the case in 2021, citing 'insufficient admissible evidence to proceed'. Calls for a public inquiry into the allegations were rejected by Morrison, who described Porter as an 'innocent man under our law'. Public outcry forced a Cabinet reshuffle, yet rather than pushing Porter to the backbench, as might be expected, Morrison moved him to the Industry, Science and Technology portfolio – and not because of the allegation, but in light of his defamation lawsuit against the ABC.

Higgins' bravery not only rocked Australia but shone a bright light on Parliament House as a workplace, illuminating the rot within. The bandaid had been ripped off, and more reports of sexism, bullying, sexual harassment and assault spilled forth. Within a month, we learned that Higgins' own alleged attacker had been accused of sexually harassing and assaulting three other women, and a video and pictures surfaced of a staffer masturbating on the desk of a woman MP and other staffers committing sexual acts in Parliament House.[14] The government's response was ineffectual and unempathetic, blaming survivors and drawing accusations of an attempt to cover up sexual misconduct.

Marching 4 Justice

This quick succession of events angered women and victim-survivors everywhere and inspired a public discussion of gendered violence and gender equality. Everyday conversations started to become deeply personal as many opened up to one another. I listened to loved ones disclose their own experiences of sexual assault and harassment, ranging from early childhood to more recently, noting they had previously remained silent because of a sense of shame and guilt. We talked about the toxicity of rape culture, the insidious effects of victim-blaming, and how our silence only benefits a system that protects perpetrators. Collectively, we felt angry yet utterly exhausted. We were fed up with a culture that prioritises the reputations of the powerful over the lives and safety of victim-survivors.

In March, over 100000 women, victim-survivors of sexual violence and allies, took to the streets of Australia to demand better, calling for an end to gendered violence in politics and society more broadly. I played a part in organising the March4Justice rally in Canberra and remember standing on the Commencement Column in front of Parliament House, looking out on a sea of people dressed in black in Federation Mall. The rage and frustration were palpable and it was evident that enough was enough. The rally commenced with a rendition of Helen Reddy's 'I Am Woman' by First Nations singer Monica Moore, as some in the crowd danced and sang along. Many, however, could only look on with tear-filled eyes, revealing the pain and suffering that survivors and their loved ones experience, shamed into silence. But, as one placard put it, 'We will not stay silent so you can stay comfortable'.

We heard from a range of speakers. Ngunnawal Elder Aunty Violet Sheridan welcomed us to country and spoke of the institutional sexism of Parliament that keeps alleged perpetrators like Porter safe; sexual assault survivor and activist Saxon Mullins called for men to re-think the behaviours that have 'helped create a toxic culture' and allowed perpetrators to thrive; CEO, author and activist Aminata Conteh-Biger posed a powerful question to the crowd: '[If] the Australian Prime Minister and politicians do not believe a white woman, what hope is there for black women?' Brittany Higgins made a surprise appearance and delivered a powerful speech encouraging us to share our truth. The collective rage and grief that had been slowly building in women around Australia for generations exploded into what one speaker, feminist activist Biff Ward, called 'the great uprising'.

Invitations to the rally were sent to every member of Parliament, but only 15 Coalition MPs and senators were in attendance. Morrison, Deputy Prime Minister Michael McCormack, Deputy Leader of the Liberal Party and Treasurer Josh Frydenberg, and Nationals Deputy Leader David Littleproud were notably absent. Morrison instead poured fuel on the fire with comments made in Question Time that day. After refusing to face the march and turning down an offer to meet privately with three of the organisers, Morrison stated that it was 'good and right' – a 'triumph of democracy' – that so many could peacefully express their 'genuine and real frustrations', because, he added, 'not far from here, such marches, even now are being met with bullets'.

In the days after Higgins' allegations, Morrison announced four reviews into the matter: the Foster Review into the handling of serious incidents; the Gaetjens Review to identify who in the Prime Minister's Office knew about Higgins' allegations; the Kunkel Review into the behaviour of the Prime Minister's media staff; and the Hammond Review into Coalition staffing issues. These were all internal and offered little of substance – what was needed was an external independent inquiry. After much pressure, and realising this issue was not going away, Morrison finally appointed Sex Discrimination Officer Kate Jenkins to lead an inquiry examining parliamentary workplace culture. The inquiry's findings, presented in November 2021, offer a damning indictment of this culture and set out a framework for change with 28 recommendations, including the advancement of gender equality and increasing the number of LGBTQIA+/disabled/First Nations parliamentarians and staffers, developing a centralised Office of Parliamentarian Staffing and Culture to provide support, creating a Code of Conduct, and professionalising management practices for *Members of Parliament (Staff) Act* employees.

The future?

If anything, 2021 has shown us that the feminist movement is far from dead and young women are leading the fight for change. Standing on the shoulders of all the feminists that came before us, young feminists are picking up the baton and driving the creation of an equitable world. We are building on the legacy of past issues and protests – often hand-in-hand with older feminists as at the March4Justice rallies – but putting our own spin on it.

Women's anger was a resolute force to be reckoned with at the ballot box. The 2022 federal election, although a battle between Morrison and Anthony Albanese, was unquestionably about gender. Morrison continued to focus on swinging male voters, with his bulldozer leadership masculinity and a blokey campaign platform, while Albanese successfully mobilised a more caring form of leadership masculinity and endorsed a platform designed to appeal to women voters, listening to our anger and campaigning on the care economy. Morrison brought a hi-vis vest and a hard hat to an unequivocally gendered election and lost. The message for the political parties is clear: ignore women voters at your own peril. This election delivered the most progressive and diverse Parliament in Australia's history, with many previously incumbent pale, stale, male Liberals replaced by culturally and linguistically diverse candidates, including a large number of women. The red, green and teal waves washed away the previously impervious 'boys' club', promising a safer and more respectful parliamentary workplace. However, while this election brings hope for the future for the first time in a long while, it does not end our fight for equality. We still need grassroots action.

Many young Australians still feel disillusioned with the current state of the world and disenfranchised by those in power, many of whom do not speak for or represent us.[15] We are still facing multiple crises, from widespread mental health issues, climate catastrophe, unaffordable housing, economic recession, low job security and high rates of casualisation. On top of that, we are dealing with a global pandemic that has already set women's rights back by more than two decades, increased the rates of violence against women, and in which young women have borne the brunt of job losses and performed the bulk of care labour. The feminist movement is not homogenous nor does it solely fight for gender equality. Feminists are fighting alongside and supporting movements that call for action on many issues, including climate, refugee rights, First Nations rights, workers' rights and increased funding for health, education and welfare. Like many of my peers, I feel as if my future has been stolen. But we have not yet given up hope.

Yes, we need more young and diverse women in politics, but, considering the way we have been treated in and by the political system, it is unsurprising that many young activists fighting for change are doing so outside of the political system. The narrative is no longer controlled by those in power, but by those on ground. Young activists, especially girls and young women, are the leaders of global movements, such as those for climate activism. Likewise, they are re-energising the movement against sexual violence and inequality.

Nevertheless, it is crucial that we acknowledge the relative privilege shared by the most visible activists, and the need for greater diversity. The system fails survivors and only gains national attention when the privileged suffer. We have heard from women who are white, cis-gender, able-bodied and middle class, but whose stories are we not hearing? In the days after the March4Justice protests, First Nations activists pointed out that they had been ignored even though they have been fighting white patriarchal violence since colonisation. Professor Bronwyn Carlson rightly observed 'a noticeable silence in Australia when victims of violence are Indigenous',[16] while Latoya Aroha Rule, a Wiradjuri and Māori Takatāpui activist, asked us to 'imagine if white women surrounded Parliament House to call for justice for dead Black women,'[17] pointing to the more than 500 Aboriginal deaths in custody (including a disproportionate number of Aboriginal women) since the 1991 Royal Commission.[18] Feminist activism must not repeat the mistakes of the past – that is, as Indigenous activist and distinguished Professor Aileen Moreton-Robinson writes, we must not 'reinvest in whiteness … feminists [are] not challenging white race privilege; they [are] exercising it'.[19]

This is the most pressing issue facing the future of feminist activism in Australia. Gender equality cannot be achieved if it simply means replacing a white man in power with a white woman in power, or if our focus is on pushing for more women CEOs instead of improving working women's conditions. We, as feminist activists, must seek to demolish *all* hierarchies of oppression, from patriarchy, capitalism, white supremacy and ableism to cis-heteronormativity. To create lasting and meaningful change, we need to adopt an intersectional approach that centres First Nations women's issues, voices and stories while amplifying the voices of other marginalised women, non-binary and gender diverse people too often silenced in these discussions. We must fight for a future that is inclusive and empowering for all and we cannot afford to leave anyone behind.

ACKNOWLEDGMENTS

In the process of editing this book, I have incurred many debts. I would first like to thank all the contributors, many of whom have been part of this project since it was first devised. You have all been incredibly patient and generous with your stories and your time. Special thanks to the dedicated staff of the Whitlam Institute, especially Andrea Connor, Fiona Pacey, acting director Eric Sidoti and director John Juriansz, and the board of the Institute for their support of this project. Thank you also to Elspeth Menzies, Sophia Oravecz and the team at NewSouth for all their hard work on the book, and to John Mapps for his fine copyediting.

I am particularly grateful to Jocelynne Scutt, who generously granted permission to reproduce an edited version of Pat Eatock's autobiographical essay first published as:

Pat Eatock, 'There's a Snake in My Caravan', in Jocelynne A. Scutt (ed.), *Different Lives – Reflections on the Women's Movement and Visions of its Future*, Penguin, Melbourne, Australia, 1986, pp. 22–31.

This book was the brainchild of two extraordinary women: the Hon Susan Ryan AO (a Whitlam Institute Distinguished Fellow), and the former director of the Whitlam Institute, Dr Leanne Smith. Together, they devised the conference upon which this book was built, and both made important contributions to the book. It is a source of tremendous sadness that Susan Ryan did not live to see the book make it into print, but that it exists at all is tribute to her tenacity, intelligence and wisdom. The book is dedicated to her memory.

NOTES

Introduction (Michelle Arrow)

1   Department of the Prime Minister and Cabinet, *The Women and Politics Conference 1975*, Volume One, (Canberra: Australian Government Publishing Service, 1977), vii.

2   See Michelle Arrow, Chapter 4: 'National Consciousness-Raising', in *The Seventies: The Personal, the Political and the Making of Modern Australia* (Sydney: NewSouth, 2019).

3   Patricia Karvelas, 'Women Are Raising the Alarm over the Liberal Party's Lack of Diversity, and the Coalition Can't Ignore Them', ABC Online, 14 August 2022, <www.abc.net.au/news/2022-08-14/women-raising-alarm-liberal-party-diversity-coalition-electoral/101327332>.

4   Paul Karp, 'Under-55s and Higher Educated Voters Propelled Labor to Victory, Study Finds', *The Guardian*, 20 June 2022, <www.theguardian.com/australia-news/2022/jun/20/under-55s-and-higher-educated-voters-propelled-labor-to-victory-study-finds>; Australia Institute, 'Women 7–10 Percentage Points Less Likely to Vote Coalition', <australiainstitute.org.au/post/women-7-10-percentage-points-less-likely-to-vote-coalition-analysis/>.

5   Frank Bongiorno, 'Good Blokes? Gender and Political Leadership in the Australian Labor Party', in Zareh Ghazarian and Katrina Lee-Koo (eds), *Gender Politics: Navigating Political Leadership in Australia* (Sydney: UNSW Press, 2021), 25–26.

6   Arrow, *The Seventies*, 23.

7   Carol Hanisch, 'The Personal Is Political' (1969, republished 2006), <www.carolhanisch.org/CHwritings/PIP.html>.

8   Nancy Dexter, *The Age*, 23 November 1972, quoted in Marian Sawer with Gail Radford, *Making Women Count: A History of the Women's Electoral Lobby*, UNSW Press, Sydney 2008, 13.

9   Susan Ryan, 'Revisiting the Revolution: Whitlam and Women', *Whitlam Institute Legacy Series*, 8, December 2020: 6.

10   Elizabeth Reid, 'The Child of Our Movement: A Movement of Women', in Jocelynne A. Scutt (ed.), *Different Lives: Reflections on the Women's Movement and Visions of its Future* (Melbourne: Penguin, 1986), 14.

11   Gough Whitlam, election speech, 13 November 1972, <electionspeeches.moadoph.gov.au/speeches/1972-gough-whitlam>.

12   Susan Ryan, *Catching the Waves: Life in and Out of Politics* (Sydney: HarperCollins, 1999), 124.

13   *International Women's Year: Report of the Australian National Advisory Committee* (Canberra: Australian Government Publishing Service, 1976), 18.

14   Gough Whitlam, speech at the opening of the Women and Politics
      Conference (Canberra, 31 August 1975), <pmtranscripts.pmc.gov.au/
      release/transcript-3874>.
15   Ryan, 'Revisiting the Revolution', 10.
16   Michelle Arrow, '"An Inquiry into the Whole Human Condition?"':
      Whitlam, Sexual Citizenship and the Royal Commission on Human
      Relationships', in Jenny Hocking (ed.), *Making Modern Australia: The
      Whitlam Government's 21st Century Agenda* (Clayton: Monash University
      Publishing, 2017), 3–34.

Whitlam and the Women's Liberation Movement (Elizabeth Reid)

1   This is an extract from a longer paper, published by the Whitlam Institute
      and available from <www.whitlam.org>. I am indebted to Murray Goot,
      Shirley Castley, Biff Ward and Julie Hamblin, who have contributed
      significantly to recreating and 'fixing up' the narrative. And to Caroline
      Summerhayes and Catherine Dovey, whose memories of those times
      have supplemented and confirmed mine and whose judgment I respect
      immensely. To Anne Gunn, Gil Appleton, Jane Timbrell and Gail Radford,
      who read and helped with the text. My sincere thanks to each.
2   *Brazen Hussies*, a documentary history of the Australian Women's
      Liberation Movement and those times, written and directed by Catherine
      Dwyer, uses superb archival footage and present-day interviews
      to chronicle and celebrate this history; <vimeo.com/ondemand/
      brazenhussies>.
3   Peter Wilenski, personal communication.
4   Pat Eatock, 'A Small but Stinging Twig: Reflections of a Black
      Campaigner', in Henry Mayer (ed.), *Labor to Power: Australia's 1972
      Election* (Sydney: Angus & Robertson, 1973), 153.
5   Gough Whitlam, speech at the opening of the Women and Politics
      Conference, Canberra, 31 August 1975, <pmtranscripts.pmc.gov.au/
      release/transcript-3874>.
6   Gough Whitlam, *The Whitlam Government 1972–1975* (Ringwood:
      Penguin, 1985), 17, 512.
7   Carolyn Collins, *Save Our Sons: Women, Dissent and Conscription during
      the Vietnam War* (Clayton: Monash University Publishing, 2021), xii.
8   Whitlam, *The Whitlam Government*, 19–22.
9   Kay Daniels, 'Report on the Women's Liberation National Conference,
      Sydney, June 1972', *Liberaction*, 3 (1972): 4–5.
10   Quoted in Hester Eisenstein, *Contemporary Feminist Thought* (North
      Sydney: Unwin Paperbacks, 1984), xii.
11   Elizabeth Reid, 'Development as a Moral Concept: Women's Practices as
      Development Practice', in Noeleen Heyzer (ed.), *A Commitment to the
      World's Women* (New York: UNIFEM, 1995), 119–21.
12   In *Brazen Hussies* the level of male violence, and police violence, towards
      women is shocking.

13   See the demands and the discussions in *Brazen Hussies* of the need for women to take control of their bodies.

14   *International Women's Year: Report of the National Advisory Committee* (Canberra: Australian Government Publishing Service, 1976), 10–11. See also Elizabeth Reid, 'Woman: Egalitarianism and Reforms', in *Equality: The New Issues* (Melbourne: Victorian Fabian Society, 1973), 4.

15   Gough Whitlam, speech by the Prime Minister – International Women's Year – Inaugural Meeting of the National Advisory Committee, Canberra, 11 September 1974, <pmtranscripts.pmc.gov.au/release/transcript-3385.

16   Activism was not new to me, having marched on the streets of London (CND) and Canberra (anti-war and Women's Liberation Movement marches); written articles on rape in marriage, masturbation and the objectification of women, the draft Criminal Code for the Australian Territories, etc.; debated abortion, sexuality, birth control, etc. at the ANU; been a founding member of the Homosexual Law Reform Society of the ACT and the Abortion Law Reform Association of the ACT; worked to establish the Family Planning Clinic in the ACT; been campaign manager for Pat Eatock, an Indigenous independent candidate for the ACT in the 1972 elections; worked on various submissions to government, including the Women's Liberation Movement/Women's Electoral Lobby submission on no-fault divorce law; and more.

17   Whitlam, speech by the Prime Minister – International Women's Year – Inaugural Meeting of the National Advisory Committee, Canberra, 11 September 1974.

18   Elizabeth Reid, 'How the Personal Became Political: The Feminist Movement of the 1970s', *Australian Feminist Studies,* 33 (95) (2018): 9–30.

19   Elizabeth Reid, 'The Draft Criminal Code for the Australian Territories', *Woroni* (9 March 1972): 8–9.

20   Susan Magarey, 'Beauty Becomes Political: Beginnings of the Women's Liberation Movement in Australia', *Australian Feminist Studies*, 33 (95) (2018): 31–44.

21   Elizabeth Reid, 'The Child of Our Movement: A Movement of Women', in Jocelynne A. Scutt (ed.), *Different Lives: Reflections on the Women's Movement and Visions of its Future* (Melbourne: Penguin, 1987), 15.

22   Elizabeth Reid, 'Creating a Policy for Women', in *The Whitlam Phenomenon: Fabian Papers* (Fitzroy: McPhee Gribble/Penguin, 1986), 145–55.

23   Iola Mathews, 'Woman's Voice in PM's Ear', *The Age*, 28 September 1973, 8.

24   Elizabeth Reid, interview by Dany Torsh, Papers of Elizabeth Reid, NLA, Box 9 MS9262/4/2.

25   Elizabeth Reid, 'Woman: Egalitarianism and Reforms', in *Equality: The New Issues* (Melbourne: Fabian Society, 1973), 2.

26   See the discussion of the potential benefits and drawbacks of maternity

leave in Carol Ambrus and Dale Dowse, 'Visions', *Canberra Women's Liberation Newsletter*, May 1973, 6–8.

27   *The Women and Politics Conference 1975*, vol. 1 and vol. 2 (Canberra: Australian Government Publishing Service, 1977), Introduction. See also *International Women's Year: Report of the National Advisory Committee,* 147–51.

28   For more details on the Royal Commission, see *The Interim Report of the Royal Commission on Human Relationships* (Canberra: Australian Government Publishing Service, 1976), vol. 1. See also Anne Deveson, *Australians at Risk* (Sydney: Cassell, 1978), 2–4.

29   Gough Whitlam, International Women's Day Reception, Melbourne, 8 March 1975, <pmtranscripts.pmc.gov.au/release/transcript-3643>.

30   Royal Commission on Human Relationships, *Final Report* (Canberra: Australian Government Publishing Service, 1977).

31   For a more detailed discussion of the Commission and its final moments, see Michelle Arrow, *The Seventies: The Personal, the Political and Making of Modern Australia* (Sydney: NewSouth, 2019), 187–93 and passim.

32   Whitlam, International Women's Day Reception.

33   *International Women's Year: Report of the National Advisory Committee*, 2.

34   *International Women's Year: Priorities and Considerations* (Canberra: Australian Government Publishing Service, 1974), reprinted in 'Women, the Family and Society', *St. Marks Review*, 80 (Dec. 1974): 22–23.

35   For the full list, see *International Women's Year: Report of the National Advisory Committee,* Part Two, Sections 2 & 3.

36   *International Women's Year: Report of the National Advisory Committee*, 74–75.

37   Whitlam, International Women's Day Reception.

38   Sara Dowse, 'The Femocrat Factor', *Inside Story*, 6 June 2013, 2–3, <insidestory.org.au/the-femocrat-factor>.

39   Gough Whitlam, speech at the opening of the Women and Politics Conference, Canberra, 31 August 1975, <pmtranscripts.pmc.gov.au/release/transcript-3874>.

40   'Child Care in Australia report March Quarter 2020', <www.dese.gov.au/child-care-package/early-childhood-data-and-reports/quarterly-reports/child-care-australia-report-march-quarter-2020>.

41   Hester Eisenstein, *Inside Agitators: Australian Femocrats and the State* (Philadelphia: Temple University Press, 1996), 50–51.

42   Adele Murdolo, 'Safe Homes for Immigrant and Refugee Women: Narrating Alternative Histories of the Women's Refuge Movement in Australia' *Frontiers*, 35 (3) (2014): 128; Gwendolyn Gray Jamieson, *Reaching for Health: The Australian Women's Health Movement and Public Policy* (Canberra: ANU Press, 2000), 306.

43   Gareth Evans, 'The Lessons', in Australian Fabian Society (ed.), *The Whitlam Phenomenon: Fabian Papers,* (Fitzroy: McPhee Gribble/Penguin, 1986), 166.

44 Gough Whitlam, election speech, 13 November 1972, <electionspeeches. moadoph.gov.au/speeches/1972-gough-whitlam>.

45 *International Women's Year: Report of the National Advisory Committee*, 37.

Women and political influences: The Women's Electoral Lobby and equal pay (Iola Mathews)

1 Michelle Grattan, 'Politicians Are Wary', in the 'Women Voters' Guide', *The Age*, 20 November 1972, 10.

2 WEL Interview Schedule, Federal Election 1972, copy in possession of the author.

3 Jenny Hocking, *Gough Whitlam*, vol. I, *A Moment in History* (Carlton: Melbourne University Press, 2008), 196.

4 Dedication, Gough Whitlam, *The Whitlam Government 1972–1975* (Ringwood: Penguin, 1985).

5 Gough Whitlam, *The Whitlam Government 1972–1975* (Ringwood: Penguin, 1985), 516.

Sisterhood (Biff Ward)

1 Helpful comments on this chapter came from Elizabeth Reid, Julia Ryan and Gail Radford.

2 Conversation with Suzanne Bellamy, 2022.

3 Conversation with Julia Ryan, 2022.

4 Luke Buckmaster, 'Strong Female Lead: Viscerally Powerful Film Lets the Gillard Years Speak for Themselves', *The Guardian*, 14 September 2021, <www.theguardian.com/film/2021/sep/14/strong-female-lead-viscerally-powerful-film-lets-the-gillard-years-speak-for-themselves>.

The personal is political (Pat Eatock and Cathy Eatock)

1 Pat Eatock, Interview by Ann-Mari Jordens, Tape 4 [sound recording] 8 sound files (476 min). Recorded on 23–24 May 2005, at Canberra, Oral History and Folklore Collection, National Library of Australia.

2 Eatock Interview, Tape 4.

3 Gary Foley, 'A Reflection on the First Thirty Days of the Embassy', in Gary Foley, Andrew Schaap and Edwina Howell (eds), *The Aboriginal Tent Embassy: Sovereignty, Black Power, Land Rights and the State* (London and New York: Routledge, 2014), 24.

4 Eatock, Interview, Tape 3.

5 Foley, 'A Reflection on the Embassy', 32.

6 John Newfong, 'The Aboriginals Embassy: Its Purpose and Aims', *Identity*, July 1972, 4.

7 Newfong, 'The Aboriginals Embassy', 5.

8 Eatock, Interview Tape 4.

9 Scott Robinson, 'The Aboriginal Embassy: An Account of the Protests of 1972', first published in *Aboriginal History* 18 (1) (1994): 49–63, republished in *The Aboriginal Tent Embassy*, 12.

10   Foley, 'A Reflection on the Embassy', 33.
11   Robinson, 'The Aboriginal Embassy', 13.
12   Robinson, 'The Aboriginal Embassy', 13.
13   Robinson, 'The Aboriginal Embassy', 14–15.
14   Robinson, 'The Aboriginal Embassy', 16.
15   Robinson, 'The Aboriginal Embassy', 17.
16   Robinson, 'The Aboriginal Embassy', 18.
17   Robinson, 'The Aboriginal Embassy', 18.
18   Robinson, 'The Aboriginal Embassy', 20.
19   Robinson, 'The Aboriginal Embassy', 20.
20   Pat Eatock, 'A Small but Stinging Twig', in Henry Mayer (ed.), *Labor to Power: Australia's 1972 Election* (Sydney: Angus & Robertson, 1973), 152.
21   Eatock, 'A Small but Stinging Twig', 153.
22   Eatock, 'A Small but Stinging Twig', 153.
23   Eatock, 'A Small but Stinging Twig', 154.
24   Eatock, 'A Small but Stinging Twig', 153.
25   Eatock, 'A Small but Stinging Twig', 154.
26   Eatock, 'A Small but Stinging Twig', 154.
27   Eatock, 'A Small but Stinging Twig', 154.
28   Stewart Harris, and Jack Waterford, 'Did the Aboriginal Tent Embassy Achieve Anything? Yes!', *Canberra Times*, 26 January 1982, republished in *The Aboriginal Tent Embassy*, 215.
29   Coral Dow and John Gardiner-Garden, *Overview of Indigenous Affairs: Part 1: 1901 to 1991*, Social Policy Section, Australian Parliament, 2011, <https://www.aph.gov.au/about_parliament/parliamentary_departments/parliamentary_library/pubs/bn/1011/indigenousaffairs1>.
30   Dow and Gardiner-Garden, *Overview of Indigenous Affairs.*
31   Dow and Gardiner-Garden, *Overview of Indigenous Affairs.*
32   Eatock, Interview Tape 5.
33   Michelle Arrow, *The Seventies: The Personal the Political and the Making of Modern Australia* (Sydney: NewSouth, 2019), 59.
34   Peter Boyle, 'Pat Eatock: The '72 Tent Embassy was about Land Rights and Sovereignty', *Green Left Weekly*, 1 February 2012, <https://www.greenleft.org.au/content/pat-eatock-72-tent-embassy-was-about-land-rights-and-sovereignty>.
35   Eatock, Interview, Tape 7.
36   Eatock, Interview, Tape 7.
37   Eatock, Interview, Tape 7.
38   Eatock, Interview, Tape 7.
39   Arrow, *The Seventies*, 93.
40   Eatock, Interview, Tape 6.
41   Eatock, Interview, Tape 7.
42   Eatock, Interview, Tape 6.
43   Arrow, *The Seventies*, 93.
44   Arrow, *The Seventies*, 94–95.

45   Eileen Haley, Facebook post commemorating Pat Eatock, 18 March 2015.

46   Eatock, Interview, Tape 8.

47   Eatock, Interview, Tape 8.

48   Eatock, Interview, Tape 8.

49   *Eatock v Bolt* [2011] FCA 1103, 28 September 2011, <http://
      www.austlii.edu.au/cgi-bin/viewdoc/au/cases/cth/FCA/2011/1103.
      html?context=1;query=eatock%20v%20bolt;mask_path=>.

50   *Eatock v Bolt*, FCA 1103.

51   *Eatock v Bolt*, FCA 1103.

52   *Eatock v Bolt*, FCA 1103.

Women and the Law (Kim Rubenstein)

1   Mary Jane Mossman, *The First Women Lawyers: A Comparative Study of
      Gender, the Law and Legal Professions* (Oxford: Hart Publishing, 2016), 14.

2   See 'Australia Women Lawyers as Active Citizens',.

3   You can listen to Jane Mathews speak about her life in her oral history at
      <catalogue.nla.gov.au/Record/5160658>.

4   See Peg Lusink interviewed by Kim Rubenstein in the Trailblazing Women
      and the Law oral history project, in particular in session 4 where she
      describes that experience and the challenges of the period, <catalogue.nla.
      gov.au/Record/6928772>.

5   For example, see the profiles of Jane Connors, Erica Feller, Lara Giddings,
      Linda Lavarch, Sue Oliver, Gail Wallace and Beth Wilson on the online
      exhibition 'Australian Women Lawyers as Active Citizens', <www.
      womenaustralia.info/lawyers/index.html>.

Whitlam, women and human rights (Elizabeth Evatt)

1   The Act came into force on 31 October 1975; CERD was ratified on
      30 September, and took effect 30 days later. The Act was held valid by the
      High Court, which enabled the highly important Mabo proceedings to
      continue.

2   Buttfield represented South Australia from 1968 to 1974; Guilfoyle was a
      Victorian senator from 1971 to 1987.

3   *Convention on the Political Rights of Women*, 31 March 1953, 193 UNTS
      135 (entered into force 7 July 1954). See also UDHR art. 21, ICCPR
      art 25, and CEDAW art 7 – calling for the equal right of women to vote
      and be elected, to hold public office and to perform all public functions
      without discrimination.

4   Australian Resources and Energy Group, 'Fair Work Commission Shuts
      out Female Talent', <www.amma.org.au/news-media/media-center/fair-
      work-commission-shuts-female-talent/>.

5   *Convention (No 100) concerning Equal Remuneration for Men and Women
      Workers for Work of Equal Value*, 29 June 1951, 165 UNTS 303 (entered
      into force 23 May 1953). Australia ratified on 10 December 1974.

6   <tbinternet.ohchr.org/_layouts/15/TreatyBodyExternal/Treaty.
      aspx?CountryID=9&Lang=EN>. The Convention was implemented
      through the *Sex Discrimination Act 1984*.

7   Nicolee Dixon, *Abortion Law Reform: An Overview of Current Issues*,
      Queensland Parliamentary Library, Research Brief No. 2003/09,
      <documents.parliament.qld.gov.au/explore/ResearchPublications/
      ResearchBriefs/2003/200309.pdf>.

8   The story is told in Elizabeth Evatt et al., *Interim Report of the Royal
      Commission on Human Relationships* (Canberra: Australian Government
      Publishing Service, 1976), 28–35. WEL had requested a Commission on
      the Status of Women before the election.

9   SA 1969; WA 1998; Tas 2001; ACT 2002; Vic 2008; NT 2017;
      Queensland 2018; NSW 2019.

10   CEDAW, General recommendation No. 24, article 12, 1999, para 31(c),
      <tbinternet.ohchr.org/Treaties/CEDAW/Shared%20Documents/1_Global/
      INT_CEDAW_GEC_4738_E.pdf>.

11   Elizabeth Evatt et al., *Royal Commission on Human Relationships Final
      Report*, vol. 4 (Canberra: Australian Government Publishing Service, 1977),
      146–48.

12   For a history of the 'Elsie' refuge, see: Dictionary of Sydney, 'Forty Years of
      the Elsie Refuge for Women and Children', <dictionaryofsydney.org/entry/
      forty_years_of_the_elsie_refuge_for_women_and_children>; and Anne
      Summers, *Ducks on the Pond: An Autobiography 1945–1976* (Ringwood:
      Penguin, 1999), 335.

13   Evatt, et al., *RCHR Report*, vol. 4, 133–34.

14   Evatt, et al., *RCHR Report*, vol. 1, 115, recs. 80–94; vol. 4, p 133 ff.

15   Evatt, et al., *RCHR Report*, vol. 1, 90, 126; vol. 5, 157ff: Rape and other
      sexual offences.

16   *Pycroft, PGA v the Queen* (2012) 245 CLR 355.

17   Declaration on the Elimination of Violence against Women 1993; GA Res
      48/104 of 20 December 1993, <www.ohchr.org/en/professionalinterest/
      pages/violenceagainstwomen.aspx>; Australian Human Rights Commission,
      Deaths from Domestic and Family Violence, <humanrights.gov.au/our-work/
      sex-discrimination/projects/deaths-family-and-domestic-violence>.

18   For example, Evatt, et al., *RCHR Report*, vol. 5, p. 4, para 8.

19   New South Wales enacted legislation in 1977 making it unlawful to
      discriminate on the grounds of race, sex or marital status in employment
      and the provision of services (with exclusions and exemptions). Evatt, et al.,
      RCHR Report, vol. 5, 59, para 324.

20   Evatt, et al., *RCHR Report*, vol. 1, 81–83, 118; vol. 6, 60–61,
      paras 331–39.

21   Evatt, et al., *RCHR Report*, vol. 1, 82, para 32; 120, para 29; vol. 5, 55,
      para 301.

22   Australian Labor Party Platform 1971, Chapter XXIII, paras 11 and 14,
      <parlinfo.aph.gov.au/parlInfo/download/library/partypol/1042679/upload_

binary/1042679.pdf;fileType=application/pdf#search=%22Australian%20
Labor%20Party%20platform%201971%22>.

23   Senate Standing Committee on Constitutional and Legal Affairs, *Interim
     Report on the Law and Administration of Divorce and Related Matters,
     Parliamentary Paper no. 255* (Canberra: Parliament of Australia, October
     1972).

24   Wikipedia, 'Celebrant (Australia)', <en.wikipedia.org/wiki/Celebrant_
     (Australia)>; ABS, Provisional Marriage Data 2020, <www.abs.gov.au/
     articles/provisional-2020-marriages-data; AIFS>, <aifs.gov.au/research/
     facts-and-figures/marriages-australia>.

25   Kep Enderby, 'The Family Law Act, Background to the Legislation',
     UNSW Law Journal, 1 (1985): 10.

26   Jenny Hocking, *Gough Whitlam,* vol. II, *His Time* (Carlton: Melbourne
     University Press, 2012), 183.

27   UDHR article 16.

28   *Family Law Act 1975*, s. 64.

29   *Family Law Act 1975*, s. 117.

30   Hocking, *Gough Whitlam, His Time*, 183–84.

31   This had been recommended by the RCHR, vol. 1, p. 111, but was not
     achieved until 1990; the referrals of powers did not cover child welfare
     issues.

32   This followed referrals of power over de facto property and financial
     matters by the states and territories, except Western Australia.

33   See Rosalind F Croucher, 'Family Law: Challenges for Responding to
     Family Violence in a Federal System', in Alan Hayes and Daryl Higgins
     (eds), *Families, Policy and the Law* (Melbourne: Australian Institute for
     Family Studies, 2014), 207–14.

'Every difficult female': Women and the Family Law Act (Camilla Nelson)

1   *Family Law Act 1975* (Cth).

2   *La Rovere v La Rovere* [1962] 4 FLR 1.

3   Women's Electoral Lobby submission to the Attorney-General,
    CS106 Family Law Bill (II), Attorney-General's Department, M132
    Correspondence Files, 1973–75, National Archives of Australia.

4   'Struggle Looms on No Guilt Divorce', *Sydney Morning Herald*,
    16 December 1973, 47.

5   'Family Law Bill Backed, Attacked', *Sydney Morning Herald*, 21 October
    1974, 2.

6   'Pernicious Attack on "the Family Unit"', *Advertiser* (Adelaide),
    10 September 1974; and 'New Bill "to Destroy Marriage"', *Advertiser*,
    11 August 1974.

7   Richard Beckett, 'Divorce: Or How to Get it Apart', *Nation Review*,
    13–19 July 1973, 208–209.

8   'Family Law Bill Greatest Blow', *Sydney Morning Herald*, 24 October 1974,
    24.

9   'Guilt is Vital in Divorce', *Herald* (Melbourne), 12 April 1973.

10   'Mock Wedding as Divorce Bill Protest', *Sydney Morning Herald*, 20 February 1975, 1.

11   'NSW No.1 Divorce State', *Sydney Morning Herald*, 14 June 1970, 3; 'Puzzle for Legal Men: NSW Divorce Rate', *Sydney Morning Herald*, 4 December 1966, 11.

12   'Man Divorced Five Times', *Sydney Morning Herald*, 9 June 1970, 1.

13   'Inquiry hears Divorce Runs in Families', *Western Australian*, 21 July 1973.

14   'Divorce Rise with Wives Earnings', *The Australian*, 16 August 1971.

15   *Canberra Times*, 26 June 1975, 9.

16   *National Times*, 8–13 October 1973, 3.

17   'S.M. Fears Ghastly Horrors of Sodom', *The Australian*, 31 July 1971.

18   'Desertion Was Main Ground for Divorce', *Sydney Morning Herald*, 10 January 1976, 2.

19   'Taking the Heat Out of Divorce', *Sydney Morning Herald*, 25 January 1973, 12.

20   Paul Marin, 'Dilemmas of Deserted Wives', *Nation Review*, 13–19 September 1974, 1531–32.

21   Marin, 'Dilemmas of Deserted Wives', 1531–32.

22   'Taking the Heat Out of Divorce,' *Sydney Morning Herald*, 25 January 1973, 12.

23   Richard Beckett, 'Divorce', *Nation Review*, 13 July 1973, 1908–1909.

24   Advertisement, *Sydney Morning Herald*, 26 October 1973, 12.

25   'Bid to Right Injustice to Defaulters', *The Australian*, 9 June 1971.

26   'Divorced Men Aided to Escape', *The Australian*, 2 July 1970.

27   'When a Law Forces a Man into Slavery', *Daily Telegraph*, 8 October 1970.

28   Elizabeth Evatt et al., *Royal Commission on Human Relationships Final Report* vol. 4 (Canberra: Australian Government Publishing Service, 1977), 4.

29   Evatt et al., *Royal Commission on Human Relationships Final Report* vol. 4, 133.

30   Evatt et.al., *Royal Commission on Human Relationships Final Report* vol. 4, 51.

31   *Matrimonial Causes Act 1959* (Cth). To obtain a divorce on the grounds of separation, the separating parties additionally had to prove that neither party had conducted themselves in a manner that might give rise to legal action based on the other grounds over the course of the five-year period.

32   Colin James, 'A History of Cruelty in Australian Divorce', *ANZLH E-Journal* (December 2006): 1–30.

33   James, 'A History of Cruelty'.

34   James, 'A History of Cruelty'.

35   *Tilney v Tilney* [1968] HCA 32.

36   Judge Selby in Senate Standing Committee on Constitutional and Legal Affairs, 'Reference: the Law Relating to Divorce, Custody and Family Matters: Transcripts of Evidence Taken on 8 June, 6 July, 21 August 1972,

30 April, 1 May, 20 July 1973', Parliamentary Papers 315, Parliament of Australia, 8 June 1972, 11.

37   Evan Whitton, 'WEL Founder Never Actually Cut a Man Up – Except with Words', *National Times*, 8–13 October 1973, 33.

38   Mungo MacCallum, 'The Women Who Govern Labor', *Nation Review*, 3–9 August 1973, 1294.

39   Letter from Ray Watson, QC, to Lionel Murphy, 4 March 1974. NAA, Attorney-General's Department, A432 Correspondence Files, 1973/7216, Part 2 [Item ID 7800666].

40   Attorney-General's Department, M132 Correspondence Files, 1973–75, CS106 Family Law Bill (II), NAA.

41   Women's Electoral Lobby, A6122, 2218, 1972–1973, vol. 1, NAA.

42   Caroline Graham, 'Australian Woman at War with Herself', *Nation Review*, 10–16 January 1975, 345.

43   On the breakdown of the traditional divisions between the public and private spheres in the 1970s, see Michelle Arrow, *The Seventies: The Personal, the Political and the Making of Modern Australia* (Sydney: NewSouth, 2019).

44   Letter from Ray Watson, QC, to Lionel Murphy, 4 March 1974. Family Law Bill 1973, A432, 1973/7216 PART 2, NAA.

45   Attorney-General's Department, M132 Correspondence Files, 1973–75, CS106 Family Law Bill (II), NAA.

46   *Canberra Times*, 22 January 1974, 9.

47   'New Style Divorce: How Does it Affect Women?' *Australian Women's Weekly*, 13 November 1974, 4–5.

48   Murphy in Senate, *Hansard*, Parliament of Australia, 13 December 1973, 2833.

49   The only other female politician was Liberal Senator Margaret Guilfoyle, elected in 1971.

50   Ray Watson, QC, in Senate Standing Committee on Constitutional and Legal Affairs, 'Report on the Law and Administration of Divorce and Related Matters and the Clauses of the Family Law Bill, 1974, Transcript of Evidence Taken in Camera, 11, 23 and 27 September 1974', Parliamentary Papers 12 (193), Parliament of Australia, 40.

51   Judge Burnet in Senate Standing Committee on Constitutional and Legal Affairs, 'Report on the Law and Administration of Divorce and Related Matters and the Clauses of the Family Law Bill, 1974, Transcript of Evidence Taken in Camera, 11, 23 and 27 September 1974', Parliamentary Papers 12 (193), Parliament of Australia, 191.

52   Senate, *Hansard*, Parliament of Australia, 30 October 1974, 2136–39.

53   Senate, *Hansard*, Parliament of Australia, 30 October 1974, 2136–39.

54   Senate, *Hansard*, Parliament of Australia, 19 November 1974, 2499.

55   The use of non-adversarial procedures encountered trouble in *R v Watson; Ex Parte Amstrong* (1976) 136 CLR 248, for example, and employment earnings were privileged following the High Court decision in *Mallet v Mallet* [1984] HCA 21. In the wake of the Family Court bombings

(1980–85), there was also a heated debate in the media and legal profession about the abandoning of wigs and gowns. See Shurlee Swain, *Born in Hope: The Early Years of the Family Court in Australia* (Sydney: UNSW Press, 2012) and Camilla Nelson and Catharine Lumby, *Broken: Children, Parents and Family Courts* (Melbourne: Black Inc/La Trobe University Press, 2021).

56   Elizabeth Evatt, 'Foreword' in Henry Finlay, *To Have But not to Hold: A History of Attitudes to Marriage and Divorce in Australia, 1858–1975* (Sydney: Federation Press, 2004), vii.

57   *Australian Women's Weekly*, 4 August 1971, 5.

58   *Australian Women's Weekly*, 'Easy Guide to Family Law, Part 5', 31 January 1979, 121.

Health and social policy (Karen Soldatic)

1   Michelle Arrow, 'Australian Women Are (Rightly) Angry. Now They Need a Plan', *The Conversation*, 5 March 2021, <theconversation.com/women-are-rightly-angry-now-they-need-a-plan-156286>.

2   Jacqueline Maley, 'Hear Me Roar: How the Female Vote Swung the Election', *Sydney Morning Herald*, 23 May 2022, <www.smh.com.au/politics/federal/hear-me-roar-how-the-female-vote-swung-the-election-20220522-p5anjq.html>.

3   Karen Soldatic, *Disability and Neoliberal State Formations* (London: Routledge, 2019).

4   Louise St Guillaume, *Newstart, Poverty, Disability and the National Disability Insurance Scheme* (Parramatta: Whitlam Institute, 2020).

5   Mike Steketee, 'Disability Insurance a Real Reform', *The Weekend Australian: Inquirer*, 12 August 2009, 2.

6   Soldatic, *Disability and Neoliberal State Formations*.

7   Karen Soldatic and Barbara Pini, 'Change or Continuity: Disability Policy and the Rudd Government', *Social Policy & Society*, 11, no. 2 (10 February 2012): 183–96.

8   Soldatic, *Disability and Neoliberal State Formations*.

9   Soldatic and Pini, 'Change or Continuity'.

10   Karen Soldatic and Anne Chapman, 'Surviving the Assault: The Disability Movement and the Neoliberal Workfare State', *Social Movement Studies*, 9 (2) (2010): 139–54.

11   Doris Zames Fleischer and Frieda Zames, *The Disability Rights Movement: From Charity to Confrontation* (Philadelphia: Temple University Press, 2001).

12   Soldatic, *Disability and Neoliberal State Formations*.

Women's health, women's welfare (Marie Colman)

1   Lani Russell and Marian Sawer, 'The Rise and Fall of the Australian Women's Bureau', *Australian Journal of Politics and History*, 45 (3) (September 1999): 362–77.

2   The first Labor universal, compulsory health insurance scheme was named Medibank, which was much changed by the succeeding Fraser Coalition government. The Hawke Labor government of 1983 introduced Medicare. Both the Social Welfare and Hospitals Commissions had an executive Chair, and part-time commissioners: for the Hospitals and Health Services Commission, all were drawn from the health sector, while the 12 Social Welfare Commissioners were not only geographically diverse but also occupationally diverse, with only one a Professor of Social Work.

3   Yes, that was the salary in 1972 of a Departmental Secretary/CEO, in the second-tier departments – a far cry from the 2021 typical $350000.

4   A fuller description can be found in the Commission's final publication, *An Idea Before its Time: The Social Welfare Commission* (Queanbeyan: Australian Government Social Welfare Commission, 1976).

5   Class A Widow's Pension applied to de jure widows, Class B to de facto widows – women who had been in a relationship for a minimum of three years. Only children of the relationship conveying eligibility were eligible for the allowances, medical benefits etc. associated with these payments.

6   Peter Whiteford, 'Debt by Design: The Anatomy of a Social Policy Fiasco – Or Was it Something Worse?', *Australian Journal of Public Administration*, 80 (2) (June 2021): 340–60; Jane Millar and Peter Whiteford, 'Timing it Right or Timing it Wrong: How Should Income-Tested Benefits Deal with Changes in Circumstances?', *Journal of Poverty and Social Justice*, 28 (1) (2020): 3–20; Peter Whiteford, 'Social Security since Henderson', in P. Saunders (ed.), *Social Security Reform: Revisiting Henderson and Basic Income* (Melbourne: Melbourne University Press, 2019).

7   Christine Sykes, *Gough and Me: My Journey from Cabramatta to China and Beyond* (Edgecliff: Ventura Press, 2021).

8   See Melanie Oppenheimer, 'Voluntary Action, Social Welfare and the Australian Assistance Plan in the 1970s', *Australian Historical Studies*, 39 (132) (June 2008): 167–82; Erik Eklund, Melanie Oppenheimer and Joanne Scott, 'Developing a Community Soul: A Comparative Assessment of the Australian Assistance Plan in Three Regions, 1973–1977', *Australian Journal of Politics and History*, 62 (3) (2016): 417–31.

9   *Education and Training for Social Welfare Personnel in Australia* (Canberra: Australian Government Publishing Service, 1979).

10 Essentially, the implementation of his election commitment for one year of free pre-school for every four-year-old.

11 Dr Gail Wilenski was also appointed to the Public Service Board as an adviser of Equal Opportunity.

12 Deborah Brennan, *The Politics of Australian Child Care: Philanthropy to Feminism and Beyond*, (Melbourne: Cambridge University Press 1998).

13 Joan Fry had previously been principal of the Sydney Day Nurseries Teacher's College, and a well-respected educator. The elements of her report dealing with workforce were admirable, but with less relation to child care.

14   *Annual Report: Public Service Board* (Canberra: Australian Government Publishing Service 1967), 73.

15   *Annual Report: Public Service Board* (Canberra: Australian Government Publishing Service 1966), 30.

16   *Annual Report: Public Service Board* (Canberra: Australian Government Publishing Service 1969), 27.

17   *Annual Report: Public Service Board* (Canberra: Australian Government Publishing Service 1975), 91

18   *Annual Report: Public Service Board* (Canberra: Australian Government Publishing Service 1972), 3.

19   *Annual Report: Public Service Board* (Canberra: Australian Government Publishing Service 1973), 3.

20   *Annual Report: Public Service Board* (Canberra: Australian Government Publishing Service 1973), 3.

21   *Annual Report: Public Service Board* (Canberra: Australian Government Publishing Service 1973), 3.

22   *Annual Report: Public Service Board* (Canberra: Australian Government Publishing Service 1974), 4.

23   *Annual Report: Public Service Board* (Canberra: Australian Government Publishing Service 1974), 100.

24   *Annual Report: Public Service Board* (Canberra: Australian Government Publishing Service 1975), 92.

25   *Annual Report: Public Service Board* (1975), 98.

26   *Annual Report: Public Service Board* (1975), 107.

27   *Annual Report: Public Service Board* (1975), 92.

Women for Whitlam everywhere: The Whitlam government and regional Australia (Margaret Reynolds)

1   Elspeth Preddey, *Women's Electoral Lobby: Australia, New Zealand, 1972–1985* (Canberra: WEL,1985), 2.

2   Gough Whitlam, election speech, 13 November 1972, <electionspeeches. moadoph.gov.au/speeches/1972-gough-whitlam>.

3   Judith Ireland, 'Whitlam and Conscription: An End to the Lottery of Death', *Sydney Morning Herald*, 21 October 2014, <www.smh.com.au/ politics/federal/whitlam-and-conscription--an-end-to-the-lottery-of-death-20141021–119esl.html>.

4   Gough Whitlam, election speech, 13 November 1972, <electionspeeches. moadoph.gov.au/speeches/1972-gough-whitlam>.

5   Margaret Reynolds, *The Last Bastion: Labor Women Working Towards Equality in the Parliaments of Australia* (Chatswood: Business and Professional Publishing, 1995), 75.

6   Jenny Hocking, *Gough Whitlam,* vol. II, *His Time* (Carlton: Melbourne University Press, 2012), 20.

7   Defining Moments, 'Equal Pay for Women', National Museum of Australia, Canberra, <www.nma.gov.au/defining-moments/resources/equal-pay-for-women>.

8   Hocking, *Gough Whitlam, His Time*, 82–83.

9   Hocking. *Gough Whitlam, His Time*, 80.

10   Hocking. *Gough Whitlam, His Time,* 81–82.

11   Gough Whitlam, 'The First Twelve Months – Statement Made in the House of Representatives by the Prime Minister of Australia', 13 December 1973 (Canberra: Australian Government Printer), 3.

12   'International Agreements', Whitlam Institute, <www.whitlam.org/whitlam-legacy-human-rights#international-agreements>.

13   Gough Whitlam, 'The First Twelve Months', 14.

14   Margaret Reynolds, *Living Politics* (St Lucia: Queensland University Press, 2007), 95.

15   Jacqueline Shea, in Robin Joyce (ed.), *Social Images 1891–1991* (Canberra: ACT Branch Australian Labor Party, 1991), 139.

16   Gough Whitlam, speech at the opening of the Women and Politics Conference (Canberra, 31 August 1975), <pmtranscripts.pmc.gov.au/release/transcript-3874>.

Just add women and stir: Revisiting the femocrat revolution (Eva Cox)

1   Hester Eisenstein, *Gender Shock: Practising Feminism on Two Continents* (Sydney: Allen & Unwin, 1991).

2   Eisenstein, *Gender Shock*, 19–21.

3   Eva Cox, *Leading Women* (Milsons Point: Random House, 1996).

4   Cox, *Leading Women*, 133–35.

5   Marian Sawer with Gail Radford, *Making Women Count: A History of The Women's Electoral Lobby in Australia* (Sydney: UNSW Press, 2008), 261.

6   Linda Hancock, *Women, Public Policy and the State* (South Yarra: Macmillan, 1999).

Out of wedlock, out of luck: Single mothers and ex-nuptial babies (Terese Edwards)

1   This chapter draws on my own work and the memory and narration of pioneering activists Rosemary West, Tricia Harper and Brenda Richards, enhanced by archival documents.

2   Tricia Harper, interview by Terese Edwards, 2022; Elaine Martin, 'Social Work, the Family and Women's Equality in Post-War Australia, '*Women's History Review,* 12 (3) (2003): no. 3 (2003445–68; Sheila Shaver, 'Class and Gender in Australian Income Security', *Australian and New Zealand Journal of Sociology,* 24 (3) (1988): 377–97.

3   David Stanton and Andrew Herscovitch, 'Social Security and Sole Parents: Developments in Australia', *International Social Security Association,* 26 (1992): 157–84.

4   Brenda Richards, 'The Scarlet Letter', Melbourne, 2019. Copy in possession of author.

5   Christine A Cole, 'Stolen Babies – Broken Hearts: Forced Adoption in

Australia, 1881–1987' (Doctor of Philosophy thesis, University of Western Sydney, 2013).

6   Richards, 'The Scarlet Letter'.

7   Community Affairs Reference Committee, Commonwealth Contribution to Former Forced Adoption Policies and Practices (Canberra: Commonwealth of Australia, 2012), Section 5.70, <www.aph.gov.au/parliamentary_business/committees/senate/community_affairs/completed_inquiries/2010–13/commcontribformerforcedadoption/report/index>.

8   Deanne Carson and Fiona Hendry, *Single but Not Alone: The First 40 Years of the Council of Single Mothers and their Children* (Melbourne: Council of Single Mothers and their Children Inc, 2012).

9   Rosemary West, interview by Terese Edwards, 2022

10   Carson and Hendry, *Single but Not Alone.*

11   Rosemary West, interview by Terese Edwards, 2022.

12   S Fitts, *A request for co-operation and support in approaching the Commonwealth Government* (Melbourne: CSMC, 1972).1972

13   Eric Benjamin, 'Acceptance for Position of Panel of Advisers', June 1971, Letter to Council of Single Mothers and her Child, National Council of Single Mothers and their Children Archives. These archives are held by the NCMC.

14   Sandy Walker, 'Minutes of the Meeting between the Panel of Advisers, CSMC and P Cullen', 11 April 1972, National Council of Single Mothers and their Children Archives.

15   Panel of Advisers, Submission to the Prime Minster, July 1972, National Council of Single Mothers and their Children Archives.

16   Peter Cullen, Unmarried Mothers Assistance, 30 March 1972, letter to Council of Single Mother and her child, National Council of Single Mothers and their Children Archives.

17   S Fitts letter to Peter Cullen, 23 March 1972, National Council of Single Mothers and their Children Archives.

18   Rosemary West, interview by Terese Edwards, 2022.

19   Tricia Harper, interview by Terese Edwards, 2022.

20   Peter Cullen, letter to Jo Clancy, 7 March 1972, National Council of Single Mothers and their Children Archives.

21   Gough Whitlam, 1972 election campaign launch speech, 13 November 1972, <electionspeeches.moadoph.gov.au/speeches/1972-gough-whitlam>.

22   Ronald Sackville, 'Social Security and Family Law in Australia', *International and Comparative Law Quarterly,* 27 (1978): 127–67.

23   Marie Coleman, interview by Terese Edwards, 2021.

24   Andrew Podger, interview by Terese Edwards, 2021.

25   Bill Hayden, Social Services Bill (No. 3) (Canberra: Commonwealth of Australia, 1973).

26   Dale Daniels, 'Social Security Payments for People Caring for Children, 1912–2008: A Chronology' (Canberra: Parliamentary Library, 29 January 2008), <www.aph.gov.au/About_Parliament/Parliamentary_Departments/Parliamentary_Library/pubs/BN/0809/children>.

27   Stephanie Charlesworth, 'Monitoring Income Maintenance Policies for Single Mothers', *Australian Journal of Social Issues*, 17 (2) (1982): 135.

28   Charlesworth, 'Monitoring Income Maintenance Policies for Single Mothers', 135.

29   Daryl Higgins, *Impact of Past Adoption Practices: Summary of Key Issues from Australian Research* (Australian Institute of Family Studies, 2010), 2.

30   Sheila Shaver, 'Class and Gender in Australian Income Security', *ANZJS*, 24 (3) (November 1988): 384.

31   Tricia Harper, interview by Terese Edwards, 2022.

32   Brian Howe, interview by Terese Edwards, 2021.

33   Marie Coleman, interview by Terese Edwards, 2021.

34   Bill Hayden email to Terese Edwards, April 2009.

35   Alys Gagnon, 'Single Mums Hope to Fly Under the Radar of the Federal Budget', *Kidspot* (Australia), 2017, <www.kidspot.com.au/parenting/single-mums-hope-to-fly-under-the-radar-of-the-federal-budget/news-story/237b4f7406841adafe5b4385ac1d5880>.

36   Kay Cook, 'Social Support in Single Parents' Transition from Welfare to Work: Analysis of Qualitative Findings', *International Journal of Social Welfare*, 21 (4) (2012): 338–50.

37   Ben Phillips and Cukkoo Joseph, *Income Trends for Selected Single Parent Families*, ANU Centre for Social Research and Methods (Canberra: Australian National University, 2016), 10.

38   Patricia Karvelas, 'Gillard Government 'Got It Wrong' on Single Parent Payments, Says Jenny Macklin', *The Australian*, 25 March 2014, 6.

39   Film Stretch, in partnership with the Sydney Community Foundation, the NCSMC and the Snow Foundation, *10 Stories of Single Mothers* (Sydney: 2014), <www.youtube.com/watch?v=LD91Eoyv1d0>.

40   Amy Remeikis, 'Melbourne Woman Complains to UN, Saying Parenting Cuts Are Human Rights Abuse,' *The Guardian* (Australia), 20 September 2017, <www.theguardian.com/world/2017/sep/21/un-complaint-parenting-payment-melbourne-cuts-human-rights-abuse>.

Media, arts and education (Julie McLeod)

1   Gough Whitlam, 'The First Year: Statement by the Prime Minister The Hon. E. G. Whitlam, Q.C., M.P., on the Achievements of the Labor Government's First Year Of Office' (1973), National Archives of Australia, <www.naa.gov.au/learn/learning-resources/learning-resource-themes/society-and-culture/gender-and-sexuality/labor-governments-womens-rights-achievements-after-first-year-office-statement-prime-minister-gough-whitlam>; Gough Whitlam, 'Achievements and Prospects in Education', *The Australian Quarterly*, 46 (1) (1974): 59–67.

2   Bronwyn Coulston, 'Women's Rights and the Whitlam Program: A Source Based Study', *Teaching History*, 50 (1) (2016): 13–17; 'Whitlam Legacy: Women's Rights', Whitlam Institute, <www.whitlam.org/whitlam-legacy-womens-rights>.

3   Gough Whitlam, *The Whitlam Government 1972–1975* (Ringwood: Penguin, 1985), 554.

4   Gough Whitlam, 'Achievements and Prospects in Education', *The Australian Quarterly*, 46, no. 1 (1974): 60.

5   Whitlam, 'Achievements and Prospects in Education', 59.

6   Whitlam, 'Achievements and Prospects in Education', 60.

7   Whitlam, 'Achievements and Prospects in Education', 59.

8   Schools Commission, *Girls, School and Society* (Canberra: Australian Government Publishing Service, 1975).

9   Peter Karmel, *Schools in Australia: Report of the Interim Committee for the Australian Schools Commission* (Canberra: Australian Government Publishing Service, 1973), 19.

10   Dean Ashenden, Jean Blackburn, Bill Hannan and Doug White, 'Manifesto for a Democratic Curriculum', *The Australian Teacher*, no. 7 (February 1984): 13–20.

Whitlam, women and the media (Gillian Appleton)

1   John S Western, *Australian Mass Media: Controllers, Consumers, Producers* (Sydney: Australian Institute of Political Science, 1975).

2   Gough Whitlam, *The Whitlam Government 1972–1975* (Ringwood: Penguin, 1985), 576–58.

3   Graham Freudenberg, *A Certain Grandeur: Gough Whitlam in Politics* (South Melbourne: Macmillan Australia, 1977), 339

4   Whitlam, *The Whitlam Government*, 581.

5   Evan Williams, quoted in *Report of the Women and Politics Conference 1975*, vol. 2 (Canberra: Australian Government Publishing Service, 1977), 224–25.

6   Michelle Arrow, *The Seventies: The Personal, the Political and Making of Modern Australia* (Sydney: NewSouth, 2019), 90–93.

7   Gloria Steinem 'Elizabeth Reid, Why I Quit, Gloria Steinem and Elizabeth Reid talk about Revolution', *The Bulletin*, 10 January 1976, 39–43.

8   Australian Film and Television School for UNESCO, *Women in the Media, The Professional Participation of Women in the Audio-Visual Media – Film, Radio and Television* (Sydney: AFTS, 1976), 21ff.

9   An exception was the ABC's Caroline Jones on *Four Corners*. In 1978, the ABC's Margaret Throsby was the first woman to read the national TV news, <www.womenaustralia.info/leaders/biogs/WLE0487b.htm>.

10   First broadcast in 1975 as an IWY initiative, it covered very frankly a wide range of topics relevant to women's concerns, sometimes too confronting for ABC management. It survived for 23 years. Ken Inglis, *This is the ABC: The Australian Broadcasting Commission 1932–1983* (Carlton: Melbourne University Press, 1983), 365–67.

11   Siobhan Moylan, Julie Rigg and Daniela Torsh, 'Media Women's Action Group', in Bridget Griffin Foley (ed.), *A Companion to Australia*

Media (North Melbourne: Australian Scholarly Publishing, 2014), 271–72. Members included distinguished Fairfax reporter, later China correspondent, Margaret Jones; *Women's Weekly* senior feature writer Kay Keavney; film writers Julie Rigg and Sandra Hall; and science journalist, later head of Film Australia, Robin Hughes.

12   Steinem, 'Elizabeth Reid, Why I Quit'.

13   Nancy Dexter, '$2 Million for the Sheilas – Surprisingly it's Not a Joke', *The Age,* January 1975, 13.

14   Inter alia, the MeJane collective (a subgroup of the Women's Liberation Movement), publishers of *MeJane* newspaper (1971–74).

15   *International Women's Year: Report of the Australian National Advisory Committee* (Canberra: Australian Government Publishing Service, 1976), 15.

16   In the absence of sophisticated media monitoring services, clipping print media was the primary means of keeping a record of media coverage of the IWY.

17   Susan Mitchell, *Margaret Whitlam: A Biography* (Milsons Point: Random House Australia, 2006), 230–32.

18   Full details of funded projects, see *International Women's Year: Report of the Australian National Advisory Committee* (Canberra: Australian Government Publishing Service, 1976), 74–113.

19   Anne Beveridge, 'No More Sex Please, Ms Greer', *Daily Telegraph*, 11 June 1975.

20   'Experimental Shorts from the Women's Film Fund', <www.artistfilmworkshop.org/experimental-shorts-from-the-womens-film-fund>. The fund was eventually dissolved in the 1990s.

21   *Daily Telegraph*, 17 June 1975.

22   Jocelyn Olcott, *International Women's Year: The Greatest Consciousness-Raising Event in History* (New York: Oxford University Press, 2017), 256.

23   'Speech presented by Elizabeth Reid to the First World Conference of the International Women's Year held in Mexico City from 19 June to 2 July 1975', held in Whitlam Prime Ministerial Collection, Whitlam Institute.

24   Among the team were Blanche d'Alpuget, Elisabeth Wynhausen, Barbara Martyn, Gordon Burgoyne and John Lahey.

25   *International Women's Year: Report of the Australian National Advisory Committee,* 57.

26   'Angry Mob of Women Marches on Newspaper', *Melbourne Sun,* 6 September 1975, quoted in *International Women's Year: Report of the Australian National Advisory Committee,* 57.

27   The government, in the throes of the supply crisis after the Morosi affair and the foreign loans (Khemlani) debacle, may have wanted to avoid further controversy. (The UN itself would have had to endorse the cancellation.)

28   Steinem, 'Elizabeth Reid, Why I Quit'.

29   United Nations Fourth World Conference on Women, Women and Media

Diagnosis, September 1995, <www.un.org/womenwatch/daw/beijing/platform/media.htm>.

30   Global Media Monitoring Project, *6th Global Media Monitoring Project: Highlight of Findings* (Toronto: GMMP, 2021), <whomakesthenews.org/wp-content/uploads/2021/08/GMMP-2020.Highlights_FINAL.pdf>.

31   Jenna Price with Blair Williams, *2021 Women for Media Report: Take the Next Steps* (Canberra: Women's Leadership Institute Australia, 2021), <www.wlia.org.au/_files/ugd/bd2988_38fee1f77f71481b91ff82163e12f3b1.pdf>.

32   *Global Report on the Status of Women in the News Media* (Washington DC: International Women's Media Foundation, 2011), 216–18, <www.iwmf.org/wp-content/uploads/2018/06/IWMF-Global-Report.pdf>.

33   Simge Andi, Meera Selva and Rasmus Kleis Nielsen, *Women and Leadership in the News Media 2020: Evidence from Ten Markets*, University of Oxford and the Reuters Institute, Fact Sheet, March 2020, <reutersinstitute.politics.ox.ac.uk/sites/default/files/2020-03/Andi_et_al_Women_and_Leadership_in_Media_FINAL.pdf>.

34   Jess Hill, 'The Reckoning: How #MeToo Is Changing Australia', *Quarterly Essay*, no. 84 (2021), provides a detailed and impassioned account of the events in 2020–21 that led to support for women on a scale unprecedented since the 1970s.

Whitlam, women and the arts (Patricia Amphlett)

1   Gough Whitlam, *The Whitlam Government 1972–1975* (Ringwood: Penguin, 1985), 553–54.

2   Ben Eltham, 'Budget Shock Decimates Australia Council', *Arts Hub*, 2 May 2015, <www.artshub.com.au/news/news/budget-shock-decimates-australia-council-248017-2348326/>.

3   Eltham, 'Budget Shock'; Dan Conifer and Michael McKinnon, 'Australia Council Budget Cuts Blindsided Peak Arts Body Executive, Documents Show', ABC News, 20 February 2016, <www.abc.net.au/news/2016-02-20/$105m-budget-cut-caught-australia-council-by-surprise:-emails/7185900>.

4   Sasha Grishin, 'Gough Whitlam's Legacy in the Arts World Needs Protecting', *Sydney Morning Herald*, 23 October 2014, <www.smh.com.au/entertainment/art-and-design/gough-whitlams-legacy-in-the-arts-world-needs-protecting-20141023-11aatp.html>.

5   Grishin, 'Gough Whitlam's Legacy in the Arts World'.

6   Grishin, 'Gough Whitlam's Legacy in the Arts World'.

7   John Gardiner-Garden, *Commonwealth Arts Policy and Administration* (Canberra: Parliamentary Library, 2009), 3, <www.aph.gov.au/binaries/library/pubs/bn/2008–09/artspolicy.pdf>.

8   Susan Ryan, 'Women of Australia', in Troy Bramston (ed.), *The Whitlam Legacy* (Sydney: Federation Press, 2013), 215.

9   Judy Jacques, personal communication with author.
10   Cate Blanchett, 'Cate Blanchett Pays Tribute to Gough Whitlam: Full
        Text', *Sydney Morning Herald,* 5 November 2014, <www.smh.com.
        au/opinion/cate-blanchett-pays-tribute-to-gough-whitlam-full-text-
        20141105–11hdb1.html>.

Jean Blackburn, girls, and their school education (Craig Campbell and Debra Hayes)

1   Committee on Social Change and the Education of Women, *Girls, School
        and Society: Report by a Study Group to the Schools Commission* (Canberra:
        Schools Commission, 1975).
2   Jean Blackburn and Ted Jackson, *Australian Wives Today* (Melbourne:
        Victorian Fabian Society, 1963).
3   Craig Campbell and Debra Hayes, *Jean Blackburn: Education, Feminism
        and Social Justice* (Melbourne: Monash University Publishing, 2019), 141.
4   Peter Karmel (Chair), *Education in South Australia: Report of the Committee
        of Enquiry into Education in South Australia 1969–1970* (Adelaide:
        Government of South Australia, 1971). See also Campbell and Hayes,
        Jean Blackburn, 148–51.
5   Jean Blackburn, interview by Tony Ryan, National Library of Australia,
        12 and 19 May 1994. Peter Karmel (Chair), *Schools in Australia: Report
        of the Interim Committee of the Australian Schools Commission* (Canberra:
        Australian Government Publishing Service, 1973).
6   Karmel, *Schools in Australia*, 19.
7   Marjorie Theobald, *Knowing Women: Origins of Women's Education in
        Nineteenth Century Australia* (Cambridge: Cambridge University Press,
        1996); Marilyn Lake, *Getting Equal: The History of Australian Feminism*
        (Sydney: Allen & Unwin, 1999).
8   Committee on Social Change and the Education of Women, *Girls, School
        and Society: Report by a Study Group to the Schools Commission* (Canberra:
        Schools Commission, 1975), 1–2.
9   Daniela Torsh, interview by Craig Campbell and Debra Hayes, 30 August
        2016. Held by Debra Hayes, University of Sydney.
10   Ken McKinnon, interview by Craig Campbell, 27 May 2016. Held by
        Debra Hayes, University of Sydney.
11   Dean Ashenden, interview by Craig Campbell and Debra Hayes, 7 June
        2016. Held by Debrah Hayes, University of Sydney.
12   Torsh, interview.
13   McKinnon, interview. See also Campbell and Hayes, *Jean Blackburn*,
        206–208.
14   McKinnon, interview.
15   *Girls, School and Society,* 155.
16   *Girls, School and Society*, 155.
17   *Girls, School and Society*, 168.
18   *Girls, School and Society*, 15.

19   WF Connell, *Reshaping Australian Education 1960–1985* (Melbourne: ACER, 1993), 514.

20   Jean Blackburn, *Ministerial Review of Postcompulsory Schooling: Report* (Melbourne: Ministerial Review of Postcompulsory Schooling, 1985).

21   Lyn Yates, interview by Craig Campbell, 27 November 2014. Held by Debra Hayes, University of Sydney.

22   Denise Bradley, interview by Craig Campbell and Debra Hayes, 9 October 2015. Held by Debra Hayes, University of Sydney.

23   Peter Beilharz, Trevor Hogan and Sheila Shaver, *The Martin Presence: Jean Martin and the Making of the Social Sciences in Australia* (Sydney: UNSW Press, 2015), 211.

24   Susan Ryan, *Catching the Waves: Life in and Out of Politics* (Sydney: HarperCollins, 1999), 213.

25   Alison Mackinnon, 'Girls, School and Society: A Generation of Change?', *Clare Burton Memorial Lecture* (Adelaide, 2005).

26   Jean Blackburn to Barry Hill, 27 November 1975. Jean Blackburn Personal Papers, National Archives of Australia (NAA).

27   Jean Blackburn to Dany Torsh, 6 September 1974. Jean Blackburn Personal Papers, NAA.

28   Ashenden, interview.

29   See Simon Marginson, *Education and Public Policy in Australia* (Cambridge: Cambridge University Press, 1993); Craig Campbell, Helen Proctor and Geoffrey Sherington, *School Choice: How Parents Negotiate the New School Market in Australia* (Sydney: Allen & Unwin, 2009); Michael Pusey, *Economic Rationalism in Canberra: A Nation-Building State Changes its Mind* (Cambridge: Cambridge University Press, 1991).

30   See Blackburn, *Ministerial Review of Postcompulsory Schooling; Schools Commission, Schooling for 15 and 16 Year-olds* (Canberra: Schools Commission, 1980), and Campbell and Hayes, *Jean Blackburn*.

31   David Gonski (Chair), *Review of Funding for Schooling: Final Report* (Canberra: Australian Government, 2011); David Gonski, 'Inaugural Jean Blackburn Oration', 2014, <www.abc.net.au/news/2014–05–22/gonski-gonskis-verdict-on-the-years-since-his-review/5469974>.

Then, now, and what might come: A writer's take (Sara Dowse)

1   WK Hancock, *Australia* (New York: Charles Scribner, 1930). Hancock's irony vis-à-vis state socialism was lost on this migrant when I first read this. What I took away from it was an endorsement, which delighted me about my new country.

2   Sara Dowse, *West Block* (Ringwood: Penguin, 1983), 4.

3   Dowse, *West Block*.

4   Avivah Wittenberg Cox, '5 Economists Redefining … Everything. Oh Yes, and They're Women', *Forbes*, 31 May 2020, <www.forbes.com/sites/avivahwittenbergcox/2020/05/31/5-economists-redefining-everything--oh-yes-and-theyre-women/?sh=6a4bffa8714a>.

Why a grassroots women's movement is vital (Ranuka Tandan)

1   Gisela Kaplan, *The Meagre Harvest: The Australian Women's Movement 1950s–1980s* (Sydney: Allen & Unwin, 1996), 37.

2   Malcolm Fraser, election speech, 27 November 1975, Museum of Australian Democracy, <electionspeeches.moadoph.gov.au/speeches/1975-malcolm-fraser>.

3   Chelsea Watego, *Another Day in the Colony* (Brisbane: University of Queensland Press, 2021), 116.

4   Nancy Fraser and Olimpia Malatesta, 'A Feminism Aimed at Liberating All Women Must Be Anti-Capitalist,' *Jacobin*, 10 February 2019, <jacobinmag.com/2019/10/nancy-fraser-feminism-anti-capitalist-99-percent-majority>.

5   Fraser and Malatesta, 'A Feminism Aimed at Liberating All Women'.

6   Erica Millar, 'Feminism, Foetocentrism, and the Politics of Abortion Choice in 1970s Australia', in Sharon Stettner, et al. (eds), *Transcending Borders: Abortion in the Past and Present* (London and New York: Palgrave Macmillan); Kaplan, 'The Meagre Harvest', 98.

7   RAG Dublin, 'Why Anarcha-Feminism?', in *Quiet Rumours: An Anarcha-Feminist Reader* (Oakland: AK Press, 2012), 14.

8   Alan Duncan, 'Behind the Line: Poverty and Disadvantage in Australia in 2022', *Bankwest Curtin Economics Centre* (2022), 7.

9   Alice Nutter, 'Make Your Own Tea: Women's Realm and Other Recipes and Patterns', in *Quiet Rumours: An Anarcha-Feminist Reader* (Oakland: AK Press, 2012), 106.

10   Romina Akemi and Bree Busk, 'Breaking the Waves: Challenging the Liberal Tendency within Anarchist Feminism', Black Rose Anarchist Federation, 6 July 2016, <blackrosefed.org/breaking-the-waves/>.

11   Amber Schultz, 'From Chaos to Triumph to Abuse: What Happened After 100,000 Pissed-off Australians Marched on Parliament?' *Crikey*, 7 May 2021, <www.crikey.com.au/2021/05/07/march4justice-fallout/>.

12   'Safety. Respect. Equity.', <www.safetyrespectequity.com.au/>.

13   Bri Lee, 'The Uneven Justice of Australia's Defamation Laws', *Saturday Paper*, 13–19 November 2021, <www.thesaturdaypaper.com.au/2021/11/13/the-uneven-justice-australias-defamation-laws/163672200012865#hrd>.

14   Dhanya Mani, 'I Was a Staffer, and So Was My Perpetrator', *Saturday Paper*, 20–26 February 2021, <www.thesaturdaypaper.com.au/opinion/topic/2021/02/20/i-was-staffer-and-so-was-my-perpetrator/161373960011138#hrd>.

15   Sisonke Msimang, 'Grace Tame and Brittany Higgins Are Supremely Admirable, and the Acceptable White Faces of Australian Feminism', *The Guardian*, 7 March 2021, <www.theguardian.com/commentisfree/2022/mar/07/grace-tame-and-brittany-higgins-are-supremely-admirable-and-the-acceptable-white-faces-of-australian-feminism>.

16   NSW Teachers Federation, 'A Quick Guide to Union Wins for Women Teachers in NSW', <www.nswtf.org.au/files/22004_womenswin_a2_ poster_update.pdf>.

17   Kaplan, 'The Meagre Harvest', 12.

18   Australian Bureau of Statistics, 'Trade Union Membership', August 2020, <www.abs.gov.au/statistics/labour/earnings-and-working-conditions/trade- union-membership/latest-release>.

19   Black Flag Sydney, 'Against Carceral Feminism: Advocating for Working Women's Freedom without the Police', *Mutiny*, 12 May 2022, <blackflagsydney.com/article/45>.

20   Workplace Gender Equality Agency, Australian Government, 'Unpaid Care Work and the Labour Market', 9 November 2016, <www.wgea.gov. au/publications/unpaid-care-work-and-the-labour-market>.

21   Benita Kolovos, 'Victoria and NSW Announce Overhaul of Preschool Education with Extra Year of School', *The Guardian*, 16 June 2022, <www.theguardian.com/australia-news/2022/jun/16/victoria-and-nsw-to- announce-overhaul-of-preschool-education>.

22   Black Flag Sydney, 'Against Carceral Feminism'.

23   Aileen Moreton-Robinson, *Talkin' Up to the White Woman: Indigenous Women and Feminism* (Minneapolis: University of Minnesota Press, 2021), 159.

24   Moreton-Robinson, *Talkin' Up to the White Woman*, xxvi.

Re-energising the revolution today (Blair Williams)

1   Carol Johnson, 'Playing the Gender Card: The Uses and Abuses of Gender in Australian Politics', *Politics & Gender*, 11 (2) (2015): 303.

2   Mary Crawford and Barbara Pini, 'Gender Equality in National Politics: The Views of Australian Male Politicians', *Australian Journal of Political Science*, 45 (4) (2010): 93.

3   Blair Williams, 'It's a Man's World at the Top: Gendered Media Representations of Julia Gillard and Helen Clark', *Feminist Media Studies*, 10 November 2020, <http://www.tandfonline.com/doi/abs/10.1080/1468 0777.2020.1842482>.

4   Julia Gillard, *My Story* (North Sydney: Random House Australia, 2014), 113.

5   Carol Johnson and Blair Williams, 'Still Lacking Her Rights at Work: The Treatment of Women Politicians in the Australian Parliament and News Media', *Australasian Parliamentary Review*, 36 (2) (2021): 110–29.

6   Amanda Haraldsson and Lena Wängnerud, 'The Effect of Media Sexism on Women's Political Ambition: Evidence from a Worldwide Study', *Feminist Media Studies*, 19 (4) (2019): 525–41.

7   Blair Williams and Marian Sawer, 'Rainbow Labor and a Purple Policy Launch: Gender and Sexuality Issues', in Anika Gauja, et al. (eds), *Double Disillusion: The 2016 Australian Federal Election* (Canberra: ANU press, 2018), 642.

8   Sarah Casey and Juliet Watson, 'The Unpalatable-Palatable: Celebrity Feminism in the Australian Mainstream Media', *Outskirts: Feminisms Along the Edge*, 37 (2017): 15.

9   Sara Ahmed, 'Feminist Killjoys (and Other Willful Subjects)', *Cahiers Du Genre*, 53 (2) (2012): 77–98.

10   Johnson and Williams, 'Still Lacking Her Rights at Work', 120.

11   Johnson and Williams, 'Still Lacking Her Rights at Work', 124.

12   Johnson and Williams, 'Still Lacking Her Rights at Work'.

13   Jess Hill, 'The Reckoning: How #MeToo Is Changing Australia', *Quarterly Essay*, no. 84 (2021): 99–100.

14   James Glenday, 'Parliament House Staffer Sacked Over Desk Masturbation Scandal Makes Report to Police', ABC News, 29 April 2021, <www.abc.net.au/news/2021-04-29/police-report-made-over-desk-masturbation-scandal/100105650>.

15   Prior to the 2022 federal election – which saw 29-year-old Greens MP Stephen Bates win the seat of Brisbane – there was not a single MP in the federal House of Representatives under the age of 30, with only two in the Senate.

16   Bronwyn Carlson, 'No Public Outrage, No Vigils: Australia's Silence at Violence against Indigenous Women', *The Conversation*, 16 April 2021, <theconversation.com/no-public-outrage-no-vigils-australias-silence-at-violence-against-indigenous-women-158875>.

17   Latoya Aroha Rule, 'My Hope for the March 4 Justice and Beyond Is that We Consider the Plight of Black Women in Australia', *The Guardian*, 15 March 2021, <www.theguardian.com/commentisfree/2021/mar/15/my-hope-for-the-march4justice-and-beyond-is-that-we-consider-the-plight-of-black-women-in-australia>.

18   According to the Australian Human Rights Commission, 11.8 per cent of Aboriginal deaths in custody were women – but 'female prisoners accounted for 11.3 per cent of Aboriginal deaths in custody but only 5.2 per cent of non-Aboriginal deaths in custody'. See *Indigenous Deaths in Custody*, 1996, 'Chapter 3 Comparison: Indigenous and Non-Indigenous Deaths', <humanrights.gov.au/our-work/indigenous-deaths-custody-chapter-3-comparison-indigenous-and-non-indigenous-deaths>.

19   Aileen Moreton-Robinson, *Talkin' Up to the White Woman: Indigenous Women and Feminism* (St Lucia: University of Queensland Press, 2000), 108.

INDEX